HEBREW WRITERS
on Writing

Intimate and eclectic, surprising and wise, this anthology offers a writer's-eye view of the last Hebrew century. Drawing from essays, letters, notebooks, poems, interviews, memoirs, and other sources, the collection provides a fresh look at well-known figures who helped shape modern Hebrew culture while also introducing a host of fascinating yet little- or never-before-translated writers. Peter Cole's selections begin in early twentieth-century Warsaw, wander through the literature's formative years in Europe and Palestine, and explore the charged complexity of contemporary Israel. In the process, *Hebrew Writers on Writing* probes the shifting cultural and political landscape from which this rich and diverse body of work emerged.

CONTRIBUTORS

S. Y. Agnon	Avraham Kook	Anton Shammas
Natan Alterman	Ronit Matalon	Avraham Shlonsky
Yehuda Amichai	Sami Michael	Gershon Shofman
Aharon Appelfeld	Amos Oz	Ya'aqov Steinberg
David Avidan	Dan Pagis	Noah Stern
Devora Baron	Haviva Pedaya	Sha'ul Tchernichowsky
Haim Nahman Bialik	Gabriel Preil	David Vogel
Yosef Haim Brenner	Esther Raab	Yona Wallach
Sami Shalom Chetrit	Rahel	Meir Wieseltier
Ya'aqov Fichman	Yonatan Ratosh	A. B. Yehoshua
David Frischmann	Dahlia Ravikovitch	Avot Yeshurun
Uri Nissan Gnessin	Harold Schimmel	Avraham Ben Yitzhaq
Lea Goldberg	Gershom Scholem	S. Yizhar
Uri Zvi Greenberg	Aharon Shabtai	Natan Zach
David Grossman	Ya'aqov Shabtai	Zelda
Shulamit Hareven	David Shahar	
Yoel Hoffmann	Yitzhaq Shami	

The Writer's World
Edward Hirsch, SERIES EDITOR

The Writer's World features writers from around the globe discussing what it means to write, and to be a writer, in many different parts of the world. The series collects a broad range of material and provides access for the first time to a body of work never before gathered in English. Edward Hirsch, the series editor, is internationally acclaimed as a poet and critic. He is the president of the John Simon Guggenheim Memorial Foundation.

Hebrew Writers on Writing (2008)
EDITED BY Peter Cole

Irish Writers on Writing (2007)
EDITED BY Eavan Boland

Mexican Writers on Writing (2007)
EDITED BY Margaret Sayers Peden

Polish Writers on Writing (2007)
EDITED BY Adam Zagajewski

Trinity University Press gratefully acknowledges the generous support of the following Patrons of The Writer's World:

Sarah Harte and John Gutzler
Mach Family Fund, Joella and Steve Mach

HEBREW WRITERS

on Writing

EDITED BY

Peter Cole

TRINITY UNIVERSITY PRESS

San Antonio

Published by Trinity University Press
San Antonio, Texas 78212

Copyright © 2008 by Peter Cole

Complete copyright information continues on page 312.

The epigraph is from *Sefer, sofer, ve-sippur,* by S. Y. Agnon
(Schocken Books, 2000 [1938]), 8.

Cover design by Karen Schober
Book design by BookMatters, Berkeley

♾ The paper used in this publication meets the minimum requirements of the American
National Standard for Information Sciences—Permanence of Paper for Printed Library
Materials, ANSI Z39.48-1992.

Printed on 100% post-consumer waste recycled text stock.

Library of Congress Cataloging-in-Publication Data
   Hebrew writers on writing / edited by Peter Cole.
      p. cm.—(The writer's world)
   Includes bibliographical references and index.
   Summary: "Drawing from essays, letters, poems, interviews, and other sources, the book
   offers a fresh look at figures who shaped modern Hebrew literature and introduces
   fascinating yet little-translated writers. Ranges from early twentieth-century Warsaw
   through the formative years of Hebrew modernism in Europe and Palestine, to the
   complexity of contemporary Israel"   —PROVIDED BY PUBLISHER.
   ISBN 978-1-59534-051-1 (hardcover : alk. paper)
   ISBN 978-1-59534-052-8 (pbk. : alk. paper)
   1. Hebrew literature—Translations into English. 2. Israeli literature—Translations into
   English. 3. Authors, Israeli—Political and social views. 4. Authorship. 5. Israel—
   Intellectual life. I. Cole, Peter, 1957–
   PJ5059.EIH43   2008
   892.4'09006—dc22   2008020815

12   11   10   09   08   —   5   4   3   2   1

Of the making of books there is no end. And if there's no end to the making of books, all the more so with stories about them, for there is not a single book in the world, not even the smallest pamphlet, that doesn't have its story — how many adventures its author, and the book itself, underwent in its making; and if we try to account for it all, we are not able.

S. Y. AGNON

Contents

Preface

The tradition of Hebrew writing on writing goes back at least some two and a half millennia to the biblical sigh of Ecclesiastes: "Of the making of books there is no end," says Kohelet (the Haranguer, as some commentators call him), who quickly follows with his signature refrain, "All is *hevel*." The King James version of the Bible, which most of us still hear, translates the term as *vanity;* but it has also been understood as indicating futility, vapor, bafflement, injustice, breath, and evanescence — definitions that point with equal precision to the practice of writing, as the work in this volume attests.

Comments on craft, advice for aspirants, meditations on purpose and vision, accounts of creation, epiphanic crystallizations in verse, release of steam — all emerge in the history of Hebrew writing on writing, even through the thickets of Talmud. Full-fledged reflection on the art, however, proliferates only with the renaissance of Hebrew literature in eleventh-century Muslim Spain. One of the giants of that period, Shmuel HaNagid, is a Hebrew writer writing on writing in Muslim Granada, though he can be heard today in Kalamazoo:

THE CRITIQUE

I'd pictured your poem like the king's daughter,
   a man's delight, a woman of pleasure;
or a burning fire set by the hearth —
   in its corners calamus, cassia, and myrrh.

And I found it exquisitely copied —
   all the vowels were precisely arrayed.

> In the past, I'd seen poems by your friends,
>   but they were obscure, while yours amazed.
>
> Your discourse flowed like the purest water
>   for ablution — but this new one's a stain.
> You've been for me like a precious son,
>   whose standards I'm obliged to maintain.
>
> So, hone your poems and their subjects,
>   and know that each in its way moves toward
> a day of judgment. And fear the critics,
>   whose tongues are polished and sharpened like swords.

Another of the period's major poets composes a full-length, idiosyncratic treatise on the art of poetry, touching, if only in passing, on the nature of talent and the importance of revision, the primacy of the ear and criteria for excellence, mediocrity's impact, the role of experience, advice for translators, and much more.

Like almost all the fully realized work in the history of Hebrew, the Andalusian poetry is fed by multiple sources. In this case the hybrid folds Arabic into a largely biblical Hebrew, as a rich and self-conscious tradition develops that will survive for over five hundred years — into Christian Spain and Provence — absorbing new influences wherever the spirit, the winds of history, and the trade routes take it: Italy, Turkey, North Africa, Iraq, Yemen, Palestine, the Balkans, and northern Europe.

Still other perspectives on writing come from the mystical tradition as it evolves in all these communities. Here, of course, the writer who matters most is fabricating on another level entirely: "The world," says the *Zohar,* or Book of Splendor, a thirteenth-century mystical compendium that many consider a kind of poetry, "was engraved and established with forty-two letters [those beginning the Book of Genesis]. . . . They were adorned with crowns in its four corners. . . . After this, the letters went out and created the world above and below, the world of unification and the world of separation, and these are the Song of Songs' mountains, the mountains of division" (II, 234a). "Language," writes Avraham Abulafia, the Iberian-Hebrew word-wizard and part-time poet (who held its, or his own, power in such high esteem that he thought he could convert the pope), "is a thing that brings to actuality what's imprinted in the soul *in potentia.*"

On the cusp of the modern era, Hebrew literature is again on the rise, this time in Italy, where it has been assimilating elements of the developing Western tradition since the twelfth century. (Hebrew was the first language other than Italian in which a sonnet was written, and there is at least one important Hebrew work in Dante's *terza rima*.) Driving this transition to the modern is a Paduan qabbalist, ethical writer, and poet, Moshe Haim Luzzatto (1707–47), who, thoroughly versed in Western learning, broke onto the local Hebrew scene at age seventeen with an accomplished work that reflects on the nature of the language and its employment. Essentially a Renaissance-style manual of rhetoric and poetics, *Leshon Limmudim* derives its name from Isaiah 50:4, which in itself constitutes another early Hebrew writer's comment on writing's ethos and purpose: "The Lord God hath given me the *tongue of them that are taught (leshon limmudim)*, that I should know how to sustain with words him that is weary." Luzzatto's goal with that volume was to train the writer, or speaker, to use words in a way that would please his listeners and prime their hearts to receive what is said.

Almost miraculously, given Judaism's reputation for divisiveness (two Jews, three synagogues, as the old joke has it), Luzzatto's work somehow endeared him to all three major and mutually antagonistic streams of emerging modern Jewish culture: the mystically inclined Hasidim related to his qabbalism; their archenemies, the rationalist Mitnaggedim, embraced his ethical work; and the nineteenth-century belletristic writers of the Haskala, or Jewish Enlightenment, considered him an illustrious forebear in their art.

These adherents of the Haskala looked to the values and models of the broader European Enlightenment — reason, good taste, and the rights of man — in their efforts to emancipate European Jewry from what they saw as its essentially stalled medieval worldview. Taking shape in the late eighteenth century and lasting until the early 1880s, the Haskala — initially in Germany, and soon in Galicia, Lithuania, other areas of the Russian Pale of Settlement, and elsewhere in western Europe as well — viewed Hebrew literature as a primary force of reform. Its purpose, in this scheme, was essentially didactic: to "enlighten" the communities of Europe's Jews. Paradoxically, the movement's spread in some ways limited its success, as the Haskala cultural program created such a powerful and assimilatory linguistic undertow that many of its students were swept *away* from Hebrew and into the complicated embrace of the

various local languages. The Lithuanian Yehuda Leib Gordon (1831–92), perhaps the Haskala's leading poet, asks in one of the more important poems of
the day just who he is serving, aware that by composing secular poetry for a
dwindling Hebrew readership, he is leaving behind not only the old world of
his pious parents — who thought of poetry as the path of death — but also the
world of his fellow reformers, who preferred absorption into German: "The
muse still makes her way to me, / and my heart still longs as my hand records /
these poems in a forgotten tongue. / What good does it do me, and what do I
seek, / for whom do I labor, these choice years, / depriving my soul of rest and
peace?" Gordon closes his 1871 cri de coeur by wondering if he might not be
"the last of the poets of Zion." He wasn't being hyperbolic: in 1797, fourteen
years after its founding, the movement's pioneering journal, *HaMe'assef*, had a
mere 120 subscribers, and *HaShahar*, where Gordon published regularly, had a
list that topped out at 700. (At their height, subscriptions to the leading
Hebrew weeklies of the day, which covered the news and therefore had more
popular appeal, rarely exceeded two thousand.)

The ultimate aesthetic value of the products of the Haskala is now a subject
of some dispute, and the long-held view of the Haskala's achievement as little
more than Starch-und-Drang is gradually being dismantled; all agree, however,
that the movement was a critical link in the chain of Hebrew, and that its synthetic ideal of a modern Hebrew humanism — where readers of the Gemara
would encounter Goethe — provided fertile ground for a major renascence
that was underway even before Gordon's death in 1892. With that modern
Hebrew revival (HaTehiyya), a new breeze enters the literature, and this
anthology begins.

One of the pivotal figures in the revival was Haim Nahman Bialik (1873–
1934), who would eventually come to be considered modern Hebrew's greatest
poet. In 1894, still seven years away from the publication of his first book of
poems, Bialik writes from a small town near Kiev (where he was working with
his father-in-law in the lumber business) to his new friend, Yehoshua Ravnitzky,
the editor of an Odessan journal that had begun publishing his work. He asks
Ravnitzky what he thinks about the verse of the day, which is to say, that of the
Haskala poets and particularly the romantic Hibbat Tzi'on (Love of Zion)
strain that had developed within that movement, and then he offers up his
own take on the contemporary poetry scene. Instead of the divine spark and

linguistic dexterity one wants in poetry, says Bialik, there is in the collective-minded work of these late Haskala writers "a spirit of vagueness and idle think-ing, of emptiness and vain musing that blossoms in the air of a hollow heart . . . apart from the lie and deceit conspicuous in all their poems, as they bewail the destruction of their people . . . and long for Zion. . . . The fraud of all these fine words is plain as day — and so, my fine soul has grown sick of them."

Bialik was working on ground that was gradually being cleared in an ideo-logical sense by essayists such as the imposing cultural Zionist and limpid Hebrew prose stylist Ahad Ha'Am ("We must liberate ourselves from the *inner* slavery, from the degradation of the spirit caused by assimilation") and his younger and distinctly Nietzschean rival, Micha Yosef Berdichevski, who, around the same time, noted that "the fundamental conditions . . . that have determined our existence to date have collapsed. . . . And the fear in our hearts is real, for we are . . . now facing a time in which two worlds are collid-ing: to be or no longer to be! To be the last of the Jews or the first of the new Hebrews." On the literary level, the pioneer work had been performed by writ-ers like Mendele Mokher Seforim — a precursor in both Yiddish and Hebrew fiction — and David Frischmann, who in many ways stands as the tutelary spirit of this anthology. Frischmann's name is rarely mentioned in the con-temporary Israeli cultural conversation, and his little-read work is not part of the prevailing (Zionist) narrative of Hebrew literature, but it is hardly less rel-evant for that difference. His independence from nationalist concerns, his maverick and finely calibrated sensibility, his deep-seated humanism, linguis-tic conscience, and flexibility within the language, along with his devotion to the possibility of what has been called a Hebrew Republic of Letters — all today are endangered values but call elegiacally from the work of this founding father.

By the late 1880s, as Frischmann neared his prime as a writer, editor, and translator, the Hebrew readership for belletristic writing had exploded. (Translation, it should be noted, played a major role in this literary renewal, with Frischmann leading the way: he and others brought into Hebrew a wide range of European, American, and Asian work, everything from Shakespeare, Byron, and Oscar Wilde to Homer, Heine, Tagore, and Longfellow's *Hiawatha*!) Astonishingly rich five- to eight-hundred-page literary journals and annual almanacs of tremendous vitality containing stories, poems, translations, essays, and scholarly articles by leading writers were regularly being published and selling many thousands of copies.

The presence of these journals was transformative. Writing much later in life, Bialik remembers discovering as a very young man back issues of two of the leading journals of the day in the attic of a neighbor's house and returning again and again to read through the stack of them: "The periodicals are not read . . . so much as licked, sucked, and drunk up thirstily till one becomes intoxicated with them. . . . It made no difference if the issue was long out of date. All the better — old wine. . . . In it I discovered the various flavors of the world."

The unique socioeconomic circumstances that led to that exponential growth of the audience for Hebrew literature did not, however, last for long, and by the turn of the century and into the middle of its first decade the pool of readers was rapidly drying up. In the wake of anti-Jewish pogroms, government censorship, and revolutionary fervor, numerous journals closed or suspended publication, and the incipient Hebrew Republic of Letters found itself threatened with extinction. The Hebrew writer was, at this point, struggling against the longest of social odds — writing in a language he did not, for the most part, speak, and losing his readership to assimilation and immigration alike. The high-modernist sophistication of the new literature didn't help matters, as it appealed only to the few.

This precarious cultural situation combined with the weight of Hebrew's past to create a nearly intolerable burden for Hebrew writers. Hebrew literature was now bound to existential questions that applied not only to the individual artist but to Hebraic and Judaic culture as a whole. The self-consciousness of the early Hebrew writers in particular was, therefore, acute, as they were working in an endangered and even suspect language, and one that would come for many to function as a kind of substitute homeland. Eventually the external crisis would pass, as new journals and publishers sprang up and old ones resumed publication (in Warsaw above all — where the Jewish community numbered, then, some 300,000, and constituted nearly 40 percent of the city's population — though also in Odessa, Vilna, Berlin, London, and Tel Aviv); the readership, however, remained quite small, and the tenuousness of the enterprise was keenly felt. "The essence of all this writing," said Gershon Shofman, now another forgotten writer, but for half a century a central figure, "is nothing but an exchange of letters between a few kindred spirits scattered across the face of the earth, most of whom don't know one another."

Soon, of course, they would know each other all too well, particularly as the literature moved away from Eastern Europe and began to take shape in the far more narrow confines of the Land of Israel — Ottoman and then British Mandatory Palestine, and eventually the State of Israel (whose greatest national product to date, in both quantity and significance, may be Hebrew sentences). The European base would continue to nourish Hebrew writing in Palestine and among a small group of Hebrew authors in the United States, up to and in some ways even through the Holocaust. For despite its Middle Eastern provenance, much of twentieth-century Hebrew poetry and prose can in a sense be considered a curious branch of European literature — as it takes up European modes almost exclusively. To be sure, there were occasional exceptions to that cultural orientation, among them the Palestinian Arab-Jew Yitzhaq Shami in the 1920s and '30s, and Iraqi-born-and-bred writers who moved from Arabic into Hebrew when they immigrated to Israel in the early years of statehood; and today Mizrahi (Eastern) writers are contributing in important ways to the reconfiguration of Hebrew's matrix. Adding to that remapping of the national imagination is the question of whether or not Hebrew writing need be "Jewish" at all, which was first taken up by the Warsaw-born "Canaanite," Yonatan Ratosh, in the 1930s. Some fifty years later the Palestinian Israeli novelist and translator Anton Shammas (b. 1950) looks at that option from a different angle.

Though Hebrew's writerly spirits are today less and less "kindred," Shofman's sense of the art as intimate exchange still holds true, and *Hebrew Writers on Writing* sets out to reflect that reality by letting these fifty-odd authors speak to, and about, each other. Throughout, this notion of connectedness informs the book, as one piece opens onto another, which turns out to be a response to a third, perhaps by a different author, who may be reacting in delayed fashion to a prod from an early mentor or teacher. As the anthology began to take shape, it developed a kind of unconscious, so that in addition to the conspicuous links between many of the pieces, subterranean ties (and tensions) across generations and aesthetic factions began to make themselves felt.

At the beginning of the twenty-first century, for instance, we find a poet of Iraqi descent, a religious woman steeped in Scripture and mystical texts

(Haviva Pedaya), adopting a position vis-à-vis Hebrew that calls to mind the stance taken up by the wild-eyed prophet of Jewish secularism, Russian-born Yosef Haim Brenner, who, writing ninety years earlier, notes that "the divine spark within us emerges only within [Hebrew's] flame" (and not that of Yiddish). How Israel's occupation of the Palestinian territories has affected its language is discussed by Aharon Shabtai and others, and aligns in chilling fashion with concerns expressed by Gershom Scholem, in a prescient letter from 1926. All this is touched on in novelist Shulamit Hareven's seminal essay, sounding Hebrew's distinctive qualities and virtues, and also its limitations. Along similar and curious lines, we see the ritual phylacteries of Jewish prayer transformed in Avraham Shlonsky's early work into a metaphor for the roads he is paving in Palestine (ca. 1920), before they wind up (literally) as a sexual aid, some fifty years later, in Yona Wallach's scandalous poem — which is hardly the response that Uri Zvi Greenberg envisioned when he called for the "untaming" of the Jew. As one might expect, nearly all these writers are concerned with the past and the nature of influence, but none is as eloquent — or at once steeply humble and proud — in limning its web as S. Y. Agnon, Hebrew's only Nobel laureate, in his very Jewish address before the Swedish Academy.

A word, then, on perspective. On the whole, the material for this anthology was gathered while Hebrew literature was, as it were, out posing for its official portrait. With its writers distracted, I felt free to rummage through what they'd left on their desks or in their files — notebooks, poems, stories, speeches, notes for talks, transcripts of interviews, letters drafted or just received (all literature, suggests one of these writers, quoting Rashi, the great biblical commentator, should be read like a letter that has just arrived) — in short, work that takes us into their world and opens onto the mystery of its creation. In making my final choices I have, for the most part, followed my nose, preferring the tactile to the theoretical, the intimate perspective to the view from on high. I've accounted for neither canon formation nor the growth of the nation; rather, to the extent I was able, I've tried to let the pieces and writers speak for themselves, regardless of the picture that the whole might — or might not — form. Throughout, vitality has been the principal consideration.

And so, for better and worse, I've chosen. One could easily imagine assembling a companion volume, with an entirely different set of selections by these same writers and many others whose work isn't included in this gathering: Mendele Mokher Seforim, Ahad Ha'Am, Y. L. Peretz, Berdichevski, Yehuda Burla, Shimon Halkin, Yocheved Bat-Miriam, Abba Kovner, Amalia Kahana Carmon, Amir Gilboa, Ozer Rabin, T. Carmi, Hanoch Levin, Yehoshua Sobol, Shimon Ballas, Dan Tsalka, Yoram Kaniuk, Yehoshua Kenaz, Batya Gur, Hezy Leskly, Yitzhaq Laor, Zali Gurevitch, Salman Masalha, Michal Govrin, Orly Castel-Bloom, Etgar Keret, and others whose work is clearly worthy.

Looking back over what I considered, and what finally ended up between these covers, I'm struck again and again by the tremendous potency and variety of Hebrew literature, but also by the fact that so little of what is richest about it is known beyond Israel's borders (wherever they are). It is my hope that this anthology will, in some small way, contribute to the broadening of our notion of what the language has done and might do, and that — politics and all — as one of the poems in this volume puts it, "Hebrew delivered will lick the walls of our heart."

Peter Cole
Jerusalem, March 2008

Acknowledgments

For their generosity and help in a variety of ways, thanks are due to Hana Amichai, Aminadav Dykman, Deborah Harris, Hannan Hever, Matti Huss, Dan Laor, Lee Maman, Matthew Miller, Moshe Ron, Robert Schine, Aryeh Tepper, Helit Yeshurun, Sassona Yovel, Noa Zilberstein, Azza Zvi, and to the translators who contributed to this volume. Special thanks to Gideon Nevo and, as always, to Gabriel Levin and Adina Hoffman.

Translators' names in what follows are identified by initials at the end of each selection. (A key appears at the back of the volume.) Unattributed translations of poetry and prose in the preface and biographical introductions to each entry are mine.

Previously published selections appear as in the work's original publication, except for obvious corrections and minor changes in punctuation and spelling to ensure uniformity of style throughout.

Throughout, ellipses in brackets [. . .] have been inserted to indicate omissions from the original texts or translations. When the excerpts are taken from volumes of letters and notebook entries, the brackets are inserted only *within* a given entry, and not between entries.

David Frischmann

(1859–1922)

A fierce critic and a pathbreaking editor, translator, poet, and writer of prose,
David Frischmann was one of the major bridging forces in the modern revival
of Hebrew literature as it emerged from the Haskala and the wan Romanticism of the late nineteenth century. Though deeply secular and not a Zionist,
he was passionately and, as it turns out, presciently concerned about the
developing shape of Jewish culture. "What is it, you ask?" he wrote in an
essay called "On Judaism." "We might subsume its entire essence in a single
word . . . the sense of *yosher* (decency, honesty, or integrity), or, better still,
an absence of the ability to do evil to one's fellow man. That is all."

Frischmann was born near Lodz and raised in that industrial center of
czarist Russia (now Poland). He subsequently lived in the major cities of Jewish
cultural activity at the turn of the century—Warsaw, Berlin, Saint Petersburg,
Moscow, and Odessa. His finest work was done as a writer of feuilletons, and
as an editor and translator. In the former he chronicled life as he knew it and
literature as he experienced it on his skin; his many translations greatly
widened the horizons of Hebrew, introducing into its matrix work by Tagore,
Nietzsche, Wilde, Byron, Heine, Shakespeare, Ibsen, and others. He was a
promulgator of no one school or line of thought: "His phrasing alone was a
kind of system and contained an entire worldview," noted Ya'aqov Fichman.

And after Frischmann's death in Berlin in 1922, Gershon Shofman wrote: "If there is still any hope for this literature . . . let there always rise to the fore in it the Frischmannian foundation, which is: Freedom of the spirit, superior refinement, flight from darkness in all its manifestations, and a deadly hatred for all that is not true."

Frischmann's moving 1913 essay about the prose writer Uri Nissan Gnessin (on whom see p. 37) offers not only a portrait of this singular author—drawn just after his death in Warsaw—but insight into the nature of writing and writers, generally, and our relation as readers to both.

For a portrait of Frischmann himself, during the last year of his life, see Ya'aqov Steinberg's "Three Who Would Console."

On U. N. Gnessin

The breeze outside was fresh, and the crowd behind his bier grew larger. The gathering was vast. Men and women, writers and readers, ordinary people. All had come. And no wonder: announcements had been posted noting the time of the funeral. And the breeze was so fresh. One man, a writer and editor, came up to me and muttered, asking: This dead writer — what, what exactly was he? . . . It's such a shame. He was so timid. And I felt the blood rushing to my face. I hadn't realized just how foreign he was to his readers, and even to many of his friends. But it doesn't matter. They've come to pay their last respects. Lord of the universe, if only they'd paid him some initial respect. . . .

I remember when I first saw him. A tall young man, somewhat disheveled, and a little shy. It would have been easier to extract a bar of gold from a mountain than to get a superfluous word from his mouth. There was nothing remarkable about him, neither great nor small. I was the editor of a journal — *HaDor* (The Generation) — and he had brought me a poem. The poem, too, wasn't especially distinguished. It was respectable enough, a well-written poem, like hundreds of others. It held no particular spark. I printed it. And then I printed another one, and another. And then he stopped bringing them. The poems vanished and so did the writer. I didn't see him again, and nearly forgot his name.

Time passed; circumstances changed. I was appointed editor of the monthly journal *HaZeman* (The Times) and received from the previous editor a large bundle of manuscripts. Among them was one called "Sideways." Since I'd decided to read the manuscripts in order, I took my time getting to it. Days went by, and then weeks. I began to wonder, Was it possible that I had buried treasure in my home and was keeping it from reaching its public? I will, though, never forget the moment I first encountered that story. Its diction was somewhat halting and heavy, and irritated me. Within a few moments, however, I was completely oblivious to — and ceased to be troubled by — these small annoyances. Once I had read some twenty lines I knew immediately that I was in the presence of not only a great and exceptional talent, but a marvelous human being. For here was a writer who was not "making" a story at all; there was nothing at all contrived about his writing. It betrayed not a hint of labor, and nothing in the way of a pose. He was writing from his heart — living and writing himself, with tears. And this, perhaps, is what talent really is, and so he was the most gifted among us. I can't say each word was a "gem." Certain phrases were already so hackneyed in our language that they left no impression. But I *can* say that each and every line of his was the beginning or climax of a lyric poem — and one that brought me near the truth. He had no notion of what it meant "to fake it," even in the best sense of the word, and writing was not the most important thing to him; it was secondary in his life, and everything he did was a kind of "occasional poem," in the truest sense of the word, as Goethe saw it. Each of his stories was just such a poem. And these occasions in him were constant, because he was a human being, and the man in him was in pain. I cannot really think of him as a "writer," as someone who could write of another person's life. And the fact is that every time Gnessin tried to write about the inner lives of others, he became a third- or even fourth-rate author, and this despite the fact that he had an extremely sharp eye, and saw and explored and absorbed so much. But anyone who has read his stories — "Sideways," and "Meanwhile," and "Before," and their like — will never forget them.

Their content? They had almost nothing in the way of content. Does a person have content? Does a life? His stories had neither beginning nor end.

Everything seemed to sway before us, rising and falling, rising and falling, now a thunderstorm and now pure skies, now a spark of light with some hope, and now an overcast day, with the heart hid in a cloud; it was all so maculate and heavy, so slow and empty and loathsome, as the heart, tortured and twisted, cried out from the intensity of its suffering — and then it would end. And all around was like a fog, or a dream — contingency. And so the titles he gave his books were fitting. Everything with him was done indirectly, or "sideways"; it was all only provisional, or "meanwhile." Everything was "before" or "beside." Just like life. "The fact of a thing in itself," in reality, does not exist, only another of his prepositions. . . . For we don't really live in fact, but in relation. . . .

Could a man like this have asked much more of life? He might well have given more, but not taken. Over the past few days he has been written about as someone who was naturally quiet. But I don't believe it. He was extremely proud: proud by nature. And people like that are reluctant to speak. A man like this knows from the outset "whom he will see and speak with and what a certain one will report and what another will have to say." And therefore, more often than not, he is silent. Moreover, he knows from the start that it's "reasonably clear just what his heart will tell him at the end of the night," and what will happen tomorrow, and the day after tomorrow, and later still, and to the end of the generations. And this is his great tragedy. Throughout his life he aspires to goodness, and greatness, and to what is sublime, and at the same time he despairs of ever reaching it. I know of no one like him in our literature, no one who dreamed as he did, and who at the same time despaired so completely. He dreamed — but he did not believe. . . .

A man like this was among us, and we barely knew him. He was just in his early thirties when he died.

APRIL 1913

[PC]

Avraham Kook

(1865–1935)

Avraham Kook was one of the major Jewish spiritual figures of the early
twentieth century. Born in Latvia, he received a traditional education in
Talmudic subjects but, driven by a strong sense of independence, he read
very widely on his own. He did not, however, turn his back on the world of
religion. On the contrary, from the late 1890s on, Kook served in a variety
of rabbinical capacities in Eastern European communities, and in 1904 he
emigrated to Palestine. Seventeen years later he became modern Palestine's
first Ashkenazi chief rabbi. In sharp distinction to other Orthodox Jews, whose
worldview was anti-Zionist, Kook saw the return to the Land of Israel as the
beginning of the divine redemption. He is, in this sense, the father of religious
Zionism, though that movement has gone in a very different direction since
its founder put forth his visionary and bridge-building platform.

Kook was a grounded mystic—a radical Teilhard de Chardin–like figure
whose mysticism combined the spiritual and the physical, and was based on
respect for both eloquent speech and that which lies beyond articulation.
Human creative energy, whether it took on the outward trappings of religion
or not, lay at the heart of his synthetic vision; it would, he believed, pave the
way to an evolving and universal perfection. The nation of Israel was to play
a crucial role in that evolution, and the writers of the Land of Israel—with
whom he corresponded on a variety of high-flown topics—were, as he saw it,

critical to the nation's utopian project. Kook wrote prolifically and lyrically
on a wide variety of metaphysical and political topics, and he was also a poet.
The short selections here—taken from several collections of his philosophical
reflections and spiritual diaries published in the 1920s and '30s—treat the
responsibility and experience of the writer in the transformation of society.
Kook's comments on the inevitable envy that writers feel for one another's
gifts and achievements are based on the Talmudic passage (in *Baba Bathra*
21a and 21b) which states that "the envy of scribes [*sofrim,* or writers]
increases wisdom."

THE WRITER'S SOUL

The literature of Israel cannot possibly flourish unless the souls of its writers are sanctified. Every writer who has not endeavored to refine his character, to purify his actions as well as his thoughts, so that his inner world might
be filled with light, and inner perfection be felt within him, along with desire
to make what is partial whole, and be filled with modesty blended with
courage — and serenity with an awakening of the heart and mind — every
such writer is obliged to better himself, to instruct himself, and to aspire to
stand at the noble height of purity and sanctification. So long as he does not
arrive at such a height, he cannot properly be called a *sofer* (a writer, or
scribe). Only the sages of old were called *sofrim* (pl.), because they would
count (*hayu sofrim*) the letters of the Torah [*Hagiga* 15b; *Qiddushin* 30a]. And
this counting of the Torah's letters raised them to a superior degree of purity
and greatness of spirit, so that the name *sofrim* suited them. And those who
would revive the literature of Israel must follow this sacred path, and come
to writing through sanctity: *And there will be a path and a way, and it shall be
called the way of holiness. . . . And there the redeemed shall walk* [Is. 35:8–9].

WRITER'S ENVY

Wisdom increased through the envy of writers is destined to lead to corruption, precisely because it was born of envy. And all corruption gives off a

stench, and this is the wisdom of writers, which will stink with the coming of the Messiah. By means of this stench its previous aspect will be erased, and the light of the soul of wisdom that is above all envy, above the wisdom of writers, will start to shine. This is a wisdom that will shine forth from a new song and a new name which the Lord will grant us. *And his beauty shall be like the olive tree's, and his fragrance like that of Lebanon* [Hos. 14:7].

On Knowledge and Originality

Insight attained on one's own — this is the highest degree of spiritual elevation. That which is acquired by study is, after all, taken in from outside, and pales in comparison with the thoughtful reflection in the depths of one's soul. All that is learned in such a manner is only a kind of profound advice concerning how best to draw the most essential significance from what is hidden within the heart, deep within the soul.

Knowledge streams forth continuously, creating and acting.

One who re-creates in supreme fashion does not renew, so much as he transfers, or translates, bringing new and vital light from an original place on high to a place where it has not been — from *a place no bird of prey has known, and on which the falcon's gaze has not fallen, and where no man has settled or passed.*

In the great revelation of self the faithful ear is formed, and the heart that is able to hear, which will not utter a word that has not been heard from its teacher, the prophets of truth and justice, in whose mouth God has placed the truth.

A Fourfold Song

There is one who sings the song of his soul, and in his soul finds all there is, and spiritual satisfaction in that fullness.

There is one who sings the song of his people, moving beyond the circle of the self, which he deems of insufficient breadth and unable to contain thought's ideal. In courage and strength he aspires to heights and holds through a love that is gentle to the congregation of Israel. With it he sings its songs and shares in its sorrow, and delights in its hope, reflecting in pure and sublime fashion on its past and its future, as he lovingly explores, with wisdom, the content of its inner spirit.

And there is one whose soul aspires further still, until it crosses Israel's border, and he sings the song of man. His spirit widens continually, to take in the majesty of man generally, and the glory of his image. He longs for knowledge that is universal, and awaits its sublime realization; and from this fountain of life he draws his thought and deepest reflection, his aspirations, his vision.

And there is one who would rise even farther, lifted until he is one with existence, with all creatures, and with all worlds, and with them all he sings. This is one who busies himself each day with a portion of song, and to whom a place is promised in the world to come.

And then there is he who ascends with all these others as one in a single chorus. All lend their voices, and all as one give pleasure with their song. Each lends another life and vitality, and the sounds of gladness and joy, of happiness and delight, of pleasure and that which is sacred.

The song of the single soul, the song of the people, the song of man, the song of the world — all within him, at all times and at every moment, are coming together.

And this completion, in its fullness, ascends to become a sacred song, a song of God, the song of Israel, in the fullness of its strength and splendor, its truth and greatness. The name Israel contains within it the song of God (*šir,* song; *el,* God), a simple song, a song that is doubled, threefold, and also fourfold. The song of songs, which is Solomon's (Shelomo), the king to whom the wholeness of peace — *shalom* — has come.

[PC]

Haim Nahman Bialik

(1873–1934)

Few poets in the history of Hebrew have possessed the fulcral power of Haim
Nahman Bialik. In a tradition that stretches back to the Bible and the great
Hebrew poetry of Spain, the middle ages East and West, Bialik stands out as
one of the literature's greatest figures, "a modern Isaiah," as one writer has
put it—though English translations of his poetry, it needs to be said, have
rarely done him justice.

   Born in 1873 in the Ukrainian village of Radi, Bialik soon moved with his
timberman turned tavern-keeper father to the nearby suburb of Zhitomir.
(In one poem Bialik recalls him studying sacred texts in the tavern while
"lushes swarmed around him, and drunks rolled in their vomit.") When he
was seven, his father died, and Bialik was sent off to live with his wealthy,
pious grandfather. At seventeen, he left home and entered the famous
Lithuanian yeshiva, or religious academy, of Volozhin (near Vilna). Like many
other students at that institution, he read Russian literature, but he also
began—secretly at first—to write poems in Hebrew. The publication of his
first poem in 1892 made him famous virtually overnight. In 1900 he took up
a post as a teacher and supervisor at a school in the vital Jewish center of
Odessa, on the Black Sea, where he worked under one of the most influential
Hebrew prose writers and thinkers of the day, and a man who had quietly
served as his mentor, Ahad Ha'Am.

9

Bialik soon became known as the central poet in the emerging revival of Hebrew literature. With his debut book of poems, which appeared in 1901, he was crowned by one of the leading critics of the day "the poet of the national renaissance." He also became a central figure on the cultural scene, playing a major role in supporting the Hebrew revival: he edited a succession of important literary journals, launched publishing ventures, and catalyzed what he called the "ingathering" of key works from the literary past—many of which he helped bring out in popular editions.

Known first and foremost for his singular poetry, which channels the tradition of Hebraic writing that runs through Jewish history (while also absorbing the foreign, especially Russian, influences that surrounded him), Bialik was also an important and gifted writer of prose. "Revealment and Concealment in Language," which was written in 1915 and published in Russia in 1917, has had perhaps the greatest impact on the generations that followed. In this essay, he ostensibly sets out to describe the difference between poetry and prose. His vision, however, quickly lifts this powerful, almost Laurentian essay onto a metaphysical and even spiritual plane, and over time the piece has acquired a kind of iconic status. Readers have seen in it everything from a universalizing symbolist statement about the nature of art and its ability to ward off the angst that underlies existence to a Russian-influenced quasi-linguistic treatise; from a personalizing and secular piece of Romantic theorizing to an esoteric and deeply Jewish mythopoetic qabbalistic work. In the latter scenario, the deep subject of the essay is understood to be the redemptive power of poetry constructed from the husks or shattered shells of fallen words. Its place in the Hebrew canon is such that an edition of it was recently published in Israel in which the essay was treated as tradition has dealt with sacred texts, locating Bialik's Hebrew in the center of the page, with commentary by a variety of writers proliferating around it.

The second essay printed here, "On the Dominion of the March," is cast in an entirely different mode and presents a somewhat stylized—albeit wholly grounded and tactile—depiction of the poetic sensibility at work. At

the same time it comprises a quiet act of resistance, giving voice to the poet's
concern for the fate of the individual in the wake of the Bolshevik revolution.
This surprising sketch by the poet was also published in 1917—after two years
during which Hebrew publications had been banned in Russia—and translated into Russian twice. (The translations were made between 1917 and 1918
and again in 1919—though only the latter was ever published. Bialik, it
should be noted, was the first Hebrew poet to be recognized in non-Jewish
Russian circles; Jabotinsky's translations of a selection of his poems went into
six printings and were praised highly by the likes of Gorky, Mayakovsky, and
Gumilev.) The sketch—some would say story—also demonstrates the degree
to which Bialik had heeded the call of, or simply lived up to the standards set
by, his mentor Ahad Ha'Am, who had criticized earlier generations of Hebrew
writers for ignoring the various historical registers of Hebrew in favor of a
biblical purity; that biblical purity, felt Ahad Ha'Am, was insufficient for the
flow of modern prose and the wide variety of situations it treats.

In 1921, with the new Soviet government again prohibiting the publication of work in Hebrew, Gorky interceded on behalf of a number of Jewish
writers, including Bialik, and asked the Soviet government to grant them
permission to emigrate. Bialik traveled initially to Berlin (where he founded
one of the most important Hebrew publishing houses of the day) and then
moved on to Tel Aviv, where he became a key personality in the development
of that city as the cultural capital of Hebrew-speaking Palestine. He wrote
little poetry after his move to the Middle East, primarily devoting himself to
his broader cultural activity. He died in 1934 while on a trip to Vienna. His
coffin was shipped back to Tel Aviv, where he was given a hero's funeral.

Revealment and Concealment in Language

Every day, consciously and unconsciously, human beings scatter heaps of
words to the wind, with all their various associations; few men indeed know

or consider what these words were like in the days when they were at the height of their power. Many of these words came into the world only after difficult and prolonged birth pangs endured by many generations. Others flashed like sudden lightning to illuminate, with one leap, a complete world. Many were paths through which living hosts passed, each leaving behind its shadow and aroma. There were words which served as receptacles for delicate and profound thoughts and exalted emotions. Some words were like the high mountains of the Lord, others were a great abyss. Sometimes all the vital essence of a profound philosophic system, its complete immortality, was hidden in one small word. There were words that laid low nations and lands in their time, deposed kings from their thrones, shook the foundations of heaven and earth. But there came a day when these same words, having fallen from their height, were thrown aside, and now people wallow in them as they chat, as casually as one wallows in grass.

Is this cause for wonder? The laws of nature are not to be questioned. That is the way of the world. Words rise to greatness, and, falling, turn profane. What is essential is that language contains no word so slight that the hour of its birth was not one of powerful and awesome self-revealment, a lofty victory of the spirit. So, for example, it was with the first man, when, taken aback by the sound of the thunder ("The voice [sound] of the Lord is in the power, the voice of the Lord is in the glory"), overcome by amazement and terror-stricken, he fell on his face before the divinity. Then a kind of savage sound burst spontaneously from his lips — let us assume, in imitation of nature — resembling a beast's roar, a sound close to the *r . . . r* to be found in the words for thunder in many languages. Did not this wild cry vastly free his confounded soul? Was a smaller measure of the power, the fearfulness, and the exultation of creative victory revealed in this echo of a spirit shaken to its depths than are revealed in the happy phrases on exalted subjects expressed by any of the great seers in moments of spiritual elevation? Did not this meager syllable, this seed of the future word, embrace a complete volume of primordial emotions, powerful in their novelty and vigorous in their savagery, resembling terror, fear, amazement, submission, astonishment, preparedness for self-defense? And if this was true, was not the first man himself at that moment an artist and lofty seer, an intuitive creator of an expression — and a very faithful expression, for himself, at any rate —

pointing to a deep and complicated inner disturbance? As one thinker has commented, how much of profound philosophy, of Divine revealment was there in that small word *I* that the first man uttered!

Nevertheless, at this very moment these same words, and a great many others like them, are being lost in language — and it does not matter. We are inwardly almost untouched. Their core is consumed and their spiritual strength fades or is hidden, and only their husks, cast out from the private domain to the public, still persist in language, doing slack service within the limited boundaries of logic and social intercourse, as external signs and abstractions for objects and images. It has come to the point where the human language has become two languages, built upon one another's destruction: one, an internal language, that of solitude and the soul, in which what is essential is "how?" as in music — the domain of poetry; the other, the external language, that of abstraction and generalization, in which the essential is "what?" as in mathematics — the domain of logic.

Who knows whether it is not for the best that man should inherit the husk of a word without its core — for thus he can fill the husk, or supply it constantly from his own substance, and pour his inner light into it. "Every man prefers his own measure." If the spoken word were to remain throughout history at the height of its glowing power, if the same complex of emotion and thought which became attached to it in its prime were to accompany it always, perhaps no speaking creature would ever attain to its self-revealment and particular illumination. In the final analysis, an empty vessel can hold matter, while a full vessel cannot; if the empty word enslaves, how much more is this true of the full word?

What is there to wonder at? This: the feeling of security and the satisfaction that accrue to human beings when they speak, as though they are really leading their thoughts or feelings beside the still waters and across the iron bridge of the Messiah, without their having any conception of how shaky is their bridge of mere words, how deep and dark the void is that opens at their feet, and how much every step taken safely partakes of the miraculous.

For it is clear that language with all its associations does not introduce us at all into the inner area, the essence of things, but that, on the contrary, language itself stands as a barrier before them. On the other side of the barrier of language, behind its curtain, stripped of its husk of speech, the spirit of man wanders ceaselessly. "There is no speech and there are no words," but only a perpetual search, an eternal "what?" frozen on man's lips. In truth, there is no place even for this "what?", implying as it does the hope of a reply. Rather there is — "nothingness"; man's lips are closed. If, nevertheless, man does achieve speech and with it contentment, it is only because of the extent of his fear at remaining alone for one moment with that dark "void," face to face with the "nothingness," with no barrier between them. "For man shall not look on me and live," says the void, and every speech, every pulsation of speech, partakes of the nature of a concealment of "nothingness," a husk enclosing within itself a dark seed of the eternal enigma. *No word contains the complete dissolution of any question.* What does it contain? *The question's conceal-ment.* It makes no difference *what* the particular word is — you can exchange it for another — just so long as it contains the power momentarily to serve as concealment and barrier. Dumb music and symbolic mathematics — two hostile kin at two parallel extremes — attest unanimously that the word is not necessarily what it seems, that it is nothing but web and woof of the void. Or rather, just as physical bodies become sensible to the eye and determinate by virtue of the fact that they serve as barriers before light in space, so the word's existence takes place by virtue of the process by which it closes up the small aperture of the void, constructing a barrier to prevent the void's darkness from welling up and overflowing its bounds.

He who sits alone in the depths of darkness, trembling, speaks to himself: he confesses his sins, or whispers a word. Why? *Because the word is a talisman which serves to divert him and to dissipate his fear.* It is the same with the spoken word — or with complete systems of words. The word's power does not con-sist in its explicit content — if, generally speaking, there is such a thing — but in the diversion that is involved in it.

Averting one's eyes is, in the final resort, the easiest and most pleasant means, although an illusory one, of escape from danger; in situations where keeping one's eyes open constitutes the danger there is really no securer refuge, and "Moses did well to conceal his face."

Who knows? Perhaps the truth is that from the time of Creation, speech has not been cast as a social vessel to pass between two men, i.e., it has not been speech for its own sake. It may have always had its source in men sitting alone, speaking to themselves, as a spiritual need, i.e., "speech for its own sake" falling in the class of "When my spirit within me is dumb, I shall speak unto my heart. . . ." The first man was not content until he had spoken *himself* aloud for himself to hear. For the sound that at the time of creation drew man's self-recognition up from the depths of the void — that very sound suddenly stood as a dividing wall between man and that which is on the other side, as though to say: "Henceforth, O man, thou shalt direct thy face toward that which is 'on this side.' Thou shalt not look *behind* thee, and if thou shouldst — it shall not avail thee, for man shall not see the 'void' face to face and live. The dream that is forgotten shall not be recalled. Thy desire shall be to the 'void' and speech shall rule over thee."

And, in truth, "knowledge and speech" rule only over that which is on this side, within the four cubits of space and time. "Man walketh in the shadow merely"; the nearer he approaches the illusory light *that is before him,* the larger grows the shadow *behind him,* and the surrounding darkness is never lessened. Perhaps, on this side, everything can be explained — strictly or liberally, but explained. What is essential is that man's atmosphere of knowledge must never for a single moment be rid of words, crowded and consecutive like the links in a suit of armor, without so much as a hair's breadth between them. The light of knowledge and speech — the glowing coal and the flame — is an eternal light that must not be extinguished. Indeed, the very area on this side that lies within the bounds of the illusory light — in the final analysis, of what importance is it compared with the endless sea of universal darkness that still remains, and will always remain, *outside*?

And again, in the final analysis, it is that very eternal darkness that is so fearsome — that darkness that from the time of Creation has always secretly drawn man's heart to it, arousing his hidden yearning to gaze on it for a brief moment. Every man is afraid of it, and every man is drawn to it. With our very lips we construct barriers, words upon words and systems upon systems, and place them in front of the darkness to conceal it; but then our nails immediately begin to dig at those barriers, in an attempt to open the smallest of windows, the tiniest of cracks, through which we may gaze for a single moment at that which is on the other side. But alas, vain is the labor of man! At the very moment when the crack is apparently opened — another barrier, in the shape of a new word or system, suddenly stands in the place of the old, shutting off the view again.

Thus, there is never an end. A word cometh and a word goeth, a system riseth and a system falleth — and the old eternal enigma remains as powerful as ever, unalterable and irreducible. Signing a note, or listing a debt in a ledger, is far from being the debt's liquidation; it merely momentarily removes the note's burden from one's memory — and no more. The same is the case with definitive speech: the assignment of names and the putting up of orderly fences around images and their associations. No reply to the question of essence is ever possible in the process of speech. Even the express reply to a question is really no more than another version of the question itself — "this is amazing" we understand as meaning "pause and think" (a form of concealment instead of revealment). If we were to strip all the words and systems completely bare to their innermost core, in the end, *after the last reduction,* we should be left with nothing but one all-inclusive word. Which? Again, the same terrible "what?" behind which stands the same X, even more terrible — the nothingness. Man chooses to tear the debt into small pieces under the false illusion that he is thus easing the final payment. When this illusion fails him, he exchanges the present word for another, the present system for another — he writes a new note to take the place of the old, and delays or gives himself more time for the final payment. In either event the debt is never paid in full.

So, a word or system declines and yields to another, not because it has lost the power to reveal, to enlighten, to invalidate the enigma, either totally or in part, but for the very opposite reason — because the word or system has been worn out by being manipulated and used, it is no longer able to conceal and hide adequately, and can, of course, no longer divert mankind momentarily. Man, gazing for a moment through the open crack, finding to his terror that awesome void before him again, hurries to close the crack for a time — with a new word. That is to say, he seizes the new talisman, like its predecessor; a proven momentary diversion — and is saved from the terror.

Do not wonder at this! The talisman is effective for those who believe in it, for faith itself is no more than a diversion. Do not the speaking creatures themselves provide an analogy? So long as man moves and breathes — he occupies space and everything is apparently comprehensible; "everything is all right." All the flow of life, all its content, is nothing but a continuous effort, an unremitting toil to be diverted. Every moment spent in "pursuit of" is at the same time a "flight from," and flight, and flight alone, is its wages. The wages of pursuit is flight. At every moment the pursuer finds his momentary happiness not in that which he attains to, but in that which he escapes from, a fact which gives him a momentary shadow of security. "For to him that is joined to all the living there is security."

But man dies — and his space becomes unoccupied. There is nothing to serve as a diversion — and the barrier is down. Everything suddenly becomes incomprehensible. The hidden X descends upon us in all its fearful shape — and we sit mourning on the earth before it for a moment in darkness and dumb as a stone. But for a moment only. For the Master of all life anticipates the opening with a closing. He immediately furnishes us with a new talisman with which to divert ourselves and dissipate the fear. Before the covering stone is sealed over the dead, the space that was emptied is again occupied with a word, whether it be one of eulogy, or solace, or philosophy, or belief in the soul's immortality, or the like. The most dangerous moment — both in speech and in life — is that between concealments, when the void looms. But such moments are rare both in speech and in life, and for the most part men skip over them unawares. "The Lord preserveth the simple."

From all that has been said, it would appear that there is a vast difference between the language of the masters of prose and that of the masters of poetry. The former, the masters of exposition, find their sanction in the principle of analogy, and in the elements common to images and words, in what is established and constant in language, in the accepted version of things — consequently, they walk confidently through language. To what may they be compared? To one who crosses a river walking on hard ice frozen into a solid block. Such a man may and can divert his attention completely from the covered depths flowing underneath his feet. But their opposites, the masters of allegory, of interpretation and mystery, spend all their days in pursuit of the unifying principle in things, of the solitary something, of the point that makes one body of all the images, of the fleeting moment that is never repeated. They pursue their solitary inwardness and the personal quality of things. Therefore, the latter, the masters of poetry (the allegorists), are forced to flee all that is fixed and inert in language, all that is opposed to their goal of the vital and mobile in language. On the contrary, using their unique keys, they are obliged themselves to introduce into language at every opportunity — never-ending motion, new combinations and associations. The words writhe in their hands; they are extinguished and lit again, flash on and off like the engravings of the signet in the stones of the High Priest's breastplate, grow empty and become full, put off a soul and put on a soul. By this process there takes place, in the material of language, exchanges of posts and locations: one mark, a change in the point of one iota, and the old word shines with a new light.

The profane turns sacred, and the sacred profane. Long-established words are constantly being pulled out of their settings, as it were, and exchanging places with one another. Meanwhile, between concealments the void looms. And that is the secret of the great influence of the language of poetry. And to what may those writers be compared? To one who crosses a river when it is breaking up, by stepping across floating, moving blocks of ice. He dare not set his foot on any one block for longer than a moment, longer than it takes him to leap from one block to the next, and so on. Between the breaches the void looms, the foot slips, danger is close. . . .

Nevertheless, some of this group, too, "enter in peace and leave in peace," crossing in safety from one shore to the other, "for the Lord preserveth not merely the simple."

So much for the language of words. But, in addition, "there are yet to the Lord" languages without words: song, tears, and laughter. And the speaking creature has been found worthy of them all. These languages begin where words leave off, and their purpose is not to close but to open. They rise up from the void. They *are* the rising up of the void. Therefore, at times they overflow and sweep us off in the irresistible multitude of their waves; therefore, at times they cost a man his wits, or even his life. Every creation of the spirit which lacks an echo of one of these three languages is not really alive, and it were best that it had never come into the world.

[JS]

On the Dominion of the March

All morning long words of a poem pulsed through me. For nearly half an hour now I have been sitting at my worktable, the pen trembling between my fingers — and the page before me is still entirely white. I have not yet determined what image to cast my heart's thought in, what meter I should give it. The rhymes, granted, are running toward me in pairs of their own volition, ready and willing to harness themselves to my "chariot," but the measure is not right. They're kicking — one pair leaps as an amphibrach, and another dances before it in dactyls.

"Isn't this," I said to myself, speaking from experience, "a clear sign that twins are stirring within you? And if so, perhaps it's best that I, and they, linger a bit before beginning to write. Poetry requires a clear head."

Putting my pen down, I got up and moved to a chair by the open window. I sat there smoking, and looking outside.

It was an ordinary summer day, a workday — just before noon. An hour at which the morning's bustle is no longer, though the evening's fatigue has yet to set in. The sun, as it does, continued to rise, and the air was soft and clean. Gates and doors and windows were open throughout the neighborhood, and people and tools, indoors and out, stood exposed to the eye in the middle of their day, each in its place fulfilling its task and lending its share to the neighborhood's atmosphere, its sounds and sights and motion, as movements slight and less slight made their impression on the air, each one in its way.

Behind the open window in the woodshop — a bare-armed carpenter is pushing and pulling his plane, which with every stroke and lunge gives off a sound like that of a dog with a cold sneezing, casting curled white shavings to the ground.

One building over, behind another window, a tailor is bent over his clattering sewing machine, which pecks ceaselessly at its own body, piercing hole after hole with its needle.

In one of the courtyards a large saw bitterly wails, as though *it* were being sliced into pieces, and not the plank beneath it.

Peddlers and street vendors send up their odd cries in the air — some pleading, others in rhyme, still others with a wit that cuts both ways.

In the darkness of the blacksmith's shop, on the right side of the street, twice-striking hammers compete with each other against the anvils with their bold and heavy blows, which fall into the street with a thud, like iron balls.

Behind a certain wall, coughs and groans emerge from the rickety rise and fall of scales being played on a broken piano. . . .

All was as the day before, and the day before that. People and tools were going over, for the thousandth time, like slow students in the local house of study, an ancient and venerable text, and one they've long known well. And, nonetheless, whoever looked closely would find that each and every one of them had his own verse in the text of the day, a verse that was his and his alone, one he was fond of and also fed up with, at once, and which he would in no way exchange for another. It was his, entirely, every ascender of every letter, and the specks above and beneath them, and the accents with which it was chanted.

"Aren't these people, in a way, also poets, each with a distinctive character of a sort, at least in the familiar sense? Even if only a hair's breadth. After all, it's impossible for people in the world not to have a 'melody' that's theirs, the particular rhythm of a given soul, that which makes a man different from his friends, even in the sound of his footsteps. . . ."

I was still turning the matter over in my mind — when, suddenly, a military band, its brass instruments sparkling, began coming down one of the streets, children running before and behind it, the blare of a joyful, exuberant march, with its broad echo and tumult bursting forth. The trumpets rang out full-voiced from their brass throats, and the drums and cymbals followed thunderously.

Into the ordinary weekday neighborhood air there suddenly poured streams of bold and powerful song, which flowed with force from the wide, glistening mouths of the brass tubes and filled it with a festive, holiday mood.

The band had not reached the middle of the neighborhood, but the sounds of the march were flooding its every nook and cranny, its courtyard and homes, and the air around them, reaching everywhere. Everything was swept up in the tumult of its waves, and nothing stood in the way.

Men, women, and children leapt up and went to the doors and the gates, craftsmen and workers crowded together, sticking their heads and torsos out of the windows, working their way to a view, like snakes slithering out of their holes, mouths open wide as they thirstily drank in the air of the clear, loud, and rhythmic lines of the song, which were repeated several times, and each time with renewed vigor and splendor.

In just another moment, as I was watching, the entire neighborhood and all that filled it — consciously or not — had joined in the chorus:

The prominent landlord, walking down the sidewalk before me, he, and also another behind him, and a third, and a fourth too — all were stepping to the rhythm of the march.

And soon the saw and the sneezing plane, and the sewing machine and its clatter, the hammer striking the anvil — all were driven by the rhythm of the march.

And just a moment later, the merchants and vendors calling out over their wares — they too were responding to the march. And the maid stirring her pot in the kitchen, and the servant in the courtyard beating rugs and bed-spreads, and the mother in the children's room rocking the crib, and the old woman by the gate on a bench, darning socks and clicking her needles — each kept time with the march's rhythm.

Even the horses' gallop, it seemed, and the wagons' rumble were set to the rhythm of the march.

And now I was certain, the watches in these people's pockets, and the hearts in their chests, were secretly ticking and beating to the rhythm of the march!

All the neighborhood voices and sounds suddenly came together in the march, turning into a single chorus.

What a herd! In my heart I grew annoyed at these people about whom only a moment ago I'd been mistaken. It took no more than the thunder of a single march, coming across them with its power, to wipe their uniqueness out in a flash. A military tune had been played loudly and passed by — and where now was the song of their souls, the particular touch of their own rhythms, that which was theirs and theirs alone? Nothing was left of it, not a trace! The band's power had swallowed them all, as a whale gulps down the smallest fish. From now on, I was sure, that march would have dominion, and reign supreme all day, and perhaps for many days, in the neighborhood, and there would be no refuge from it.

"No!" I said to myself in conclusion, "these people are no better than the beasts of the field. True character, that which does not surrender, and which is not swallowed up, and cannot be diminished by hordes, the unique and sole legacy, the divine share from God on high, belongs to poets alone."

A moment later, after I'd returned to my desk, my spirit suddenly rose. And within a secret pleasure — which was, in truth, not entirely free of pride, in that (as the prayer has it) "my portion did not resemble theirs, and my fate was not like that of the nations" — there descended upon me, it seemed, the divine presence; and that share from God on high was suddenly revealed within me in all its power. The rhymes rolled out beneath my pen, like lentils, and all were lively and fresh and radiant, as though they were straight from the Muse's hand.

Blessed be the Lord of Poetry! My heart's stirrings at last had found their singular and natural form. . . .

But imagine my amazement, as I cast my eye across what I'd written — and behold, nothing remained of either the dactyls or the amphibrachs. It was all of a single measure — immaculate trochees, just like the rhythm of the march.

[PC]

Sha'ul Tchernichowsky

(1875–1943)

Sha'ul Tchernichowsky was in many ways the great outsider poet of the
modern Hebrew revival. Though deeply concerned about Jewish life and
the fate of the Jews, his verse is rooted in the Hellenistic and European
tradition; he also translated widely from world literature (often from an
intermediary language), opening Hebrew's gates to pagan poetry in various
guises and becoming what one critic has called an almost mystical medium
for the vital and foreign. Among the results of that openness are strong
Hebrew versions of *The Iliad* and *The Odyssey, Gilgamesh,* Plato's *Symposium,*
the Finnish *Kalevala,* and work by Anacreon, Goethe, Shakespeare, and
many others.

Born in the rural village of Mikhailovka, in a by no means exclusively
Jewish region of the southern Ukraine, Tchernichowsky was raised in the
home of pious parents who were nonetheless open to the modernizing
influences of contemporary Jewish cultural movements. His education was
broad, covering both Hebrew and secular subjects, and as a young man
Tchernichowsky took a special interest in European languages. He studied
medicine in Germany and in Switzerland, and throughout his adult life
scraped together a living as a doctor, largely in rural communities, but also
in St. Petersburg during World War I and after, when he worked for the Red
Cross. In 1922 he left Soviet Russia with the wave of Jewish émigré writers

whose exit had been arranged by Gorky. He settled in Germany, where he lived for the next nine years (with his Russian Orthodox Christian wife), and in 1931 he received a commission to edit an encyclopedia of medical terms in Hebrew, Latin, and English, which enabled him to settle in Tel Aviv. His ten-volume complete works were published between 1929 and 1932.

In addition to a deep connection to the natural landscape and a heroic and nearly pantheistic worldview, Tchernichowsky took from his immersion in Greek literature, and world literature generally, a profound feeling for myth, form, and classical structure. He introduced a number of Greek meters and genres into Hebrew and made extensive use of motifs from a variety of ancient cultures. Among his best-known poems are his idylls of Jewish life in the Ukraine (one, in dactylic hexameters, is called "Dumplings," another "Circumcision"), a concatenated cycle of sonnets to the sun, and the emblematic "Before the Statue of Apollo," all of which effect a unique synthesis of Hellenistic and Hebraic or proto-Judaic impulses. That synthesis would go on to have a sustained impact on the emerging literature.

"In Place of a Letter" was written on July 25, 1906, to Tchernichowsky's old friend and one of the leading Hebrew critics and scholars of the day, the Revisionist Yosef Klausner, who had taken the poet to task for "passing virtually in silence over the pogrom in Kishinev and, moreover, remaining completely silent after the awful slaughter of October 1905"—despite the fact that over a thousand Jews were killed and some forty thousand homes destroyed in those events. Tchernichowksy's silence is all the more striking when contrasted with the outrage that courses through Bialik's corre-spondence and his "poems of wrath" treating the same occurrences. The horrors of the day notwithstanding, Tchernichowsky turns his response to Klausner into a defiant poetic creed in which he puts forth his distinctly Nietzschean view of "writing as victory." The letter, Klausner later wrote, "might serve as commentary" to all of Tchernichowsky's work as a poet.

In Place of a Letter

My dear Yosef,

I am not going to write you a letter. What I will write is in place of a letter and in place of letters that were not written, and which wanted to be written, and which should have been written.

But on one condition: that this matter will never be mentioned or touched upon when you come to speak to me face to face.

You want to know what I write and why I don't write, and so on and so forth. Perhaps it's best if I begin, as they say, "in the beginning," and clarify, first of all, why I write.

I write because I'm alive, because I feel at a given moment the song of life. And if you find a poem of mine that was written and signed in a certain place and at a certain time — know that at that moment and in that place I felt the song of life.

Life itself, as we find it embodied before us everywhere, is filled with shame and filth to the point of suffocation. But the content of life, its essence, and mystery — is poetry, the most sublime song of songs there is or might be.

And this is not just any poetry, or song, but a song of victory. The victory of matter over chaos, of being over nothingness, of life over death.

The universe — eternity — the infinite — all are death, while all that is embodied in matter, all that takes on form and is real, is a victory of the moment, but also a victory of life over death.

And each one of us, everything that is alive, is tantamount to a poem, or when he senses that poem — to a poet. And the truth of the matter is that we must all be poets of life, poets of victory, upholding the song of the victors. But the mire of the world, the poverty and the strain, make us forget and drown the soul in a sea of refuse and malice and cruelty and foulness of every sort.

Therefore, there are in the world victors and those who are vanquished. And since the victory is that of a given moment, and is not something that will last, and since existence is death, so the vanquished comprise the greater part of the world.

The vanquished outnumber the victors in the world of individuals, in the world of society, and in the world of poets.

Why are some people destined to one fate and others to another?

I take up the song of the victors. And as a victor, I want to make my way in the world.

But the Jew makes his way in the world and takes up the song of the vanquished.

Wherever you find a sign or trace of the Romans — upon the Romanian plains, in the Rhine Valley, along the rivers of Switzerland — there is a mark of Roman victory, the victory of those who came to subdue.

And wherever you find so much as a hint or indication of Jewish settlement, you will find a faithful sign of defeat and subjugation: the persecuted forced to wander to that place by a decree of history.

And so, by birth I was destined to take up the song of the vanquished.

But the Jew in me, too, would take up the song of the victor.

The days of Kishinev, however, are an affront to the Jew in me.

And I — that sum total I refer to as "I" — take up the song of the victors. And each and every poem of mine, written and signed in a certain place and at a certain time — bears witness: in that place, and at that time, I was among the victors.

And I have still one other quality:

I have pride. And because of that pride I will not tell of my victory. Let alone of my defeat.

And so I know nothing of the song of the vanquished. My downfall is a sign of my weakness.

And if you find a poem of mine, and it too is among the songs of the vanquished, let this be a sign that I defeated it as well.

However, when I am truly vanquished — I have no song. For the vanquished have no poetry — apart from the dirge.

And when you come to ask why I go on, I will answer: Because I still believe in my victory-to-come, and believe that in whatever place I have been as one who was vanquished, I will return, and march across it victorious.

[PC]

Devora Baron

(1877–1956)

"She brings things together," said Ya'aqov Steinberg, "with the lightest
touch and without the slightest indication of effort, as though with eyes
half shut she were weaving through the force of an age-old heritage." That
heritage was, by and large, the one reflected in the world of the Lithuanian
shtetl, and not the Land of Israel—and this despite the fact that Devora Baron
was deeply committed to Zionism and emigrated from Belorussia to Palestine
at the age of twenty-three. For whatever reason, Baron returned in her
work again and again to the matrix of her Lithuanian childhood and the
home where she had been raised by her rabbi father, who was regularly
called on by the community's needy for advice and support. Family, an
unusual knowledge of traditional sources (for a Jewish woman at the time),
and empathy for the less fortunate were conspicuous in her work, which
has been described as nineteenth-century in style. In addition to her own
fiction, she translated work by Flaubert, Chekhov, and Jack London, among
many others.

Baron began placing her stories in European Hebrew periodicals while still in her twenties, though her first collection didn't appear until she was forty. All told she published some thirteen volumes of stories and novellas. Her husband, a prominent Labor leader, edited *HaPo'el HaTza'ir* (The Young Worker—arguably Ottoman Palestine's most important Hebrew journal), for which Baron served as the literary editor. During World War I she lived in Egypt, where she may have contracted the mysterious disease that would leave her bedridden for some thirty years.

The aphorisms that follow are drawn from a collection titled *By the Way* and were recorded by Baron's daughter.

FROM *BY THE WAY*

Writing a story is like building a house. When a person lays the foundation and erects the walls, he may think the work is done. This isn't the case, as the essential part of the labor involves applying the finishing touches — determining the colors of the walls and floor tiles that will match them, the doors and windowpanes, the distance between them, and so on — for if those elements aren't handled well, what worth will the house have as a whole? And the finer the home-owner's taste — the more he aspires to perfection, and isn't content with the result. So it is with the writer. Once he has sketched out his work, he thinks that the principal effort has been accomplished, and so he feels proud; the dissatisfaction and irritation come later, when he starts revising and perfecting what he's written.

Writing a short story is like building a house. Writing a novel is like building a city.

About a certain Hebrew writer:
His writing is like the waters of a muddied spring. When you look into them as they flow, you can't really tell anything about them. However, if

you put a bit of that water into a clear dish, then you see how muddy and foul it is. So with this writer's writing — if you read his stories and essays you sense none of this; only when you read an extract or quotation, then you understand their true nature.

When the novelist writes, he doesn't necessarily have something in mind with each little thing; he writes as the spirit moves him to. Later the critics come with their heaps of interpretations and explanations. The writer — they say — meant to prove X, the writer meant to prove Y, etc., each critic in his own way, and according to his own understanding.

The writer cannot always burn with the holy-fire in his heart, though he should write only when that fire is blazing within him; for only then will his writing reveal his true talents and qualities.

It's better to wear clumsy and ugly shoes than to walk barefoot; but it's better to refrain from reading a book and listening to music altogether than to read an inferior book or listen to bad music.

The power of the great writer is, as it were, the power of God (the Holy one blessed be He) — to breathe living spirit into inanimate matter, for the writer takes a personality and makes him a "type" in his book. The prototype passes out of the world, while the type lives on forever.

Sustain me with books, refresh me with dictionaries, for I am in the throes of translation . . . [while translating Flaubert's *Madame Bovary*].

What is a good story? When you read it, you feel that you have to linger a while after each and every clause, as with sipping a vintage wine, and when you finish reading, as when you finish drinking, you feel yourself slightly intoxicated.

They (Hebrew literature's "young guard") don't know the art of condensing, nor do they understand that more is sometimes less; they heap descriptions and empty verbiage on top of what matters, until one can't see the forest for the trees.

The exquisite poetry of the Song of Songs has been so used and imitated over the years by talented and talentless poets that when we come to read the biblical text itself today, its words seem banal, and we can no longer feel their true impact.

The poet must see just the shell of things, their external aspects, and not expose what lies within them, their content — meaning the body and not the soul. For example, the poet shouldn't act like a doctor and dig around in a person's intestines or his spinal cord, and so forth. He should see the person's body as it appears outwardly — in all its beauty and glory, in its perfection.

[RTB]

Gershon Shofman

(1880–1972)

The first modern writer of Hebrew prose whose style was determined by
modernist notions of function alone, with nearly all trappings and traces
of inherited expression having been stripped away, Gershon Shofman was
a master of the epigrammatic essay and the fictional miniature. In their
utter lucidity, ruthless accuracy, and compression, his sentences, said Ya'aqov
Fichman, resemble scientific definitions. As Fichman saw it, there was a kind
of moral vigilance behind Shofman's ability to resist the more conventionally
lyrical temptations of language, and the style produced by that resistance
and vigilance resembles that of the Bible in its ability to subsume what has
been omitted under the shape of the little that does get said. He possessed,
wrote Fichman, the power of the Jewish poet, who looks long at the world
and then gives succinct expression to what he has seen, allowing a thousand
things to go by unremarked upon, in order to trap the thousand and first,
which under his gaze is seen to contain the entire world. Little wonder, then,
that Shofman's work is rarely mentioned in the garrulous culture of early
twenty-first-century Hebrew.

Shofman was born and raised in Belorussia, received a traditional religious education, and read widely in Russian and Hebrew literature. His first
volume of stories was published in 1902—the same year in which he enlisted

in the Russian army—and two years later he fled to Galicia (Poland), where he stayed for nearly a decade before moving to Vienna and later to an Austrian village. His collected writings appeared in four volumes between 1927 and 1935. Shofman emigrated to Palestine at the age of fifty-eight, eventually settling in Haifa, where he lived until his death.

A New Word

*The thing people most fear
is a new word of their own. . . .*
— DOSTOEVSKY

The writer had sensed it even as the lines were still being formed: this word was likely to make things difficult for him. He felt it vaguely. And only now, late at night, the night before his article was due out in the morning paper, did it occur to him: "What have I done?! . . ."

There was in this word something obstinate; something that crossed the line of what was acceptable. This rebellious word was likely to annoy his readership. How did he let it get away?

What could he do? Why was he always, always catching his awful slips of the pen after the fact, when it was too late to do anything about them? Tonight, he already knew, he would get no sleep.

But maybe, just maybe, it might still be possible to do something about it? He dressed and ran to the printer's. It was midnight. Maybe? He went in and gazed at the manager, as though at someone who held life and death in his hands. He turned to him, like a supplicant:

Would it still be possible to substitute one word for another?

No. The page is already set. It's impossible.

Isn't there some way that . . . ?

The only thing I can do for you — is to scratch out the word.

It was done. And the writer, calmer now, went home and slept soundly.

Coward! For once in your life you set down a new word, a word of your own — and now you've erased it!

You Won't Find It!

On the subject of writing you won't find anything satisfying among the critics and writers of "essays." For even the best of these are, in the end, outside, groping in the dark. But the poets too, and the great poets, those with sharp minds as well, when it comes to speaking about the nature of poetry and creation, do not say what needs to be said. With the former, it's because they don't know what it is, and with the latter — because they don't want to speak of it, and can't, on account of a certain instinct in them that keeps them from revealing their secret. . . . In his book *What Is Art?,* Tolstoy talks about everything you could possibly want, but not about art itself. About this and that, but round and round the heart of the matter. After all, even in the essays of the poets themselves, you won't find what you're looking for.

For the Elders Have Died

The writer in his youth, with his first steps, is reluctant to accentuate his "I" and prefers to appear in the third person. There is here, apart from the ordinary failings of the young, a measure of attractive modesty — of not presuming to instruct his teachers, the famous writers, who are also more advanced in years — a kind of bashfulness and fear of appearing superior before the elders.

Only with time does his confidence grow. Then he won't be ashamed to speak in his own name, in the first person. "Truly, I say to you . . ." And this is not just because his "I" has managed to develop and mature, but also because in his mind's eye he no longer sees the famous writers, his elders, whom he still to a certain extent reveres. *For the elders have died.*

The Ancients

The ancients, it always seems to us, were closer than we are to the truth, to the root of being and its mystery. We are, as it were, cut off from something, we've grown distant from something, and strayed. After all, we study their books with tremendous interest.

Even in relation to ourselves, we tend to think in secret that in our youth we knew more than we do now. And often, at a moment of truth, we turn to that first "I" in us and say: We're trying very hard to remember what we used to do in situations like this. . . .

The source of power in a spiritual sense — for man and mankind. Once, in our prime, our spirits knew a freshness, which now is gone; and there was, once upon a time, a freshness known to the ancients, which is no longer with us, the belated.

Say "Poet," Not "Craftsman"!

In the characterization "craftsman," there is, always, consciously or unconsciously, a hint of something pejorative. It leaves a bad taste. Craftsman — which is to say: a person whose spirit in no way rises above that of others, and may in fact be beneath them, though he knows how to turn a phrase. From here, it isn't far to the artisan of hollow deception, the forger.

At the same time the true poet despises craftsmanship, and virtuosity, the preoccupation with form. "Say what you have to say, freely or in frugal fashion, and the language will open out on its own," wrote Ahad Ha'Am. Lay bare, poet, your soul to its root, and the ideal form will emerge. The poet winds the watch from within, the craftsman turns its hands. [. . .]

In Two Worlds

In order for the poet to create, he must live in both the quotidian world and the world of the poem. Form requires a plain foundation. He seeks to enchant the quotidian in him by means of the poetic.

Maupassant tells of a painter who sat in the fields painting a certain landscape, finished his painting, and found himself so utterly enamored of the work of his hands that he leapt up and showed his painting to the cows that were grazing nearby: "Look, see what I've done!"

To show, to show oneself — that's the principal drive here. The poet in a person seeks to show his vision to the man of the world within him. After all, the latter's role is every bit as important for the work as that of the former.

And so one can imagine that there are in the world great poets who have created nothing precisely because of that greatness, which is to say —

because they are all poetry. The man of the world, the profane man, is lacking in them entirely — and so they have no one to show.

On the Nature of Graphomania

Though I intend to dwell here on the obscure poem, which is increasingly prevalent among our young poets, I would like to note, in passing, that graphomania is, by and large, not an affliction of the young in particular, nor is its sign obscurity. There are poets advanced in years whose writing, be it poetry or fiction, is simplicity itself, and who are nonetheless born graphomaniacs! Neither age nor simplicity can ward off this calamity.

Now let us return to the obscure poem with its seven seals. Each time I come across one, and this happens frequently, I begin to wonder: How does this creature live? What's behind it? What's the point?

Inasmuch as this curious phenomenon isn't merely a trick that the writer consciously plays, one can assume that there are three distinct possibilities at work here: (a) the existence of a common code, a kind of literary conspiracy, known only to the conspirators themselves; (b) a dim emission of something in the soul of the writer, the thread of an experience, a feeling or thought, to which the writer imagines he'll best be able to give expression in this fashion. After all, this is a deeply private and personal matter — a man, as it were, talking to himself — and only due to the lack of a critical faculty does he fail to grasp that the subject couldn't possibly engage others, even if they understood it. There is behind this assumption an exaggerated faith in the modest "I": if I'm here, everyone's here! (c) But there is still a third possibility — and this is worthy of special consideration — namely: that there is a cult of nonunderstanding in itself. Obscurity for obscurity's sake. Admiration and awe in the face of the obscure and impenetrable. The young man reads the "poem," is amazed by it, awed by the prospects of its very impenetrability — and desires to make one like it. His greatest desire is to write something that he himself will not be able to comprehend. That's what he longs for. Someone has tossed into the space of the world a passage of Hebrew claptrap speckled with vowels and diacritics — "then all the flock bore speckled . . . in their image, after their likeness" (Gen. 31:8, 1:26). And many, nonetheless, read these works and, understanding not a thing, shrug their shoulders — and admire them! It's a kind of psychosis — let the learned, whose art this is, take note!

Most amazing of all in this peculiar mess is that each graphomaniac -poet immediately finds his graphomaniac-critic, who places the wreath on his head and encourages him to continue on this path —

What have we come to?!

POETS OF A FALSE GOD

They resemble those who are hard of hearing. Every moment one runs to the door, opens it, and finds that no one is there. He thinks he heard a bell. But when they really ring, and knock on the door, he doesn't budge.

[PC]

Uri Nissan Gnessin

(1881–1913)

Uri Nissan Gnessin was born in the Ukraine and raised in small Belorussian towns, where his family moved when he was still very young. His father, a rabbi and a scholar, saw to it that all of his children were given a first-rate Jewish education. He also had them tutored in Russian—both the language and the literature. Eventually Gnessin would add German, French, Greek, Latin, and English to this mix, so that with the Yiddish of his childhood and the Aramaic of his traditional studies, he knew at least nine languages. (He would go on to translate extensively from the work of Lermontov, Shestov, Heine, Byron, Baudelaire, and others.) In a somewhat bizarre conjunction of fates, the adolescent Gnessin attended the same small-town yeshiva as Yosef Haim Brenner (the school was run by Gnessin's father); the two aspiring writers struck up what would become a lifelong friendship and rivalry, and they soon began editing a succession of literary journals together. The contrast between them could not have been greater. Gnessin was tall, fair, remote, melancholy, and refined; Brenner, as one writer has described him, was "unruly, feverish, common," with wild, glowing eyes and a biting social wit. Gnessin's highly refined work turned inward; Brenner's prose was rough-cut, and he criticized his friend (in a letter written in 1900) for indulging in "art for art's sake" while "the world was sick."

Gnessin's early poetry and fiction were epigonic and gave no indication whatsoever that he would soon become one of Hebrew literature's greatest prose stylists and, some have said, among the most innovative European authors of his time, anticipating work by Proust and Joyce. By 1905 he had come into his own. In a memorial essay about him, David Frischmann recounts the unforgettable moment of first coming across Gnessin's mature work (see p. 2). Marked, above all, by the prepositional nature of his sensibility, Gnessin's signature style "twists and turns," as poet and novelist David Vogel put it, "zigzags digressively into hidden paths; strains to illuminate the dark corners of the soul, the microscopic folds impenetrable to the naked, conscious eye; pursues with an expressive net the slightest momentary shades of emotion and sensation at the moment of their dynamic flow, just as they are being forged." The best-known work of this "poet in prose," as Vogel called him, is the short fiction of his so-called middle period, including "Sideways," "Meanwhile," "Before," and "Beside," all of which appeared in literary journals and were published in book form only after his death.

Throughout his all-too-short life, Gnessin wandered incessantly in Belorussia, Poland, and the Ukraine, but also to London and Genoa, and then on to Ottoman Palestine for a brief spell before returning to Europe. He died in Warsaw, of heart failure, a few months after his thirty-third birthday. The short selection of his letters that follows—treating the subjects of passion in poetry, the soul's relation to the things of the world, and what literature is built of—should be read in conjunction with Frischmann's portrait of the writer.

FROM *THE LETTERS*

Letter #7, to Sh. Bikhovsky

SUMMER 1900

Faithful Brother

Recently I've had the good fortune, though only intermittently, of receiving a letter from you. I am, however, not complaining. I'm very pleased about the literary evenings that have been established in our city: after all the cleverness and hair-splitting, we must admit that everything *we have,* everything that is for our souls, for the *private* soul within us — and woe to him who has such a thing, though it is in any event better than the nothingness facing that thing "we have" — has given us only that progress about which we're used to complaining when our hearts turn sour at the sight of dreadful reality. And so I say, the fact of this makes me happy. [. . .]

As for me there isn't much to speak of. I am now reading various books, among them also Schiller in the original. I think little, and write even less; I attend various literary evenings, talk, argue, split hairs with other people and with myself — what, is there anything here out of the ordinary? Everything, one might say, is as it was. [. . .] What else? I very much regret that I let Sokolow print my second poem in the annual volume. It no longer pleases me at all; though there are many — including Yosef Haim [Brenner] — to whom it seems good. And about my poetry in general? The less said the better. Not long ago they dedicated one of the literary evenings here to Yosef Haim's book. I wrote up an account for Yosef Haim of all the things that were said there. In a word: it was all good, all fine — and all empty and inflated. . . . We must act, therefore, if possible, as though we don't feel a thing. In this respect, as I see it, a righteous fool is better than a cunning lout. . . .

Because thoughts like these are liable to suck all the marrow out of our youth, all the vitality out of our soul — and this we need, we need it very much, it is needed, simply, for our private existence: *I feel, I feel it:* in any event the heart must boil, the soul must *storm, the blood must seethe,* and if not — then you are dead. You are even *worse* than dead, *worse.* . . .

And during these days, this is what I wrote:

> . . . And if
> in your might you stole
> seething poetry from me
> without mercy —
> my eyes like a beggar's
> will not moisten,
> for the flower that was dispossessed
> once again you'll plant!
> Not the poetry of the skies,

Lord of the evil eyes,
this, your hand, has removed from my heart —
grief within me —
a malignant leech, at least
like the depths now churn!

Whether it's poetry or sorrow — it's all the same: but let something *boil* in the heart; let it not be dry, let it not be empty, let it not be cold as ice! . . .

Letter #33, to Hava Darvin

YEKATERINOSLAV, 20 OCTOBER 1904

[. . .] And this is what I wanted to say to you about reading together. Gulya, in her letter, dreams about your reading with one another. I don't know what you think about it; I am not an advocate of such reading. What the reading of good books can give — is only the sounding of one's own soul. However, if I do not read alone, then that feeling is dulled, and if it isn't entirely lost, surely it loses all its charm. The depth within it becomes a glancing *across the surface* of things, and the essence of the content is lost. It becomes something else entirely. For example, to clarify together the words of the book, after you've already worked out your own idea of them, which you acquired while reading *by yourself* — certainly that will do no harm. But the reading itself must be freer and deeper than what can be attained while you are reading with someone else. Your thoughts and your feelings and even your dreams, which reading arouses in you at that moment, should sense no hindrance before them. They must be free; and wherever they lead you, they lead you — but you must know then that your own thoughts and your own feelings and your own dreams have paved the way to that place. You, therefore, have fortified that place, you and no one else. If, however, while you are reading some other person is sitting at your side, someone in whom those very things can arouse (in the heart of the other, which indeed beats *near you*, if beneath another chest and lock) entirely different thoughts and different reflections; and even if we assume — though we cannot in any case say so with certainty — even if we assume that these words also arouse the same thoughts and reflections in the other person that they raise within you, the images of those ideas *and the forms* of those thoughts are nonetheless and without a doubt different and other, since the other person has a different psychic and emotional makeup than you do. If that person sits at your side while you read, then you and she will not be free, because each woman will get in the way of her companion's wings, and the reading will no longer be what it should. You've wished, Hava, to be *samastayatelone* [independent] with your body, so be free in your soul as well.

The main thing is freedom in all you do. They tell you fire is red; very well. But you must look at the fire with your own eyes. Perhaps your eyes will sense another shade or the shadow of a shade. Eyes are different. They must be. [. . .]

Letter #71, to Israel-Noah Sprintz

HOMEL, MAY 1906

Greetings to you Is. N.

You ask me: Where do I plan to go and when? — and I don't know how to answer you, because I, too, know not a thing. If there were a little more sympathy in my heart for our Ivan, I would now set aside some time to translate "Sideways" and "Meanwhile" together with him into Russian — perhaps I would get a few rubles from that, but first of all I don't have that much sympathy for him, and second, even though we translated Peretz's "Fable" with success, I don't know whether his Gentile soul would be able to translate such things. True, I would be the translator, but you know the rule, *Az a katz ken oikh kalye makhen* [a cat too can give you a hernia], and especially when it comes to things belletristic, and this sort of literature, which is built entirely on halves of words, which when they're not in their proper place, mean not a thing. [. . .]

[JG]

Ya'aqov Fichman

(1881–1958)

Lyricism permeated not only Ya'aqov Fichman's poems and plays but also
the many finely drawn and admirably open sketches of other writers that
he produced over the course of his long career. Lyricism, and a spirit of
self-sacrifice—for Fichman worked tirelessly throughout his life as an editor,
translator, and promoter of others' work. Born to a modest family in rural
Bessarabia (then southern Russia, now Moldavia), Fichman received a
traditional religious education, which he broadened on his own. He left
home at an early age and, struggling to make ends meet, wandered
between many of the usual way stations for an aspiring Hebrew writer
at the time—Odessa and Warsaw (see the second excerpt below), Vilna
and Berlin. He settled in Palestine in 1912.

Fichman's work seemed to polarize readers—especially the writers
among them. Yosef Haim Brenner spoke of the "tender, transparent sorrow"
that came through his landscape poems (his principal mode), and others
have noted the way in which his sadness quietly complicates the lyric impulse.
That same tenderness, however, was at times construed as softness, and
some took him to task for the essentially subjective and creative—rather
than corrective or theoretical—nature of his criticism. Still, his essays on
a wide array of topics are passionate, astute, and warm. After Fichman's

death, poet Natan Alterman wrote: "They called you soft. A man of compromise. . . . / But we always knew—there's a softness in which / the valid lies, free of all declamation, / and the foam which is its refuse and dross."

On the Role of the Poet

You ask about the poet's role at the present hour? The role of the Hebrew poet during these fateful days is critical in the extreme: a feeling of responsibility for what he does and does not do weighs upon him in such a manner that the problem — in as much as we labor to understand it — can only be resolved by the individual; each one of us must seek a solution, not according to any general rule, but rather in his own way, in accordance with his own nature.

You know that I see poetic creation as an entirely free process, as a natural growth that cannot be judged in any way from the outside — in the sense of "Awaken not, nor stir up love, until it pleases" — for any act of coercion in poetry risks taking the life out of it. In prose one is able, at least to a degree, to steer the course of the writing when the moment calls, and sometimes we even manage to coerce ourselves. At times divine inspiration attends the writing, though it is least likely to greet those who, wringing their hands, await it . . . but in poetry all of this is far more complex. Here one should not insist; and this is the heart of the matter — divine inspiration, as it's called, is dependent upon a kind of silent anticipation of the momentous hour wherein we shall be fit to sing. Here obstinacy suggests a lack of discernment — and also, at times, poetry's desecration.

The matter is especially grave when it comes to occasional poetry. Those who make demands of it every day, even every hour — in loud tones — in the end gain little of what they sought. The profound impressions and active participation in the events of the day — however essential — still do not qualify the poet to engage in genuine occasional poetry, nor in satirical poetry that strays beyond the bounds of the popular feuilleton. Poetry is something more than this, and without this "something" it isn't worth the bother. All of us are capable of writing, with greater or lesser skill, verse based on the events of the day; but this is remote from poetry, and only he who truly understands can tell the difference between the mere thrill or excitement of rhyme, and rhyme that cuts to the very heart of time, a rhyme in which are concentrated the full intensity of pain and the power of dissent.

Whoever enjoins us in these times to disown experience that is not directly linked with the events of the day, does so at his own risk, and threatens to cause serious harm. Such an attitude is liable to inundate us with worthless poetry even when the writer is expressing his most sincere feelings. Words do not necessarily depend on feelings. Poetry is not the product of mere excitement, it is rather the result of deep observation — of a longer or a shorter duration at different times — but whatever the case, it is never a fleeting experience that hasn't quickened the blood with song. The reaction to any event, whether in poetry or in prose, is the business of journalism. And indeed, there are poet-journalists who have been trained to respond swiftly, as a matter of course; but poetry is different in its very essence. It cannot be produced on a regular basis without risk to its very being. One must prepare oneself by turning away from all events born of the moment — to strive toward poetry with all the implements of the soul, which is precisely what is barred from us when we anchor on a different shore. In this matter one should always remember that while in Kishinev, in the wake of the pogroms, and between composing "On the Slaughter" and "The City of Slaughter," Bialik wrote [the lyric poem] "With the Sun.". . . No. Those who forbid us to look at a blossoming tree or a passing cloud (even in these times!) impose on us a deceitfulness in art.

The poet will not listen to them!

The poet who is sincerely concerned with the true work of art will sing whatever God places in his mouth and in his heart. He will not close his ears to the bitter cry of his brother. He will live the tragic life of the hour with the utmost intensity. He will turn his heart to the fate of his people, to the fate of all humanity. Not in order to write a new poem in response to every horrific item he happens to read in the paper, but in order to live with his wretched brothers. He will pray with every drop of his blood for salvation, for deliverance, and curse roundly with the fervor of his crushed soul; but he will do so only when he sees himself, and the hour, as fit for poetry — without any external demands. Poetry has nothing to do with quantity, and its influence ends precisely when it ceases to be an event, a thing of surprise. It is never swayed by the moment. At times we await it for days on end. At times — without warning — it comes and knocks at the gates of our hearts, and great bitterness finds expression as though on its own, for poetry requites as does the fruit of the tree.

I have always said, and again I say it: we are not all qualified for this kind of poetry, which the hour imposes upon us — and for the most part, the lyric poet responds belatedly. Ripens to it belatedly. And it befits him, and poetry, that he not grasp at song, just that he does his duty: his paramount duty is to be faithful, to come equipped not with all the instruments of song, but rather with all the soul's instruments — to sing from the fullness of his blood, the fullness of his heart.

[GL]

The Polish School

Early one September morning in 1903, I stepped down from the train at the station along the Vistula River, worn out and weary from nights of travel, in order to try my luck in the Polish capital. I'd come from the south, the landscape in which I was born and raised, and behind me there hovered darkly my first disappointments, which I'd amassed over several years of study, as an external student and novice in literature, in the southern "city by the sea" — which had been dear to me, and which I'd loved and feared in equal measure. As I walked slowly with my pack toward Jewish Warsaw that morning through the faded dust, reddened now in the sun of the summer's end, [. . .] my heart, for one reason or another, was beating softly. The fear of what might be didn't descend on me. When, a few years earlier, I entered the gates of Odessa, my heart pounded with anticipation. Before the giants of that city, whom I'd come to meet, the fear mounted. Names like goads: Mendele, Ahad Ha'Am, Bialik. . . . The mere thought of them filled the heart with apprehension. In Warsaw, I didn't know whom I'd encounter. [. . .] The heart here was turned not toward certain people, but toward the city itself —

the city of the budding Hebrew literature, of Hebrew publishers, papers, and journals — Tushiya, Ahiassaf, *HaTzofeh,* and *HaTzefira*. [. . .]

Bohemian life is what drew one to this metropolis. The "gentler spirit," which made us all — Poles, Lithuanians, and Ukrainians — a single caste, though it wouldn't be long before some would turn to Yiddish, and some to Hebrew; some would grow in strength, and others lose heart, and quietly abandon the battle. For now, however, that spirit held sway over the entire company, and the air was filled with the tremendous desire of youth. [. . .]

Such was Warsaw's influence. In Odessa, not only for Ahad Ha'Am, but also for Bialik, the poem was first of all an accounting of the world, while in Warsaw, it was first of all the song of the world. [. . .] In this sense Odessa was "rabbinic," a little chilly, whereas Warsaw was "Hasidic," airy, full of melody. [. . .]

Poland served, therefore, in the context of the young literature, as a liberating element, as it did in the early days of Hasidism. It cracked the shell — undermining the entrenched and confusing every style of writing as it sought out channels for the hidden vitality in things that ran counter to what was routine, or fixed — all that the Odessa of Mendele built on, relied on. Hasidism wasn't just another example of form, or formulation, but a subversive and restless spirit of renewal. And we, the students of severe Odessa, felt [. . .] that something within us was being dislodged. Even we, who remained loyal till the end to our masters in the south, [. . .] couldn't help but feel that here were stores of spirit. [. . .] Mendele, Bialik, Tchernichowsky sought to sculpt and polish Hebrew, like marble. Warsaw, which rejected all that was sculptural, believed only in the heart's pulsing, the heart's shudder. It dispensed with all that ancient modeling in favor of a blossoming, of enthusiasm, of relentless rejuvenation. Odessa encouraged. Warsaw rebelled.

[PC]

Yosef Haim Brenner

(1881–1921)

"A bitter, moody, thickset, sloppy . . . Russian Jew, a Dostoevskian soul continually oscillating between compassion and rage," as Amos Oz has put it,
Yosef Haim Brenner was an irascible writer with a gift for friendship, and from
early on in his career he was virtually worshipped by his peers as a prophet of
Hebrew secularism. The role, it seems, came to him naturally. Living in poverty
and celebrating simplicity, he hated both the high road and the high hand,
according to Ya'aqov Fichman, and he embraced the downtrodden soul. Like
his followers, he "gave up the small happiness for the great sorrow"—the
sorrow of truth.

Brenner was born in a small town in the Russian Pale of Settlement and
raised in a religious home. By the time he was a teenager, however, he had
shed the trappings of religion and joined the Jewish workers' socialist party,
the Bund. Marxism soon gave way to Zionism, and, after serving for three
years in the Russian army, he deserted and eventually made his way out of
the country, initially to Germany and then to London, where he lived for four
years in the East End, working as a printer and editing an important Hebrew
journal he'd founded. (He had also worked in Yiddish.) In 1909 he settled in
Palestine. He was brutally murdered in Jaffa during the Arab riots of 1921.

Although he was known for his rugged, uncompromising style and his apparent disregard for form, Brenner was in fact, as critics later noted, a radical writer who, in breaking through formal prose conventions, was searching for a form of his own—one that would give expression to the bleak vision he held within him and the devastating psychosocial critique at its heart. "My craft requires a certain coolness," he wrote, "while I am on fire." Instead of the smooth surface that plasters over the cracks in the wall, observed Fichman, Brenner evolved his style from the cracks themselves.

In addition to his numerous novels and short works of fiction, Brenner produced a torrent of literary and cultural journalism (under a variety of pseudonyms). The essay that follows is drawn from that occasional work. The controversy it treats—the emotional, spiritual, and political implications of a Jewish writer's choice of language, the historically charged if limited Hebrew or the vernacular, proletariat Yiddish—was central to the culture's concerns at the turn of the century.

Pages: From the Notebook of a Hebrew Writer

They come to us with a question, and in the name of life: What has Hebrew to do with life?

Or no! They don't come with a question, they come with conviction, they come in a fury: It's a fetish! We don't need this dead language!

This dead language — indeed, there is no need for a dead language. It's odious to try to summon the dead, to seek to establish contact with them, a disgrace for a free people to worship a language that has died, to make gods out of a handful of words, which human beings do not need — What, however, can we do, if in this dead language we have a literature that is three thousand years old, and is not dead? What can we do, when, if we erase this dead language entirely from the book of our life, if with our own bare hands we destroy all that our spirit has acquired throughout the generations? What can we do with this dead thing, which has the peculiar characteristic of having been used by speakers of Arabic and early Spanish, like Shelomo

Ibn Gabirol and Yehuda HaLevi, and speakers of Polish and Russian, [. . .] for writing and creating books in, and sometimes in it alone?

They come in the name of life, but what is that — life? Is it a secret that life in the ordinary sense of the word has no need of literature? That life in the ordinary sense needs only fillets and crescents [Is. 3:18], cafés and circuses? That the literature of life in the ordinary sense is nothing but large sheets of paper with big advertisements about big businesses and eating and drinking and dancing?

We are dealing with masters of the spirit here, with living masters of the spirit, and with masters of the spirit among the Children of Israel —

And still I might understand all their arguments if the Jews were just a single entity, dwelling within their own land, and actually speaking Old German, mixed and muddled with Semitic and Slavic elements — then, at least, there'd be a reason for the outcry: English too is nothing but a *jargon*! So the Jews speak a Germanic *jargon,* in their own spirit! Why do we need the "burden" of the Holy Tongue?!

Now, however, now that all of us are shoved into various ghettos in Europe and in America, in Asia and in Africa, and every ghetto has a jargon of its own — now for the children of the ghettos in the West, even the jargon of Mendele is only another language that has died; it could never be the language to connect and unite our downtrodden people. And so, Yiddish has no right to say: "I am the national language, the language of the nation's soul, the language of the nation's spirit, the language of the nation's creation." Why, then, are you shouting?

Alas, they say there. Alas for those sons of men, in a place where deep sorrow roils, they come proudly with their hearts high, confident in their attack —

Here — sorrow and pain, pain and sorrow. Here, deep powers and talents are scattered; they crumble and disappear, are lost, born to a nation scattered across the seven seas, a nation that has no center to its life and to its deeds; a nation attended at every step by opposition and contradiction, and unnaturalness, and by all sorts of imposed disruptions; a nation that isn't a nation, but the incarnation of a nation. That incarnation, which has seven languages in its mouth, has not yet broken the iron pen with which its books were written during its first incarnation. And when a son is born to it, a son and not a daughter, and he speaks correctly or incorrectly all the languages of the day, his mother tongue is Yiddish, but the language of his books is Hebrew, and not Yiddish, so long as he remains within the camp!

Here — "Very great is the pain and very great is the shame"; here — tortures of hell and protests against a bitter fate, a fate that is evil and cruel; here — a stamping of the foot and shouting, Why? Why do all those souls, the creative spirits in every generation, and of every nation, why do they have their mother tongue as the language of their literature, and we, we Hebrews, have to continue the life of our literature within a language that's dead?

We have lost a great deal, we Hebrews, a great deal. For a single sensation or emotion, for a single thought, for the shadow of a single imagining, we might find a word, and find it, in fact, within this dead language, but thousands and thousands of others are hidden behind a cloud, perish in smoke, dissolve into chaos . . . the twilight of life and its fluttering, the prattling of children, young women's cries of joy, old women's stories, and the conversations of madmen — all of these things secondhand, secondhand. . . .

Lost worlds! And bitter doubts, and much weeping, and tremendous awakening within the silence: Will our days of siege be long? Will we finally cease to begin with *as if* and *as it were*? Is it within our power to bear fruit that's worthy of us? Will it ever be possible for "those who sell their senses to the Hebrew language forever" to work as Tolstoy and Dostoevsky and Ibsen and Hauptmann have — and create as they do?

Here — loss and tremendous devotion fight with all their weapons, and these men come with such conviction: Jargon — and nothing else! Yiddish — it's all here. [. . .]

Liars! Because they answer us with deception, those frivolous people; in vain, you ignoramuses, you muster the temerity to say: the Holy Tongue! The language of religion! — as though the generation that died in the desert were truly concerned with matters of ritual impurity and purity [. . .] as though the Halakhic responsa on matters of Sabbath observance and writs of divorce, on abandoned women and ritual baths, written by the rabbis of America in their *Gazetin* were not in jargon.

And apart from those Halakhic responsa, if the most important Jewish religious books, if Maimonides' code and the responsa of Rabbi Asher, and other medieval Halakhic codes were not written in the Holy Tongue — our faces, the faces of free people who write in Hebrew, would not pale for that reason. For we have not a shadow of faith in the God of our sixteenth- and seventeenth-century ethical tomes — *The Beginning of Wisdom* and *The Two Tables of the Covenant* — and not even in the God of the medieval Spanish *Duties of the Heart* and the Provençal *Examination of the World*. A thousand miles from us is the religion of Babylonia's Amoraim and the Land of Israel's Tannaim, and, no less so, the religion of the later Ashkenazic commentaries. We write in Hebrew, however, because we must, because the divine spark within us emerges only within that flame, because this spark does not flare up, does not fully come into being except in this language and not in any other, and not even in the jumbled, lovable language of our mothers, which we speak each day.

"What will the Hebrew language give us and add?" — In what language, spoken from time immemorial among the Jews, has this bitter protest about that language not been heard — that language which is dead and not dead, forgotten but not forgotten? Two millennia of exile — and in which year of all those years has that question not been asked? Yet in what year of all those years has nothing been written in this tongue?

Moreover: Now, at this time, even without the jargonists telling us, we know that the situation of our national literature is worsening. Our nation has lost hope for itself because of all of its tribulations. It is doubtful, however, that the power of Yiddish is great enough in its Russian manifestation to become a single language for us all.

Indeed, for them, for those who are content with their lot, who are certain that they have done a great thing, none of this matters. It's enough for them to retain jargon as what, according to the Bund's program, will be the leading language of the future — and when push comes to shove, also for their comrades who shout, in the Marxist dialect, "Territorialism." We, however, we, whose suppressed cry, "The Land!" comes from us not in order to observe the materialist-historical commandment of proletarianization, but rather because we fear, in the greatness of our agony, national extinction, the elimination of the Jewish people; because our eyes are open and we see the possibility of absolute loss and with it also the loss of our language, [. . .] we say: "True, our Hebrew literature in recent times, as it appears, is gradually ceasing to be the torch that sheds light for all of us, ceasing to be our pillar of fire and cloud, and if there are a few more years like this, if there are a few more years of slackening spirit and lack of redemption — our Hebrew literature will no longer be the great treasure of the soul of our nation. However, unlike you, who take glory in thinking that life is on your side, we, the Hebrews, know that the current is against us — that our path is hard, and that life is coming to extinguish our soul. However, we young Jews, the sons of ancient Hebrews, we in whose hearts the world has been placed by the scribes of Judea and its visionaries, from the days of Micah and Jeremiah to [the Haskala writer] Peretz Ben Moshe [Smolenskin] and after; we whose souls were revived and enriched by Hebrew, who have no remnant without it, for whom it alone is the source of life, part of the secret of our being, and bound to all our bones — *we do not want this.* Never, therefore, and in no way, will we be reconciled to this evil thing; and never, therefore, and in no wise, will we be able to be silent and see the field destroyed for the surviving remnant. *We will be the last to remain upon the wall.*

JANUARY 1906

[*JG*]

Avraham Ben Yitzhaq

(1883–1950)

Though his entire oeuvre consists of only eleven published poems, Avraham
Ben Yitzhaq is a legend in the history of Hebrew poetry and one of its most
admired figures. Born Abraham Sonne in Galicia (Poland) in 1883, Ben Yitzhaq
lived for the better part of three decades in Vienna, where he was close to
some of the era's most prominent men of letters, including Hermann Broch
and Elias Canetti. The latter devoted a long section of his memoirs to Sonne,
who, he said, "inspired an addiction such as I have never experienced for
any intellectual." With the Nazi invasion of Austria in 1938, Sonne fled to
Palestine.

Often described as the first truly modern poet in Hebrew, Ben Yitzhaq
evolved in his poems a fusion of the gentle and severe, the remote and the
near—a high Hölderlin-like pitch of spirit and a sensibility finely calibrated
to register even the simplest, most delicate of moments and things. All this
is transmitted within Ben Yitzhaq's cadence and quiet music, his intensity,
his clarity.

"Blessed Are They Who Sow and Do Not Reap" is Ben Yitzhaq's most
famous poem. It was also the last poem he wrote—at the age of forty-five,
after a twelve-year silence. For the remaining twenty-two years of his life,
Ben Yitzhaq wrote nothing. As a result, readers have tended to see in this
poem a final statement about his own production—though recent critics

53

have proposed beside it a broader, more political reading. Nonetheless, it remains a powerful statement of one poet's perspective on the relation between perception and expression—and perhaps the renunciation of the desire to express.

Blessed Are They Who Sow and Do Not Reap

Blessed are they who sow and do not reap —
they shall wander in extremity.

Blessed are the generous
whose glory in youth has enhanced the extravagant
brightness of days —
who shed their accoutrements at the crossroads.

Blessed are the proud whose pride overflows
the banks of their souls
to become the modesty of whiteness
in the wake of a rainbow's ascent through a cloud.

Blessed are they who know
their hearts will cry out from the wilderness
and that quiet will blossom from their lips.

Blessed are these
for they will be gathered to the heart of the world,
wrapped in the mantle of oblivion

— their destiny's offering unuttered to the end.

[PC]

Ya'aqov Steinberg

(1887–1947)

Details of Ya'aqov Steinberg's life are hard to come by. He was born into an impoverished family in the northern Ukraine, and at an early age seems to have rebelled against its traditional ways. At fourteen he fled to Odessa, where he met Bialik and other prominent Hebrew writers. Two years later he moved to Warsaw, and with the outbreak of World War I, he emigrated to Palestine, where he lived for the rest of his life.

Often considered a leading figure in the symbolist school of Hebrew poetry, Steinberg was clearly influenced by Baudelaire, Verlaine, and the Russian writers of his day. Within the embrace of elusive "correspondence," Steinberg developed a hard-edged and deliberately archaic Hebrew style. He was preoccupied with the verse line, which he saw as the vanguard of cultural salvation and the ultimate expression of individual presence. For centuries, he said, Jews had produced an essentially rhetorical literature; only the discrete and well-cut line, reflecting both the achievement of ancient Hebrew verse and a honing of the aesthetic sense, could serve as a bulwark against the formless torrent of facile talk, from which nothing vital would come. Hebrew poetry, he wrote, "embodied the last remnant of Jewish integrity and directness."

His lucid, ascetic lyrics apart, Steinberg was best known for his essays, which often contrast the authentic and the specious. "The Malingerers"— the term in Hebrew indicates both hypochondria and the psychological condition in which an imagined illness is also feigned—offers a devastating look at literary fraud, and how the work of true creation is avoided by pretenders to inspiration. The second essay treats a problem familiar to all who write.

THE MALINGERERS

Art can, in many ways, be compared to a disease: in order for it to be fully realized it needs considerable time to mature, just as many days are required for its influence to be eradicated. We are all well acquainted with robust but weak-tempered people who feign being sick, their so-called illness coming as suddenly as it goes away without leaving a trace; these are peculiar patients, whose blood heats up as soon as they take to their sickbed. No dizziness precedes the onset of symptoms; there is no concealed distress. In the hidden recesses of the blood — which is to say, the soul — almost nothing has changed. And yet, the eye displays all the external signs: the flaming whites, the imploring, whimpering, mysterious gaze. Moreover, these pseudo-sufferers are unsparing in their demand for treatment. They sometimes contort their faces just to be pampered or arouse sympathy.

Consider, for a moment, the malingerers in literature. Some among them are easily recognized: these are the innocent, believers more than believed, the mocked who are, in fact, far removed from any infirmity. In the world of the writer they represent a large and powerful tribe, and recount in sundry tongues their painless afflictions. There are periods in literature when most writers belong to this category. The impression they convey is exceedingly strange: picture a hospital where people in the full flush of health cling to every bed and post! Such a literature, when studied closely over many years, blunts one's imagination far more than the sluggish pace of a solitary life. The entire world seems diminished and sentimental. These writers, to whom one foolishly has grown accustomed, are but flies to their own selves. They're quick to brandish their thin pens over any subject or theme — and accustom one, as well, to a confused view of the world, based on longing and a constant yearning to fall sick or be saved. The ordinary weakness of the human heart — to seek out pretexts — is then experienced tenfold. The universe, which the healthy perceive according to a few, if clear and obvious, principles, becomes a network of hieroglyphs, comprising line after line after line. Whoever wants to subsume under a single category both the literature of such malingerer-pretenders and its insidious influence should summon in his memory the countless volumes of religious law and manuals of moral instruction produced by Jews from the end of the Middle Ages and up to the beginning of the Age of Enlightenment. Their effects on the spirit of our forefathers persist to this day.

The matter of these writers — feigning illness day after day en masse — reaches far and wide. But let us set aside such concerns and turn our attention to the writers of truth: even they on occasion fall prey to the pitfalls of malingering. Here recognition is difficult, because talented writers take pains, as best they can, to hide from the eye of the reader their own emotional limitations in the act of writing (even as every now and then they deliberately leave in formal flaws, to suggest the presence of bewilderment — in the midst of a passionate effort). And yet, it is very easy to imagine the development of such a writer, who begins writing under the heartfelt pressures of youth and talent, then continues, in the prime of his life, to write, as it were, out of speculation alone, on subjects wholly within his command. The beginning is, as has been said, in youth. Every writer possessed of a soul is capable during this period of making a discovery of one sort or another — in nature, in life, in creation. This occurs on its own, and is perhaps the first and clearest sign of the gifted — the ability to register, at the very outset of his writing life, something that is entirely his, and then to thoroughly integrate that with the precious vitality of temperament contained, to such a degree, in the vesicles of youth; and with this compound to sustain his pen for numerous days. For many days, indeed. But not for a lifetime. After the ordinary confusion of youth come the days of middle age; the heart pounds away in strength, silently and without complaint. But how can anything be created if the soul is not perplexed, if the eye's desire is subdued and the heart is stirred only when reading a book, or in response to life's vicissitudes, when loss or gain is incurred? From this one can infer: The writer has ceased to exist. And here lie the crossroads: the person, the man who is bold, who goes in fear of the shame reflected from within his soul, will procure for himself something that renews him, he will restrain himself, and learn from nature; he will draw upon the abundance of a second and third youth — in short, he will follow the path of toil and truth. On the other hand, there are many — and these of course form the majority — who foolishly believe that to develop a writer's talent means to instruct oneself in the act of writing. Such instruction is, on the whole, applied with success since it occurs as one matures, when diligence grows stronger. What these people lack — those who lie and are lied to — is the demand of the soul. Their soul lays no claim on them, although they write quite well. From memory, and out of speculation. They who in their youth were overcome by the sickness of creating malinger with such accomplished ease: the ink of speech comes first, which the hand then commits to paper, so that they're gripped by a light, feverish shiver, which resembles almost in equal parts the pressure they once felt in the heart at the hour of artistic creation.

There is no greater proof of a literary period's failure than finding numerous writers who over the course of many years return to their own vomit, desecrating — from a parched throat, a dulled soul, and the satiated belly of middle age — the song of their youth. This is a period in which honor has gone into exile — unknowingly, it hardly bears saying; for through such a time of inadequacy the writer's style need not necessarily be inadequate. The failure is revealed only in this: that many of the most important writers are concerned with idle matters. Writers, whose beginnings had been so promising, for them and for literature, endlessly repeat themselves, out of habit, drooling colorful words from mouths made red with the lipstick of the hour. What an impression is left after reexamining the words of such writers! From each one of them you expect to hear at any moment a sort of chortle, as if to say: Don't I make a good impression? Haven't I bared myself sufficiently, so as to seem just like one whose soul is perplexed, oppressed, or stirred? You will not hear the laughter behind this confession, of course; everything runs smoothly — both the form and what fills it. But as you're reading, you sometimes recoil in anger: Will there ever be an end to this fraud, to this writing based on utter speculation and the short-lived coercion of the soul — whose passion has left him inflamed?

1934

[GL/PC]

THREE WHO WOULD CONSOLE

In the café, under a cloud of smoke, three men were sitting together, and with them was the writer David Frischmann. Outside, a heavy winter's night hovered, thick with fog. It was nearly midnight, and in the high hall of the café the large chandeliers had already been turned off. Out late, the men were sitting under the circle of light cast by a single lamp on the wall, and they were smoking, and talking intermittently. Only Frischmann, who even during this winter, the last of his life, would pass the latter parts of his evenings in the café, sat silent, abstaining from his cigar; his hands, as a result, seemed so empty, and his entire figure too seemed so utterly detached, so sad and set apart — and indeed, at that wondrous hour, there sat Frischmann, full of sorrow and still — without the smoke rings from his cigar, which always formed a kind of mask over his face, and without that obscure and nearly natural irony, which always filled its furrows. The company's talk turned to the matter of writers' lives, as though all three, without meaning to, were trying to arouse some sort of interest on the part of the elder writer among them. They appeared to, and Frischmann suddenly murmured:

"What good is it — all this literature . . ."

At a dark and ponderous hour of the night, when the thoughts of the heart are thoroughly spent, it sometimes happens that a single desperate utterance serves as a spark to send up a flame through that dry chaff. Frischmann's sudden remark roused at once all three and rearranged, as it were, the orders of their hearts; their final moments of meeting at the gloomy café were suddenly turned into an occasion with a single purpose: to console the elder and sorrowful Frischmann, who sat there with hands denied their cigar. . . .

One of the group started in, saying:

"We beg of you, Frischmann, not to belittle the fine things you've done, things you've accomplished that remain with you still; even if you'd written nothing but feuilletons, that would have been enough — for with them you fulfilled, as the hour required, all the wishes in your readers' hearts. In their time, the wise would seek them out with greater interest and reverence than they evinced for any other kind of work. And isn't it said: He who fulfills the wishes of his own generation is as one who fulfills the wishes of the ages."

Frischmann rubbed one hand against the other, bowed his head, and said not a word.

Then the second one turned to console him:

"How can a writer complain when he has sent out into the world even a handful of fine stories? Works of literature are all like clouds. If they hold any good within them, they empty out that abundance and vanish without a trace; and how much more so if they don't. Between the reader and common sense they come for only a moment, and then they're forgotten, their whereabouts no longer known. The form of the story alone is clear, an organic kind of construction in which a second generation as well will settle the creatures of its imagination; therefore, the generation to come also pays the tax of memory, and the teller of tales is not forgotten."

Frischmann cast his eyes on the speaker — eyes bulging with age and the torments of illness, and the need to smoke: then he lowered his head further still and did not respond.

The third then started in, prefacing his remarks by saying:

"In the hour of his despair, a person resembles a wealthy man who has lost all that he once had: if you come to console him, beware, lest your words not ring true. Before you sits a man who once had it all, and now he has nothing. What good could the meager amount you would offer him do? You're bringing him only further humiliation, and summoning memories he has no use for. On the other hand, comforting words backed by substance are helpful; they restore a person to himself, without having to rely on a specious pact made between strangers, which will, in any event, not endure. Now, I too have something to say. It is a parable, and I will tell you its meaning as well. So listen:

"A certain rich man lost all that he had, and there came to him three friends to speak to his heart. The first one started in, saying:

" 'Why mourn forever over wealth that is gone? In the pen behind your house I saw a fine-looking cow; the milk she gives is enough for you to make a living for the rest of your life.' — So spoke the first friend. But the man in mourning slapped his hand and complained even more bitterly:

" 'Why do you come to mock the poor? Before, when I was wealthy, the fact of my owning a cow was too insignificant for me to even have taken note of.'

"Then the second tried to console him: 'If your entire treasure is gone, at least your house still stands before you. It's built to last for many days, and it's large, and there's nothing to keep you from selling it to strangers for a steep price. So why are you worried that want has come?'

"The man slapped his hand once again, and muttered in anger:

" 'Why do you aim your words like arrows at my heart? Even if they paid an exorbitant price for it, that would be nothing beside the precious things that were taken from me, and which I can never get back!'

"And then the third, too, said what he had to say, and spoke from his heart:

" 'Why do you say: Once I was rich, but now I have nothing? On a finger of your hand I see a precious gem, set in a ring, and it looks to be priceless, in terms of both its beauty and worth. Perhaps one of the world's great men will come along, a member of a royal family, whose eye will long to place it within his crown; then you'll be able to name your price, as the spirit moves you. For who could place a value on such a jewel, which will last forever, and then say, Have I asked too much? And so, take comfort; for your wealth is great today as well.'

"And the man took comfort. And now, I will tell you what this means:

"One of you sought to comfort our friend with the thought of his feuilletons, which are read today and forgotten tomorrow. The second reminded him of his stories, which — although their form is enduring — are gradually fading from memory and will soon vanish beneath the dust of oblivion. I came third, and recalled for him the poems that David Frischmann has written. Now the individual poem is like the single gemstone, whose worth is determined by its beauty and importance. Like the stone, it lasts forever, and there will come along a person, in a generation we cannot imagine, whose eye will suddenly be drawn to a single, small poem, the remains and trace of a writer far removed from him, and he will take great pleasure in it, and from within it project his own longing. Therefore, no mouth could put a price to the value of this single poem. And whoever believes in his heart that he is a poet — will find comfort!"

For a moment, there was silence. Frischmann stuck his hands in his pockets, as though he were looking for a cigar; then a memory came through him, and over his face — for an instant — there hovered the hint of a sad smile.

He got up at once and said:

"You've comforted me. But now let us go, for the midnight hour has come."

1925

[PC]

Yitzhaq Shami

(1888–1949)

Like the other writers in the early part of this collection, Yitzhaq Shami was
raised in a multilingual environment. The languages of his home were not,
however, Russian and Yiddish but Arabic and Ladino. Shami was a Jew born
in Hebron to a Sephardic mother and a Syrian silk-merchant father, who was
known in Arabic as "ash-Shami"—the Damascene. The well-off father led
an essentially peasant lifestyle, and his business brought him into close contact
with the women of the area, from whom the young Yitzhaq learned a great
deal about life among the Palestinian villagers. This would become one of the
dominant subjects of his fiction. After studying both Hebrew and Arabic at
religious school in Hebron, the rebellious Shami left the family for a teacher's
seminary in Jerusalem. There he adopted Western dress and began a life of
wandering—teaching (in Tiberias, Damascus, Hebron, Bulgaria, and Haifa)
and trying to write.

Wrongly pigeonholed as an ethnographic writer, Shami in his extraordinarily vivid and gripping work brought to light a world that is normally
hidden from Hebrew as he evolved a singular synthesis of Western and
Eastern modes of writing. Maintaining contact with the source of his inspiration, however, proved almost impossible for the depressive and doubt-ridden
Shami, and for much of his writing life he was caught between two worlds—
the traditional Arab-Jewish society in which he was raised and the more
modern literary culture of his day. His meager output (only seven stories)

is, perhaps, rooted in that tragic predicament. Nonetheless, the little that he left behind distinguishes him as a powerful artist and has led to his being called one of the most significant Palestinian writers of the twentieth century.

LETTERS

HEBRON, SUNDAY, 1 ADAR 5786 [15 FEBRUARY 1926]

To the poet Asher Barash, blessings and greetings.

Dear Friend,

I have received your letters. What could I possibly say, what excuse could I offer, when the failure of my silence is always before me? I have not kept my promise — not for any lack of desire, but because I simply was not able.

After all the tribulations I experienced at the end of the fall, I am now so exhausted and utterly incapable of sitting at my desk for even a few days that any attempt to do so seems to me pointless and absurd. I erase and write, and erase again, and the words sound insipid and cannot possibly convey the depth of the grief that dwells within me.

Nonetheless I will try to make my way back to life and to writing — awaken not, nor arouse [love until it please . . . Song of Songs 3:5]. The time will come, and sooner than you think.

It isn't *erasure* I fear. I have already been refined and passed through the furnace of pain at its border, and have given up all that's ephemeral; nonetheless, please wait for me a few weeks more.

With great respect and a blessing,
Yitzhaq Shami

To David Avissar

HAIFA, 18 HESHVAN 5695 [27 OCTOBER 1934]

A man hears a familiar melody a thousand times, and hundreds of times his ears absorb a certain rhyme, and still, its essence and beauty escape him.

Suddenly, waking one morning from his night's slumber, that same rhyme comes to mind and, like lightning in the darkness, illuminates the hidden places of his soul, and he understands what it means, and its mystery and majesty, its glory and profundity, are revealed in all their terrifying awesomeness.

A few days ago something similar happened to me. When I opened my eyes in the morning, aching and languishing, troubled and annoyed, depressed and tortured, as always, I found myself humming an old Arabic song: *ma hadan ila hadan* ["there's no one for one" — which is to say, each man for himself] — a street tune that drivers would sing, and one that gramophones scratched out endlessly, seemingly without the slightest hint of poetic worth, and, nonetheless, the depth of it struck me. The utter aloneness of *ma hadan ila hadan.*

For years, most of his life, a man lives under the illusion that he has friends and soul-mates, that he sits among his people, that there are those who understand his spirit and share his sorrow, and participate in his fate, *ma hadan ila hadan.*

For man is like the tree of the field, sending out roots all around him, principal roots and branching off-shoots, roots on a slant — and they are the secret of his being and sustenance. *Ma hadan ila hadan.*

But so it is. At a man's most critical hour, the hour of his death, he dies alone, even if he's surrounded by sons. One has to accept that loneliness, to get used to it at the end of the day, as the shadows of evening fall. . . .

What Honi the Circle-Drawer said comes to mind as well. "Either companionship or death" [*Ta'anit* 23a]. For all around him, when he woke from his sleep of several generations, life was bustling, people were scurrying along and going about their various kinds of business. In the house of study the sages and students were studying still; nothing had changed. The sun rose in its glory, but within his soul it had long gone down.

MY LITERARY REMAINS

My literary remains are meager and scant. The source of my creativity, in the wake of the events and obstacles I faced, was not a gushing spring that restored the soul, but a spring of hard stone, which carved no way out for itself. Deep within it raged, and only on occasion, and drop by drop, did it moisten its smooth wall, before once again being swallowed back down.

Must all who are endowed with the power to create bear on their backs a heavy burden of scrolls in their walking the long path of eternity? My burden is light, and I will not be bowed beneath it with every step I take.

So as to make the work of my friends and children easier, if they see fit to gather up my scattered remains, I hereby record the following items. [. . .]

[PC]

S. Y. Agnon

(1887–1970)

Mythmaking ran through the heart of everything that S. Y. Agnon did. Born Shmuel Yosef Czaczkes, in eastern Galicia, he adopted the name Agnon with the 1908 publication of his first story written in the Land of Israel, "Agunot" (loosely, "separated souls"), taking it up regularly as a pen name after that and officially making the change in 1924. The birth of this hero of Hebrew literature was also cast in grandly fictionalizing terms, as 8/8/1887 (the actual date of his birth) became in the writer's mythopoetic universe the magical and symbolically charged number 8/8/1888, which happened to be—he claimed (incorrectly)—the Ninth of Av, according to Jewish tradition the date of the destruction of both the First and Second Temples, and also the day on which the Messiah would be born.

Immersed from an early age in traditional Jewish texts (his father prayed with a Hasidic sect, while other family members opposed them), Agnon read voraciously in all of Hebrew literature, sacred and secular. In addition to that and his household Yiddish, he added, like many other Hebrew writers at the time, several other languages (in this case German and Aramaic). After a short period of wandering through small Galician towns and to Lvov and Vienna, he left Europe for Palestine in 1908, settling in Jaffa, but also spending time in Jerusalem. In both cities he met and worked with some of the major Hebrew writers of the day, including Yosef Haim Brenner, and in later years he formed a strong bond with Haim Nahman Bialik. Agnon returned to Europe in 1912, settling in Berlin, where the businessman and publisher Zalman Schocken became his patron. These were formative years for the writer, suspended as he was between the land of his birth and the homeland he longed for, and during this time he read widely in European fiction (in German translation). He married in 1920, eventually moving to Bad Homburg; in 1924, a fire destroyed his home, his vast library, and all of his manuscripts, including a novel in progress and many poems and sketches. With his wife and children Agnon picked up and resettled in Jerusalem, where he lived until his death in 1970. He published scores of stories and tales, several major novels, and important anthologies of traditional writing, and his collected works run to eight volumes. Another fifteen books of his fiction, letters, papers, and gatherings of an assorted nature have been published posthumously.

Widely acknowledged as the greatest writer of Hebrew fiction, Agnon was, beyond the cliché, a legend in his own lifetime, and his name continues to stand for a kind of Hebrew ideal, in which the fullness of the Jewish past is brought through art to bear on the modern world. No other Hebrew writer has exploited the registers of traditional Hebrew as Agnon has in his utterly singular prose, though this renders him somewhat "old-fashioned" to young Israelis today, and—as Gershom Scholem noted—a writer "at the crossroads," a classical master and the last of his line rather than the herald of a new age. At any rate, his artistry has not been surpassed.

Entering an Agnon story or novel is like stepping into the ocean: one instantly senses the colossal forces at work—the way in which each sentence, semantically and structurally, resonates within and implies a much greater whole. His traditional materials notwithstanding, Agnon also loads his work with scathing satire, political commentary, and recognition of disturbing antinomian drives. A religiously observant man through much of his life, he was hardly a conventional person or writer; if anything, religion opened him to the world in all its fullness and complexity, as Amos Oz's portrait of him suggests (see p. 255).

In a far more diplomatic but nonetheless impressive way, Agnon's 1966 Nobel address—delivered at the banquet that followed the prize ceremeony in Stockholm—embodies that sense of extensive connectedness and influence, along with the author's acute consciousness of the layers of Jewish history that are present in him at all times. To read Agnon is to participate in that history, and to transcend it.

The Nobel Prize Address

Our rabbis of blessed memory said it is forbidden for a person to enjoy the things of this world without first reciting a blessing over them. Whether one is eating a piece of food, or taking a drink, he has to recite a blessing before and after the act. The scent of grass, or spices, or of good fruit calls for a blessing over the pleasure. Likewise things one has seen — the sun in its cycle during the month of April, a tree's first coming into blossom, or sturdy trees and beautiful creatures: each calls for a blessing. And so too the things one has heard.

Because of you, distinguished gentlemen, one of the blessings for a thing one has heard has come my way. It happened that the Swedish envoy came to my home and informed me that the Swedish Academy had awarded me the Nobel Prize. As is incumbent on one who has heard good tidings, for himself and for others, I recited the blessing: "Blessed be He who is good, and who doeth good." "Who is good" — that the beneficent God put it in the hearts of the learned members of this illustrious academy to bestow this great and esteemed prize upon an author who writes in the sacred tongue. And "who doeth good" — that he has favored me so that I might be chosen.

And now, having come this far, I will recite still another blessing as befits one who has seen a king: "Blessed art Thou O Lord, King of the universe, who has given of His glory to a king of flesh and blood." And to you men of great learning I offer the blessing: "Blessed be He, who has given of his wisdom to flesh and blood."

It is said in the Talmud (*Sanhedrin* 23a): "The discriminating men of Jerusalem would not sit down to dine unless they knew who their companions would be." And so I will tell you who I am, that you have agreed to have me at your table.

As a result of the historic catastrophe in which Titus of Rome destroyed Jerusalem and banished Israel from its land, I was born in one of the cities of the Exile. But I have always seen myself as having been born in Jerusalem. [. . .]

I was five when I composed my first poem, out of longing for my father, who had gone away on a business trip. [. . .] I wrote many more poems, but none remain — as during the First World War a fire destroyed my father's house, in which I had left the manuscripts. The young artisans, the tailors and shoemakers, who used to recite my poems while they worked, were killed in that war as well, and those who were not killed then — some were buried alive together with their sisters in a pit which they dug for themselves at the command of the enemy, and most were burnt in the crematoria of Auschwitz together with their sisters, who had adorned our town with their beauty, and who, with their sweet voices, had sung my songs.

A similar fate awaited the books I later composed. All were burnt in a fire that destroyed my home in Bad Homburg while I lay ill in the hospital. These included a novel some seven hundred pages long, which had already been announced and the first part of which was about to appear. In that fire everything I'd written from the time I left the Land of Israel and went into exile was destroyed, along with a book I wrote together with Martin Buber, as well as some four thousand Hebrew volumes, most of which I'd inherited and some of which I'd purchased with money set aside for my daily bread. [. . .]

Who have my masters in poetry and literature been? [. . .] From whom have I drawn sustenance? Not every man remembers each and every drop of milk that he drank, the name of each cow whose milk he imbibed. [. . .] In my writing I have been influenced first and foremost by the Bible. From its books I learned "to combine" letters. Then the Mishna, Talmud, Midrash, and Rashi's commentary on the Torah. The next influences were the medieval halakhic commentators, the holy Hebrew poets, and the medieval philosophers led by Maimonides, of blessed memory. From early on I also used to read every book in German that came to hand. [. . .]

I was influenced by every man and every woman and every child who happened my way, both Jews and non-Jews. The conversations of people, the stories they told, were engraved in my heart, and some of them came up into my pen. The same is true of the scenes of nature. The Dead Sea which I used to see from the roof of my house each day at the break of dawn, the Brook Arnon in which I would bathe, the nights which I used to spend with pious men at the Wailing Wall — all of these gave me eyes to see the Land of the Blessed Holy One, which He gave us, and the city upon which He established His name.

And in order not to slight any creature, I must also mention the animals — the beasts of the field and the birds of the air — from which I learned. Job has told us: "Who teaches us more than the beasts of the earth, and maketh us wiser than the fowls of heaven?" [35:11]. Some of what I learned from them I have written down in my books. But I fear that I did not learn as much as I should have. For when I hear a dog barking, a bird piping, a cock crowing, I do not know whether they are thanking me for what I have said of them or whether they are calling me to account. [. . .]

May He Who gives wisdom to the wise, and salvation to kings, increase your wisdom without measure and exalt your king. In his days and in ours, may Judah be redeemed and may Israel dwell in safety. May a Redeemer come to Zion, and may the earth be filled with knowledge and with joy everlasting for all its inhabitants, and may they take pleasure in peace abundant.

[SH]

Rahel

(1890–1931)

Tall and striking, the daughter of a Russian upper-middle-class family,
Rahel (née Rachel Bluwstein) is in many ways the poster child of the Zionist
immigrant-writer: she not only chose to abandon her native country, culture,
and language for a far more difficult life in Palestine, but made of the gesture
an art that celebrated the landscape and self that merged there. Its close
brush with sentimentality notwithstanding, Rahel's spare, elegiac verse broke
through the more bookish literary register that characterized even the best
Hebrew poetry of the day and, instead, embraced a supreme simplicity.

Rahel arrived in Palestine when she was nineteen, planning a short visit
before going on to Italy to study art and philosophy. She was, however, so
taken with what she found that she chose to stay and study Hebrew while
working the land and, as she put it, "painting with the soil." She soon moved
to a settlement on the Sea of Galilee, where she met one of the major Zionist
philosophers of the age, A. D. Gordon, who preached a Tolstoy-like doctrine
of honest, physical labor. It was on his advice that she went to Toulouse,
France, to study agronomy. While abroad she contracted tuberculosis. Back
in Palestine she settled on a kibbutz, but her worsening illness posed a threat
to the community, and she spent the last decade of her life wandering—from
Jerusalem to Safed to Tel Aviv, and finally to a sanatorium in Gedara, where
she died at forty-one. Her grave along the shores of the Sea of Galilee, with

its book of her poems in a container beside her tombstone, soon became, and has remained, a site for Zionist pilgrimage.

On the Order of the Day

It's clear to me: the order of the day in poetry is simplicity of expression. Simple expression, which is to say: the ancients' scarlet robe of lyrical feeling, immediate expression, before it has time to cover its nakedness with garments of silk and gold; expression that is free of all that is literary; expression that touches the heart with its human truth; that restores the soul with its freshness; that can ingrain itself in memory, to accompany us though our daily lives and suddenly sing out from within us.

Doesn't this simplicity of expression, or at least the striving toward it, characterize most of the poetry of our time, from the Russian (Blok, Akhmatova, Yesenin) to the French (Jammes and Charles Vildrac)? Even to the point of pushing aside hallowed rhyme and the stanza, even to the point of recoiling from the employment of ordinary musical rhythm.

Leafing through B.'s new book of poems, I thought: "My god! How has he managed to evade that order of the day?" Detachment from the terrain of the times should be condemned no less than detachment from the physical terrain. The broad expanses of eternity leave us uneasy, so we look for a corner where we might distinguish ourselves.

B.'s sonnets have been smoothed over. His landscapes are painted with a sure hand; his palette is rich. The only thing missing from it is the color of the times.

T. has a path of his own; his image emerges from between the pages of his book, the image of a man by the side of the road, of twilight's sorrow, of brotherly compassion. Not a single false note grates on the ear. Yet he too, though less than B., ignores the directive of the day.

And then you pick up Shlonsky's *To Father-Mother* and you read, and reread, and it's right to "forgive" him his illusions, for his gift is in being so much of his times. There is, I believe, no room here for argument: simplicity of expression and a flood of imagery and metaphor. How is that possible?

For metaphor (which is used in more than just the fiery language of our country's wordsmiths), metaphor can be the unmediated result of a poetic worldview — which is to say: the eye is deployed in one way and not in another, and emotion bursts from the womb in this guise, like "children of fortune," born with silver spoons in their mouths.

Simplicity of expression is not always coupled with expressive skill, although it always makes up for its lack. [. . .] And there is, too, when it comes to expression, skill that fails because it lacks simplicity, and this transgression cannot be expiated. Indeed the path to simplicity is hard. On one side, the prosaic lies in ambush, and on the other — ornateness. It turns the tables on all our ordinary notions. Recognition of its rightness comes to us unmediated, through a cry of surprise, like that which was uttered by Jacob our forefather, when he woke in what he would call Bethel (the house of God): "Surely the splendor of the new was in this place, and I saw it not."

1927

[RTB]

David Vogel

(1891–1944)

Russian-born David Vogel led what is perhaps the most difficult material life of any of the authors in this anthology. He lost his father early and was on the move from age thirteen. In 1909, hoping to perfect his Hebrew, he settled in Vilna; he was arrested there and, for a short while, imprisoned for evasion of army service. He then made his way to Lvov (Lemburg) and to Austro-Hungarian Vienna, which was out of the Russian army's reach. At the beginning of World War I he was imprisoned in Austria as an enemy (Russian) national, and upon his release in 1916 was forced to scrounge for a living, relying on soup kitchens and often going hungry. He worked intermittently, mostly as a teacher of Hebrew. After several years of hand-to-mouth existence, he entered into a disastrous marriage with a non-Jewish woman (which would become the subject of his only novel, *Married Life*), and both he and his wife developed tuberculosis and spent time in a sanatorium. He moved to Paris on his own in 1925, then four years later left for Palestine, where he lasted only a year before returning to Europe. He eventually resettled in Paris, which he loved, and where he wrote the fiction that would lead to his being called "the last European master of Hebrew prose." He was imprisoned as an enemy national once again during World War II—

this time in France, because he was Austrian. Three years after his release, when France fell, he was arrested by the Nazis and sent, it seems, to a concentration camp. He was never heard from again.

Apart from *Married Life,* a crushing but brilliant monument to stasis and stultification, Vogel published a powerful, rich, and supple novella, *Facing the Sea,* several other stories, and one book of poems, *Before the Dark Gate,* in 1923. His restrained, elliptical poetry was, says Dan Pagis, "strange and alien to the Hebrew readership of the 1920s and 1930s," though it did have a few choice admirers, among them Yosef Haim Brenner, who noted its distinct and gentle rhythms. Bialik, however, dismissed him as a "blurrer of boundaries." Vogel's soon-to-be-haloed reputation as a poet started to take shape some ten years after his death, as literary tastes changed and, in time, a new generation discovered his work.

Vogel's Hebrew diaries, which run from 1912 to 1922, begin before he had written any poems and end before he wrote the fiction for which he would be remembered. Their overall bleakness notwithstanding, the excerpts that follow show him in the slow, desperate, doubt-ridden, and extremely painful process of evolving a singular style, something that—as he put it in a 1931 lecture—far from being grounded in exterior or lexical innovation, "begins only with the appearance of personality."

FROM *THE EDGE OF DAYS: JOURNALS*

SUNDAY NIGHT, 9 HESHVAN 5673, KOMARNO
[12 OCTOBER 1912, POLAND]

Today was a kind of beginning. I started teaching a group of fourteen-year-old boys. I'm occupied with the group for two hours: the salary—isn't much. In general, I kept busy most of the day, because I was reading a book.

A few memories. [. . .]

I rented a room in Munastirski Street, a very small, private room, one by two. I'd study a little and starve a lot and wait for Henya's visits, and Henya would come to visit me, and, to an extent, disperse the clouds of my rotten situation; she'd appear for a while then disappear, leaving behind her soul, her softness in the cold and disturbed room. Ha. I was, then, a young man who, hungry and original, read and studied — who took no one else into consideration and was allowed to develop an addiction to his feelings, to observe them; and now I've become, as it were, practical, a teacher with a steady job, someone with the prospect of earning money, and who can, for the moment, make do with the bit of honor accorded to him by the town idiots. . . . The times have changed! I have a hard and boring winter ahead of me — without a single book to read — and no money saved. Since I left Vilna and stopped reading, my progress has come to a halt, and one could also say: I've regressed; my life was stopped in the middle, and the devil knows when I'll be able to spin the threads of my life forward, to start from the place I stopped in Vilna.

Sunday, 9 March 1913, Vienna

I'm back home now. I had dinner with my student Z. (a precocious young man who has read all of German literature; he takes care of me, and is trying to help me get settled here), and with his friend G. — both mature and cheerful. My lodgings are next to my student's, and when we said goodbye to G., he told me that G. was a tremendous talent, but that this wasn't yet for public consumption — and I felt an awful pain in my heart. And I still feel bad. It's simple: I'm jealous. . . . Nothing draws me like literature; I would like to be counted among the writers. Perhaps that's nonsense, and childish, but I can't get free of that feeling. Always, when I imagine my future, I see myself as — why should I deny it — a writer. . . . Sometimes it seems to me that I would be able to paint some sort of picture, or write a story, that wouldn't be all that bad, but . . . to hell with it! One shouldn't talk nonsense. And in any event the question of "bread" worries me greatly. If I weren't so preoccupied with trying to make some money, I'd try to write something.

Monday, 17 March 1913, Vienna

Recently my life has become enveloped in books. Sometimes, when I grow tired of reading, I go out to walk around a little, and after a while, when my loneliness begins to make itself conspicuous, I return to my books. Just books. . . . I'd like to be a little closer to G. and to my pupil Z., so the acquaintance might give way to friendship — and I can't. The relationship — is friendly, but it still isn't free; there's something forced there. We talk about different things, but there's a boundary between us. This afternoon I went into "Orthodox House," the restaurant. I go there, incidentally, every day to meet these acquaintances of mine, and also to see the daughter of the owner of the restaurant, a pretty young woman whom I find attractive. Today I met G. there, as usual, and spoke with him. Afterward Z. came in and started to talk with him about another acquaintance, a writer, and about literature. I wasn't able to take part in the conversation and felt the distance between us. I felt a kind of jealousy for G. because Z. was so close to him, and I was jealous of Z. because G. was devoted to him. They have something in common, and I'm far from both. So a kind of sorrow came over me, and when I left them, I felt a certain pressure in my heart. The whole world left me alone and I sank back into a book. On Saturday I had an argument with G. about people who philosophize about life. He has scorn for them, since they help neither themselves nor anyone else. He, too, was like that some time ago, but now, "thank God," he's risen above that "superficial" philosophy. [. . .]

Recently I've started feeling a hidden need for love. I don't want to be just an observer from the side; I, too, want to take an active part in the festivities. . . . As for participating in life — I know that my personality hasn't yet been revealed. Deep down, I feel in myself something that isn't in others, that it's impossible that my talents should reach the level of a teacher and go no further — and at the same time, it's clear to me, or appears to me, that there is no greatness in me whatsoever — and then — a horrible pinching feeling in the heart. I can't accept the fact that I am, after all, one of many.

FRIDAY AFTERNOON, 21 MARCH 1913, VIENNA

Things are a bit difficult. I don't have any sense of life — this I realize as soon as I encounter it face to face. Ha-ha. Over the past few days I've become closer, as it were, to life as it really is; I walked for hours and tried to flirt with pretty women, but it's obvious that I'm just not fit to live a natural, healthy life. A man of the book. . . . I'm not like everyone else — that's a fact; the way the masses live, the falseness of their façades, repulses me — instead I'm drawn to what's within them; but it's hard for a person who has no healthy sense of it to approach that inner substance. My peculiar life has made me rot, and now I'm cast between two fires: I do not wish to die, but I am not fit to live like everyone else. . . . It's clear to me that environment is everything: I don't seek out company, but when will my situation change? I remember: in Vilna once an acquaintance told me that I needed love, and, in fact, he wasn't wrong. I have no god. . . . I feel my nerves increasingly on edge from day to day. Ultimately, I'm still young, twenty-two years old, but where is my desire for life? Sometimes, when I start moving around warmly, imitating others, I immediately feel the artificiality of it all, and give up on the entire charade. I'm not healthy. But what will be the end of me? Is death the only answer? Obviously, when things reach that point, I'll kill myself; but I don't want to die just yet. We'll see what happens!

SATURDAY NIGHT, 12 APRIL 1913, VIENNA

Most of the day — reading. Lately — bad weather, and that's had a bad effect on me. Until today I've been eating for free in the people's soup kitchen, and tomorrow the hunger starts. But for now, I'm not worried. This week I suffered at the hands of the authorities, who won't let me live in Vienna; that makes me very sad. It might be that in time they'll permit me, but for now — unpleasantness. Actually, over the past few days I've been quite satisfied with my situation. It seems that my acquaintance G. is coming closer and closer to me — and that makes me very happy. Also, the books that I've been reading recently — Ibsen, Maeterlinck, and others — are giving me considerable pleasure. As for killing myself, I'm not thinking about that now — Why? I no longer want to die. Period. As long as possible — I'll live! My mood has changed because I see my friend G. and speak with him almost daily, for an hour or half an hour — and that alleviates the feelings of loneliness and gives me energy to sit longer in my room and work. I like my two acquaintances G. and Z. very much — possibly because I don't have any others. One way or another, they're worthy of respect. They satisfy the demands that I make of a friend. My world just now is empty of women. . . . One girl, with large, beautiful eyes, occupies a narrow place in me, but that isn't important. . . . I've forgotten about Henya almost completely of late. I'm too lazy to write her, and there's also nothing left to write about. She's begun ceding the place she occupied in my heart. . . . She herself is to blame: she mocks writing. I'm busy most of the time with reading, and sometimes I feel a pinching sensation because I'm not giving myself up to my thoughts. Even real, daily life interests me greatly! — but I still can't give up the books. I have to read a great deal now. I realize that I've hardly read any literature that's worthy of the name — not to mention philosophical and scholarly literature. I'm thirsty — as cultured people of a familiar sort like to put it, for knowledge, for light. . . . The day is short, and there's so much work to do. Now I'm entering a world that's foreign to me, a foreign life and a foreign language — a transitional period. I feel bad about my Hebrew, that I have nothing to nourish it with; I have no Hebrew books, and the Zionists in Komarno haven't sent on my belongings — evil spirits that they are! I don't know what I should do. The absence of my things is palpable! Though to a certain extent I've already gotten used to it. And I have someone sharing my room — a small man. . . . He has something in common with S. . . . I can't stand him. I plan to change my quarters next month and get rid of that idiot. Ha! Strange that it's been my lot to meet — of all people — men like that in my life. But — to hell with it!

SATURDAY, 24 MAY 1913, VIENNA

The hunger won't let up; there's no way out. If I can survive it until September, perhaps my situation will change — How to survive? When I find someone to borrow small change from, I eat. . . . But to work — that I do not want to do — even if I had the physical strength for it. It occurred to me that it would be good for me to travel to Bukovina — yes, to Bukovina, of all places! — to Czernowitz or a nearby town — and live there for a while. In the meantime, to learn German better, to read German literature, and then — even to stay there a few years — if only there were a way to make a living. I'd be prepared — since I already have a decent knowledge of the language and its literature, and in general studies — When I come to Vienna the hunger isn't as certain and necessary, because I have more options. Apart from that, I'd like to improve and develop my literary talent — because ultimately I won't give up, and don't want to surrender and doubt my talents. What's within me hasn't yet been revealed — not enough of it; I haven't yet found myself, and it isn't yet clear to me what I am. But that there's something in me — that is beyond all doubt.

It's interesting, the heart hurts and it's clear that this isn't some minor illness — and just now I want to live. But I'll stop writing about my heartache — It only makes things worse.

THURSDAY, 28 AUGUST 1913, VIENNA

Movement. — A congress and convention of the Union of the Hebrew Language and Culture. I've had the privilege. Yes: I have had the privilege of seeing our greatest authors and poets. . . . Ha! I too have the poets' soul. Still, it's doubtful that it will be put up for sale on the market. . . . I have it. . . . That I'll never doubt; but it's possible that I might limit my merchandise, and bury it in a corner — and not pour forth from my soul.

SATURDAY, 4 OCTOBER 1913, VIENNA

A month has gone by already, and I haven't written anything. I haven't felt like it. I moved to another room and have already secured a few lessons, but there's still cause for complaint; it's still impossible for me to settle down and work. But my situation's excellent compared to what it was: at least I've got a grip on things. I'll have to move, because I need to find a separate room. I can't live with a family.

SATURDAY NIGHT, 23 FEBRUARY 1918, VIENNA

I'm writing. But not because I've become wiser with time. Maybe because I've grown more foolish. Nothing has changed. Also the constant hunger. It just changes shape. Everything disgusts me. As before. Even though I've been crowned a poet. With supreme grace. There's nothing to all that exalted talk, just as there wasn't before this. And Ilka. She's speaking of marrying me, which is to say — that I should take her as a wife. According to the law of Moses and of Israel. She deserves it. She still doesn't know me. Despite the numerous times we've quarreled and made up during the time of our friendship. She thinks of me as a solid person. Poor thing that she is. Now illness has come across me as well. A single illness that includes all. That weakness of the limbs and flaccidity of mind. Endless headaches. And that desire for life that was in me, despite those seizures and spasms, is gradually running out. Apathy toward everything. And the war! If it weren't for that, perhaps the movement would ease up. The wandering. I've also begun to miss the solitude. People's company is hard for me. And sometimes Ilka's company. Even though I'm fond of her. I've grown fond of that girl. There are many ways to a place. At first I felt sorry for her. Now, too. However, I love her. And aside from solitude I nevertheless have needs. — The ruin of ideas. Nothing has been clear to me even as much as a hair's breadth since I was released. Nothing. Now I stand before this world like someone whose mind is as befuddled as before. I don't understand a thing. Not even myself. And I'm nearly twenty-eight years old. Or perhaps we should try to pass the time with what is possible, without a way out. And again "to-do-away-with-oneself." I don't understand the whole "celebration," and so on. Even after having read Schopenhauer's theories.

MONDAY, 25 MAY 1919, VIENNA

Roughly a year has passed since I stopped writing. Because of the presence of another soul to open up to. And because, because of laziness and distraction. I've gone out of myself. Because I've entered someone else. I've become an exterior, and there is no interior. And so the absence of writing is natural. And again I'm awaiting change. In any event. And although I am devoted to her, to Ilka. But I was afraid to take her as a wife. Legally — ha. Because of the need for sex, which developed with habit, and because I need another soul, and because I love her. And because — that's what she wants. Because my health has collapsed and the "melancholy" has increased, and I can't breathe. I can't. But there's need for another soul. You've gotten old, Mr. Vogel, you've gotten old! Prepare the shrouds! And Vienna's stifling. There's no air to breathe. My entire life calls for departure from the big city. Departure to a meager, isolated tent at the edge of a distant forest, where I could live in tranquility, far from that whole crowd, that crowd of so-called writers, which stinks up the entire place with its rot and mold. Even if I don't have much contact with them. Far from all that walks on two legs, without exception. And if Ilka comes, she comes. Everything intrinsically connected to the nature of the city irritates me. Nauseates me. The necessity of looking like an ordinary person grates against my nature. Life with many, even with two, reduces the individual's qualities.

[JG]

Esther Raab

(1894–1981)

An important figure in the emerging literature of the language, Esther Raab
was the first modern Hebrew woman poet born in the Land of Israel. Her
verse is marked, as poet Harold Schimmel has noted, by the "strange inten-
sities" and "astounding propinquities" of a strong, idiosyncratic voice and is
reminiscent of Emily Dickinson's in its unorthodox, fractured syntax, and its
sources—the Bible and unromanticized nature. The daughter of one of
the founders of Petah Tiqva, the earliest Jewish agricultural settlement in
Ottoman Palestine, Raab herself—unlike the vast majority of Hebrew poets
of the time—was born into the language and worked the land for a good
part of her early years, and later in the Galilee at Kibbutz Degania. At the
outbreak of World War I, she was employed intermittently in her hometown
and neighboring settlements as a farmer, day laborer, and schoolteacher.
In the early 1920s she moved to Cairo, where she married her cousin, a Jewish
merchant. She returned to Palestine in 1926 and built a home in "little Tel
Aviv"; there she hosted and formed close friendships with the leading
Hebrew writers and painters of the burgeoning city.

Raab's close connection with the land was embodied in her poetry,
which—its metaphysical tilt notwithstanding—is essentially earthly,
gestural, and above all painterly in its direct apprehension of her physical
surroundings. *Thistles,* the first collection of poems by Raab, appeared in

1930, and her second was published only some two decades later. A final volume, *Last Prayer,* came out in 1972. Editions of her collected poetry and prose were published after her death.

Words Like Rare Birds

[. . .] The basis of poetry for me is music. Before I became a writer, I played the violin. I had a pretty voice, loved singing, and I thought I would be a musician or a singer.

Later, a different madness suddenly took hold of me. A friend of mine visited from Paris where she had seen Isadora Duncan dance. She described her to me and I thought to myself, I could be just like her. I had an attractive body, I was young and . . . my body would express itself through dance. So I started looking for a dance teacher. I found some old ballerina and soon grew tired of the whole thing.

Still later I thought, I'll write. It grabbed me, but what agony, it was true agony — trying to express myself in that way, I who didn't have the patience to sit in school, through ridiculous classes in math and physics. . . . I only liked nature studies, and Bible class. I had excellent teachers, and often repeat that fact, and always must, for those teachers provided a tremendous foundation for my poetry. [. . .]

So, first of all it's about the music. Later, there's always a process that precedes the writing with me, which — it corresponds, something corresponds, and I hear voices, indistinct voices, but slowly they take on the shape of words, words that aren't yet intelligible. This used to happen to me on waking, in that morning moment between sleep and wakefulness, that's when it was. Sometimes even in a dream, suddenly a single sentence — like a motto — would sing out from someplace, I don't know from where, exactly as I say in the poem: "There are words like rare birds / flying toward me; / coming from somewhere / beyond consciousness — / a trail of light in their wake; / some are bright and others dim / like embers whispering; / some ring out like a distant bell — / others are black and deep as a grave. / I'll never know where they come from. / Rustling like strange and fleeting birds — /

with a touch from another world, / miraculous . . ." — they just come, I don't question it, I don't even like looking into it, and don't know how it happens, I haven't read the psychological literature.

And so, first it's a word, then a single sentence, and I start nurturing it, circling it and creating an ambience. There's a great deal behind this, but I don't want to say more about it, it's hard to say more about it. Suddenly I'm writing the first stanza, yes, four or five lines, six lines, and then this stanza creates another, it becomes a type of *pendentif,* you know, one thing leading to another, one thing dependent on another, I know I haven't finished, I need more, not for the lines, you see, but for myself, I need to fill more in, I feel I haven't let out what I should have, so I begin again, and increasingly, it comes together, one thing emerging from another, an image from another image, as I never imagined it would unfold, and suddenly there it is — a poem!

But it's raw material, I feel it is still raw material, I haven't yet raised it to the level I can raise it to, and I know I can, so I begin erasing one line and writing another in its place, a different word; suddenly one word creates two new lines which I hadn't even thought of, the word is so heavy (in terms of content) that two new lines are formed. . . .

Then I let it be. I let a week pass before I approach it again, and by then it has taken on a different appearance, like that of an old acquaintance, who's grown distant, but . . . is also calling out to me, something in it is still calling me. I begin to rework it, until I find the problem: "What word is this? Why did you put that there? That's in the wrong place!" — I revise some more, and this can continue for two weeks. Finally I'm satisfied: I see something polished before me, I've expressed what I wanted to (more or less), and it resembles the images I saw, the internal and external images both, it resembles them and is also elevated to the level of poetry, poetry in the truest sense of the word. There it is.

As for influences, I can't say there have been very many. I am, after all, a kind of wild-vine (that's what I call myself in secret). But there were some, of course there were; there was Verlaine, and then Rimbaud, the French poets certainly, but not to a critical degree. They were a source of sustenance more than influence.

Actually there was a little-known poet who influenced me greatly, coming to me exactly when I needed him. This was Walter Calé — few remember him — a quiet and lyrical symbolist who wrote one book and then disappeared.

In those days I admired [Avraham] Shlonsky and [Yitzhaq] Lamdan also, but I wasn't influenced by them. I can't say I wasn't influenced by Bialik — who wasn't influenced by Bialik? He was the very foundation of the language, and of style too. [. . .]

That's it. What else can I say? I've trod among thistles and thorns; I *am* thistles and thorns. I've been pricked by the bramble bush on my way to gather figs. The influence of Arabic was also significant back then. We used certain Arabic words, and I sang Arabic songs — that was for me an important thing, I had a very beautiful voice. We ate yogurt and figs, we sang Arabic songs, and we learned a new-born Hebrew, emerging from Jerusalem, from Eliezer Ben-Yehuda, and my kindergarten teacher said: *At mashira kol kakh yafeh* ("you send-forth-song so beautifully"). At that age I didn't know Hebrew grammar, but instinctively I felt that something was wrong. Somehow I just knew she shouldn't say "you send-forth-song."

The language was in that nascent state. And now I'd like to boast. Once I said to my friend: "There are a multitude of beautiful things in the world" (*yesh hamon devarim yafim ba'olam*) — while in those days no one yet used the word "multitude" (*hamon*), and now that word belongs to the multitudes.

1973

[RTB]

Uri Zvi Greenberg

(1896–1981)

One of the leading modernist figures of twentieth-century Yiddish and
Hebrew poetry, Uri Zvi Greenberg was a prolific writer whose poetry and
personality blew like a cyclone into pre-State Palestine of the 1920s and
'30s and violently reconfigured its cultural landscape. Greenberg was a
major player on the political scene as well. He began as a fiery Labor Zionist
but soon became disillusioned with that movement's mainstream secular-
humanist leadership and found himself drifting toward—and eventually
going beyond—the maximalist and militant platform put forth by Ze'ev
Jabotinsky, leader of the Zionist Revisionist Party, which the poet eventually
joined.

This was but one of several revolutions that Greenberg underwent.
Born in eastern Galicia and descended from a line of charismatic Hasidic
leaders, he was raised in Lvov (Poland) and received a traditional Hasidic
education. He began writing at an early age. He was drafted into the Austro-
Hungarian army during World War I, endured a terrifying encounter in the
trenches on the Serbian front, then observed equally brutal and frightening
scenes during the anti-Jewish pogroms a year later in Poland.

The horrors Greenberg witnessed shocked his poetry out of the Romantic
haze it had drifted in, and not long after the war his work exploded into a
barely bridled expressionism that took on a Jewish nationalist hue. Immi-
grating to Palestine in 1923, Greenberg identified with the down-to-earth

ethos of the Zionist pioneers, and his poetics developed accordingly. While his frontal assault on Bialikian lyricism—the prevailing taste at the time— offended many, Bialik himself came to the young poet's defense, recognizing the power and genius of his Hebrew.

Greenberg's poetry moved through a number of subsequent phases, including, for a time, a return to shorter and quieter lyrics, but the gap between poetry, politics, and prophecy gradually dwindled. With his 1930 collection, *The Belt of Defense and Word of the Son of Blood,* his Revisionist worldview was articulated in the sharpest fashion: "I despise the peace of those who surrender, brokered by coercion, / over mounds of dead Jews and the stench of blood," he wrote—and "The Jewish soldier prays for your peace with a rifle, / May its barrel be sweeter than an organ's song."

The overtly fascistic elements of the poetry he wrote between 1930 and 1937 (the latter date marks the publication of *The Book of Indictment and Faith*) left Greenberg ostracized in Palestine; his books were removed from the stores and no longer published (though writing at times, he traveled frequently to Europe and turned his attention to the Revisionist program to rescue its Jewish community). In the wake of World War II and the exter- mination of most of European Jewry, Greenberg's poems again began appearing in print, and critics speak of his writing life as being divided into two halves: everything he wrote before World War II, and the poems he published after the war. *Streets of the River*—in which national grief and response to the Holocaust take precedence over all the internecine struggles reflected in Greenberg's other work—was published in 1951 to wide acclaim and is considered one of the finest books of its period.

After serving as a member in the first Israeli Knesset, from 1949 to 1951, Greenberg withdrew from political life, married, and devoted himself to his writing; over the next twenty-five years or so he continued to write powerful poetry in a variety of modes, informally publishing sections of what is now considered to be a long metaphysical song of himself. These many changes notwithstanding, Greenberg remained an essentially ultranationalist, messianic poet—one who considered Israel the homeland of the Jewish people exclusively. While he viewed the foundation of the state in 1948 with mixed feelings—regretting the compromise he believed it entailed—he also saw it as a vital element in his people's redemption and divine election.

The poem that follows forms the conclusion to his major 1928 poetic manifesto, "Against 99," and is, as such, addressed to the ninety-nine of every hundred poets and readers of Hebrew who, as Greenberg sees it, hold to the old-fashioned model of the poet as aesthete. Greenberg defines the purpose and mission of the Hebrew poet in the age of the pioneers against them and their outmoded ways. The poets who are settling the Land of Israel, he says, require a radical reorientation, which in turn calls for a radically new poetics.

The Poet in the Teaching
of the Untamed Jews

You who weep over white sheaves of paper, over which one might
    write truthful letters to friends far away —
Or join letters-of-fire in the name of the blood's purest grief,
    which will go on burning in the souls of men, like prophecy's
    chapters;
You whose souls and hearts and lives are as nothing beside the
    weight of the hymn, with its honey and wine and tear,
Who long for me, the untamed poet, to go with you, that with
    you I might sing my poems, before the crowd, as the teaching
    of the Hebrew aesthete demands —
Verily, I say to you: Go and close your windows, so that your
    hearts, aquiver like mercury, will not spill as I pass by in the
    gold of the desert wind, which to me is like a robe — about my
    burning body —
To the blacksmiths as the iron goes red, I will lend a hand, and to
    those who wander into the wilderness, after their finest beast.

But like the camel led through these sands, silently bearing its
    burdens, and with the tongue of its bell ringing — night and
    day its surrender — this I will not be,
But like a bull at dawn, bellowing to be released to the sun.
    One man goes to his work until evening, and another goes
    to hunger,
And at night, here, I'll join the sea in its heft and fear, and like it
    I'll lie on this ochre ground,
And sometimes I will resemble a dog with all my yearning and
    compassion;
I will not sing in blessed rhyme: my heart's gates are open . . . So
    long as I can't do this truly, my heart is a graveyard to men in
    pain;
They long for a homeland for themselves within the homeland
    itself;
Let them enter into me, as into a tavern or sanctuary —
And for the seventy years of my life, if I live, I'll join them and
    walk at the head of this column for which I've yearned, in
    search of the well of Hebrew prophecy —
Lacking any earthly bread, I'll drink from the grace of the world
    on high, by twilight's glow I'll gnaw on the melon's red flesh,
    and this will be my evening meal;
My lips will drip with the prayer for the dead, for so many beaten-
    down and poor, like me in the Land of Israel,
And the bodies' sigh in these shacks at night I will hear as the
    groan of boats on the waves.
This is the law of the poet, in the teaching of the untamed Jews.

[PC]

Gershom Scholem

(1897–1982)

"A historian who remade the world" is how Cynthia Ozick characterized the
essentially elusive Gershom Scholem, who was one of the greatest scholars
of the twentieth century and a man of prodigious talent. While he virtually
created the subject of Qabbala and Jewish mysticism as a serious area of
study, his influence has been felt far beyond the confines of the academy
and to this day extends into the realm of literature and the arts. (Borges,
for one, rhymed "Golem" with "Scholem.") Literature played a critical part
in Scholem's own life, especially in his formative years, and he wrote
(distinctive and dark) poems from his teens on. He was, however, primarily
known as a masterful writer of prose—mostly in German, but in Hebrew as
well. Scholem was extremely close to Walter Benjamin, and the two writers
shared an abiding interest in the dynamics and metaphysics of language.
In the meditation that follows, which was written in German and is in fact
a letter to the great Jewish theologian Franz Rosenzweig, that interest
intersects with Scholem's profound disillusionment with Zionism and leaves
us with a chilling portrait of what was happening—and would happen—to
the Hebrew language.

Scholem was born in Berlin in 1897, into a secular bourgeois household.
He studied in Germany, receiving his Ph.D. in 1922. A year later he settled in
Jerusalem, where he worked initially as a librarian. For many years he was

Professor of Jewish Mysticism at the Hebrew University. His groundbreaking books include the magisterial *Major Trends in Jewish Mysticism* and *Sabbatai Sevi: The Mystical Messiah* as well as *On the Kabbalah and Its Symbolism, From Berlin to Jerusalem,* and *Walter Benjamin: The Story of a Friendship.* He died in 1982.

Thoughts about Our Language

The land is a volcano, and it hosts the language. People talk a great deal here about many things which may make us fail — particularly these days about the Arabs. But another, more serious danger than that of the Arab people threatens us, a danger which follows of necessity from the Zionist enterprise. What will be the result of updating the Hebrew language? Is not the holy language, which we have planted among our children, an abyss that must open up? People here do not know the meaning of what they have done. They think that they have turned Hebrew into a secular language and that they have removed its apocalyptic sting, but it is not so. The secularization of the language is merely empty words, a rhetorical turn of phrase. In reality, it is impossible to empty the words which are filled to bursting with meaning, save at the expense of the language itself. And indeed, this *Volapük,* this ghostly language spoken in our streets, precisely represents that expressionless linguistic universe which alone may be secularized. But if we pass on to our children the language that we have received, if we, the generation of the transition, revive the language of the old books that it may be revealed to them anew — will not the religious power latent therein one day break out against its speakers? And what will be the image of the generation toward whom its expressions are directed?

We live with this language as on the edge of an abyss, yet nearly all of us walk there with confidence, like blind men. Does no one fear that, once our eyes are opened, we or those who follow us will roll down into it? Nor can we know whether the sacrifice of those lost in the abyss will suffice to cover it up again.

The creators of the Hebrew renaissance believed in the magical powers of language with a blind, almost fanatical faith. Had their eyes been open, they would have been unable to find in their souls the demonic courage to revive a language within an environment in which it could only become a kind of Esperanto. And yet they walked — and continue to walk — on the edge of an abyss, as if in a trance — and the abyss is silent. They pass on the old names and signs to others, to the youth. At times, when, in the course of a totally unimportant speech by an anonymous speaker, we hear a religious term, we shudder — even if it might have been meant to comfort us. This Hebrew language is pregnant with catastrophe; it cannot remain in its present state — nor will it remain there. Our children will no longer have any other language; truth be told, they, and they alone, will pay the price for this encounter which we have imposed upon them unasked, or without even asking ourselves. One day the language will turn against its own speakers — and there are moments when it does so even now; moments which it is difficult to forget, leaving wounds in which all the presumptuousness of our goal is revealed. Will we then have a youth who will be able to hold fast against the rebellion of a holy tongue?

A language is composed of names. The power of the language is hidden within the name; its abyss is sealed therein. After invoking the ancient names day after day, we shall no longer be able to hold off their power. We have awakened them, and they shall appear, for we have summoned them up with awesome power. True, we speak inarticulately, in a ghost language. Names walk about in our sentences like ghosts. Journalists play with them, pretending to themselves or to God that it is really meaningless. But at times the holiness of our language leaps out and speaks to us from within its spectral degradation. Names have a life of their own. Were it not so — woe to our children, who have been abandoned to emptiness.

All those words which were not created arbitrarily and out of nothing, but were taken from the good old lexicon, are filled to the brim with explosive meaning. A generation which has inherited the most fruitful of all of the holy traditions, our language, cannot live without tradition — even should it wish to do so a thousandfold. When the power inherent in the language, when the spoken word — that is, the content of the language — will again assume form, our nation will once more be confronted by the holy tradition as a decisive example. And the people will then need to choose between the two: either to submit to it, or to perish in oblivion. God cannot remain silent in a language in which He has been evoked thousands of times to return to our life. The inevitable revolution of a language in which His voice is again heard — that is the only subject not discussed here in the land, because those who renewed the Hebrew language did not believe in the Day of Judgment which they set up for us through their deeds. Would that the lightness of mind which guided us on this apocalyptic path not lead us to destruction.

1926

[JC]

Avraham Shlonsky

(1900–1973)

Avraham Shlonsky's work marks the move *away* from a Hebrew poetry rooted in Europe and *toward* a genuinely "Land of Israel" modernist mode. Shlonsky was an indefatigable polemicist, translator, lyricist, editor, and writer for the theater who, it has been said, set the tone for his generation. Born in the Ukraine at the turn of the century, he was raised in a Zionist, religious family. As a teenager he was sent to school for a year in Palestine, then completed his studies in Russia during World War I. In 1921 he came to Palestine for good, working in construction with a group of young pioneers. In one of his ecstatic, quasireligious early poems, he refers to himself as "the road-building bard." Elsewhere, as part of his transformative agenda, he calls for "free love between words, without the canopy and marriage vows of the holy text."

Shlonsky, who was by nature temperamental, was best known for having led the inevitable rebellion against Bialik's classicism. He translated into Hebrew both Russian modernists such as Yesenin, Mayakovsky, and Blok and classic works by Pushkin and many others. In his sonorous poetry, he yoked traditional imagery to contemporary contexts, yielding once-celebrated images such as "the roads winding through the land like tefillin" (phylacteries) and "the light wrapping the land like a prayer shawl." Although extremely popular during the poet's lifetime, Shlonsky's verse now seems quite dated, and it is rarely turned to by readers and writers. The prose of his journals, however (and curiously), still feels fresh.

The selections below are taken from two key periods in the poet's writing life.

"Every man has his own desires" — this is the measure of truth according to which a person of merit needs to adjust and extend the shape of his soul to its natural limits.

How? — He breaches the fenced and fences the breached, in the sense of "the right hand rejects and the left draws near," he builds and expands worlds and this is the lust for life in the sense of the "gnawing in the pit of the stomach" that detests stasis and loves to peel back layers and put on a new skin in order to peel it back again — and again to put it on . . .

Permutations! Permutations! Permutations!

> Every heart and its aspiration —
> and to each — ten thousand ills

— for such are the trials of creation, the torture of all who would "cast a glance" [at paradise]. And he who is greater than his friend — so too is his urge greater, and therefore one is stricken and loses his mind, one loses faith and becomes a heretic, and one dies an exemplary death.

And this, and only this, is the measure of truth a person will choose for himself, and live or die by. Life and death in which there is valor and splendor.

Life is disfigured by the forbidden and configured by the impossible.

The forbidden — weakens, the impossible — excites.

Desires seethe, seethe and coalesce, and turn into principles, and your model: plaster mixed with water (percolating and percolating and hardening until you have nothing that can break it apart).

It isn't always necessary to knock something down if it hasn't been understood by others.

Not everyone succeeds in not being understood.

There are times when rhyme in a poem — is like a derrick for an eagle: the broken-winged need it, the mighty-pinioned — despise it.

1943–1950

What a curse — to be a writer in a language that hasn't been spoken for generations. A tongue that has no great-great-grandfathers. To always have to create something from nothing (and even something from something). By means
of literary association. From books. And not from life. For how long?! Blessed
are you, O infants. Mischievous Hebrew children — you are a comfort.

But what joy in the past — in the sources. Each time you examine them —
a new discovery. Even what you knew appears before you like a flash of lightning. And so long as this luster is concealed in the scrolls and not in the folds
of life, in the mouths of speakers — this will be "a living exception." Only
today I rediscovered the Talmudic expression "Bring the sun to the city"
[*Ta'anit* 10b, i.e., come at dawn]. How graphic! That is: he enters the city with
the sun. If only the nation spoke like that — for this verse has a twofold and
fourfold splendor. And so — so it is, nevertheless, the dust of books, learning,
expertise, the growth pangs . . . of a nation, the growth pangs of a language.
Reviving the living.

How should I handle Eliaz? He is so sad and . . . such a boor. After all, this
man doesn't have the least bit of talent for bearing his own sadness! He
"wasn't made for this." He deals with sadness as though it were an accident,
or hard luck, as something completely unnecessary. Almost like "a missed
lunch." A sad and hungry bear. But a very nice bear. Perhaps precisely
because of this burliness, this health which is unwilling to give up on itself.

Strange: people are identifiable largely by their sadness. Truly, precisely: in
their talent for bearing their grief. Look at your friends, and how they're sad,
and you'll know who they are!!

Lea [Goldberg], when she is sad — gets offended. The sadness itself
descending upon her gives offense. As though she saw it as a lack of courtesy
on the part of Providence in relation to her. "A transgression of propriety and
decency." And her face, which grows childlike when that happens, has the
look of a little girl who has been offended, as she starts to pout.

And sadness in poems? This alone is not enough. Poetry built out of sadness smacks of "careerism," it seems to me, for many poets. Compensation
for virtue. A seeking of reward for what is required — that's what it is. A

poem!! I'm sad — lo and behold I've written a poem because I was sad. The *reward* of sadness. No, no. This is why I despise *moist,* physiological tears (in poetry). The poem needs to *freeze them.* Not to weep, so tears stream down — but rather, to cast forth ice like hail, to crystallize, to hew — to build. To build — and not to weep! "A cry-baby lyricism" — *anti-poetry!*

Expressionism tried to flee from the cry to the outcry, and the result was a *scream,* the raising of the voice, a din. And as a result the physiological tears were not neutralized, so much as falsified. They begin to harden, but although they're no longer moist, they're still sticky. It's forbidden to relinquish poetry's measure of nobility. And what is nobility if not restraint, a mask, a cruel strictness with regard to what is exterior and the maintenance of distance. Erupt — but inwardly; contained fire — but *in the bones.* And not in one's expression. Not, at all costs, in the features of the face! Ah, the face flush from weeping . . . but once again I'm tumbling down this slope of an argument with myself over poetry. Alas, poets, poets, you are incorrigible!

What can one do? People are able to conjure ideas that are greater than they are, greater than their ability and willingness to realize them. Later on, small people come onto the scene to realize ideas that the great dreamed up.

This disproportion in human history is costly for us. And there is only one solution: to establish a different regime, in which a person will not be prevented from being as great as he should be — so that he'll succeed and practice what he preaches.

Poems are not what a person wants but cannot say, so much as what he can say but doesn't want to. Here is the secret of form! Here is the "camouflage," the modesty that honors what is worthy (let's say: the sublime, the secret, the beautiful, the just). Here are the origins of rhythm, of rhyme, of all exploration. The dissatisfaction with a received mode of expression. Here too is the flight from the hyperbolic, from superfluous skill. Here is the ascent to a different form of simplicity, one that is the child of great wealth, which is selfless.

Forms? What are they? To me it seems they're a kind of protection. Thus, for instance, the ropes and pickaxes that mountain climbers use, which the justifiable fear of heights invented, and the fear of having to scale summits. A person cannot simply climb a mountain — there are dangers on its paths, dangers that don't exist in the valleys. This is what I was alluding to in one of my poems, in the verse: "Here — the twisting path is courage turned into silence."

And again: forms. This game. This noble pretense, for poetry isn't content, but a standing at the edge of content; "any minute now" . . . and you step back, absent yourself a bit from God. Am I being banal if I allow myself the obvious comparison: to Moses who succeeded in seeing only the back of God? In the sense of "No man may see my face — and live!" . . . Poetry is life — it is the great encounter between the will to live and the fact that one will inevitably die.

I once thought:
    Man, as we know, is a creature of habit. And habit, of course, "is second nature." And it is a pity that man endures and repeatedly experiences numerous afflictions and trials, and consequently becomes accustomed to them. And this is the secret of culture. While death strikes us only once. What would happen if man didn't die just once and became accustomed to death?! All of culture, all of poetry, all of life! — would change utterly as a result.

Memory isn't the vessel and advocate of the past's equity. It is also its prose-cutor. History, of course, is memory of the past, but not for its own sake. Here culture comes into the picture — to the extent that it involves moral fiber and grandeur — and this is memory of the *future*.
    Memory was given to us not for static knowledge, or knowledge for its own sake, but to enable us to draw lessons and plan our actions.

— Secular culture! — I said to someone or other. And my interlocutor countered:
    — Is it possible? You, the poet?!
    I continued, saying:
    — Yes, secular culture — that is, a culture whose sacredness is not drawn

from God who exists in any event, who rules with a high hand and thwarts the realization of man's finest dreams, but a sacredness that draws from the *yearning* for God, from the permanent, inexhaustible ability of man to make himself a God in his own image, in the image of his greatest dreams. The dreams *change*! (And maybe they don't change, but are, instead, perfected?)

— Talent, talent . . . The main thing is talent. . . .
— Yes, we've heard, and that too is right . . . of course, it's right. But if we keep in mind the magnitude of the danger, which is to say, talent alone, without the higher guidance of an idea — we can say, when it comes to this union of idea and talent, with Clausewitz on the preparations for battle: "An average measure of courage combined with extraordinary talent yields greater results than an average measure of talent combined with extraordinary courage."

The Good Poem

What are your criteria for evaluating a poem? What signs might indicate a good poem?

Courage with regard to the coexistence of form and content, and equal rights for the old and the new, the silent and the clamorous, the rhymed and the unrhymed, the light and the severe.

Singularity. Just as the final syllables of the rhyming lines do not make the rhyme, but rather the entire stanza with all its components, so too neither does the ideational, descriptive, or narrative surface constitute the real content of the poem. The singularity of the structure, of the combination of the words and the melodic qualities of what is said and what is not said — this is the test. Good poems are like those "lean cows" in Pharaoh's dream that swallowed the fat cows, the many poems that were not sung — or that were sung and discounted in the poet's heart — and "one could not tell that they had consumed them," for they ate — and remained lean.

Better a translator of useful things than a writer of idle chatter.

The Union of Writers, in its present climate and framework, with its bank balance and spiritless black market, is in its way a city of refuge to which all can flee who have murdered a story, poem, or the like — accidentally, it goes without saying. For no one murders poems willfully — that is: no one sets out intending to commit murder. After all, he is certain of his considerable talent. . . .

— You're going in the name of the Union of Writers?

— No, I am not going in the name of *writers*. I'm going in the name of literature, and that, of course, is what I represent.

[GL]

Avot Yeshurun

(1904–1991)

"A writer should write only when he has a nail in the foot," Avot Yeshurun
is reported to have said, "and I—always do." And so it has seemed: though
he didn't publish his first book (*The Wisdom of Roads*) until he was thirty-
eight, a torrent of poems followed, gathered in collections that began
in strength and continued to evolve through the power of his final two
magisterial volumes, *Master of Death* (1990) and *I Have Not Now*, which
appeared posthumously.

The literary pack rat of modern Hebrew, Yeshurun from early on in his
career scurried across the landscapes and languages of pre-State Palestine
and Israel, bringing, as he put it, everything he found: "Not all that glitters
is gold," he writes, "but I pick up / everything that glitters." Much of what
gives off such a distinctive glint in his verse is drawn from his native Yiddish
and the Arabic he grew close to while working the land as a young man;
in addition to his highly idiosyncratic Hebrew, bits of Polish, Russian,
Hungarian, and German are also thrown into the mix. His English translator,
Harold Schimmel, has written of "the pungent thingness of the objects in
his poems," and the phrase applies to the poet's work as a whole, for words
there are very definitely objects, and objects first and foremost words—in
the mouth, as shape and taste and sound. All of which is another way of
saying that Yeshurun is the most tactile of poets.

That physical sense of language and lineage extends even to his name. Born Yehiel Perlmutter in a western Ukrainian village in 1904, Yeshurun was raised in a family whose Hasidic roots went back many generations. When he was five, the family moved to Krasnystaw—a Polish town that figures prominently in the poet's work. Apart from his traditional religious education, he was privately tutored and read widely in Yiddish, Hebrew, and world literature (in Polish translation). He began writing poetry in Yiddish. In 1925 he emigrated to Palestine, where he worked in construction and as a watchman, swamp dredger, and fruit picker, among other things. With the founding of the State of Israel, he changed his name to Avot Yeshurun, which means, literally, "the fathers are looking."

The wholly sui generis style of poetry that Yeshurun developed is rhythmically distinctive and bursting with neologisms that carry a powerful emotional charge. The poet he most resembles, in a sense, is Uri Zvi Greenberg—the two shared the catastrophe of the Holocaust as a subject (both lost entire families in the war)—though no one could be further from Greenberg's nationalism than Yeshurun, whose poems on Arab–Jewish coexistence were decades ahead of their time.

The extraordinary quality of Yeshurun's poetry was matched, it seems, only by that of the man himself, whose cantankerous eccentricity and power come through clearly in the 1986 interview that follows. The interviewer is his daughter, Helit Yeshurun, the editor of *Hadarim*—arguably the finest Hebrew literary journal of the past quarter century.

How Do You Get to the Poem?

I never do. I get to a stirring and an agitation, to words that are split and crushed—until a thing moves toward itself, one crushing toward another, and the words make phrases and that makes a poem. I don't know how to pick up pen and ink and write a poem.

A person from time to time finds himself abandoned by himself, by his personal sense of confidence, his sense of connection to his surroundings, and he longs to be brought back to himself. I didn't say to be alone. To be brought back to himself. When he does that, he's restored at once to the initial landscape of his life, his childhood. And this "initialness" is linked with something sublime, something invisible. A child is in distress. A child has no hope. A child is in a difficult situation. And out of this situation you begin to say as much with words. You begin to scratch out lines. Naturally you'll change them later, or write others, but what you have in that first line — that's what will be in the poem. The poem in its essence is already there in that initial line. In a single word of that first line all of its magic already lies, that radium, which emanates across what follows. From within that drive, within these accelerators, you arrive at all sorts of expressions, which seem on the face of it to lack all connection, but each and every word is the poem, the poem in one form or another, maybe more or maybe less, though this you won't know until many years later. To this very day I don't know if a version I've chosen of a given poem is the right one. The poem follows out its own dynamic, until the stanzas make a building. A kind of construction.

A person is always writing a poem. The middle of the poem is also a beginning. You write. Whatever you write, you're writing. You have nothing. Not even a piece of fabric. But you start making yourself a suit. You don't know what you'll sew with. You need to take measurements. What measurements does the tailor take? The line, the length of the line. You write a line — until it's a line. This line is already the poem. In fact a person doesn't write a long poem at all, he writes a single line. That single line brings him into a battle with whatever it is that weighs on him, until it gives in, until for a moment it lets him be and he stops writing, though he hasn't finished. No one has ever finished. Not Shakespeare, not Goethe, not Alterman, not Bialik. He writes and writes, sewing that suit, following the lead of that single line. The second line derives from the first. The same measurements. And all that comes your way in life between the composition of that first line and the second, all that has happened to you in your life, and in the world — if you feel the world and are responsible for it — enters into the mix and troubles you and makes things complicated and weighs on you and preys on you, and enters into your search for the second line.

After that second line you have to fill out two more lines, at least, if you want to make a stanza, and four lines is the poem's structure. You have four lines — a building. The second line looks for the third. And here, the life that has entered your life, the life of the poem that is influenced by your private life, all that happens to you, enters into the search for the third line. Therefore the third line is so different from the first. You have three worlds. Though they aren't different; they're all part of an individual's single world. You don't write a poem for the sake of the poem. There is only a single line, and then the great struggle for the second line and how to make the third and how to make the fourth. [. . .]

Let's say a poem is "about something," that it has a subject. Is that subject imprinted in it?

A true poem as I see it can't be considered in terms of its subject matter. A poem is a body enveloped by a soul, a subject enveloped by a poem. The poem dissolves the need for a subject. This is how it happens: after you've written a poem, you see that it drew its nourishment from a direction you hadn't envisioned. Whatever you prepared for it in the way of a meal, it had no need for. It ate its own food. Not because it rejected what you'd prepared for it; it just didn't need it. Don't your poems have subjects, you ask? They do, but the poem itself is what determines them, according to the line of its life, the direction it takes. [. . .]

Does it ever happen that a poem leads you to write things that you didn't mean to write initially?

I don't set out to write things that I mean to write. I set out to write things that are groping about in the dark.

Is the mood that's revealed in a poem the one you knew of when you started to write?

I'm in a constant state of inflammation, a steady fever. It doesn't matter. [. . .] A poem gets used to being a poem. Used to its comfortable situation and sometimes to its uncomfortable and tragic situation — of being a poem. But this habituation to being — in itself works against the poem. Because a poem ushers in something new, which wasn't known or felt by anyone before. A poem doesn't come to express a given or known situation or state: Love, envy, death. [. . .] What is the pure lyric *about*? A state. What state? The poem needs to bring itself and its state with it, and the state that brought its state about: the poem. What is the state that caused the poem? The poem got used to the fact that this state is called love, longing, attraction; this is habituation, the habit that is death for the poem. [. . .]

Do you consciously gather "material" for poetry?

The materials take shape with the groping. Before I deal with the poem? Sometimes I write down certain expressions or my thinking turns up something of interest without joining it immediately to thoughts of a specific poem that I'm writing or will write. Maybe I'll use it, or maybe I won't. I jotted it down without thinking of it as potential material for poetry. After the ship has sailed, the material might turn out to have been a stowaway. [. . .]

How would you describe your relationship to the words at the time of writing?

If there are a few words that are destined for me to fall in love with, they'll never sleep in peace, or eat in peace, or even take off their clothes; they'll always be dressed, and sleep in their clothes, and they'll never be sure if they'll finish the night where they started it or sleep in the same place. That they won't be brought during the night from one bed to another. None of them will know where its bed is. Why? Because a man's mind is twisted. And a poet's sevenfold. He looks for himself in words, and will not leave the word he loves. When he goes out searching, he takes this word with him. "Maybe you'll sit here; maybe you'll be more comfortable over here; maybe here you'll have a better neighbor." One's always moving. Because a poem, to begin it in the morning — in the morning, like a bird one morning — there's a bird here that sings to me, and I don't know if it's a hen being slaughtered or announcing its presence and dominance here in the landscape. From early in the morning it sends up a sound like a hen being slaughtered, and so it continues throughout the day, with long breaks, until the evening. Every day I hear it from a different direction, farther away or nearer, which is to say, it moves around. And whatever is slaughtered sends up its cry until it realizes what's happening. Either it's being slaughtered, or else it's looking for a mate. That's how it is with the poem. With words. The words are that bird. These words build the poem and make it bear fruit. They distribute stamens across its lines, until they take on meaning, grow stronger, and build the poem. And then the poem is poured and cast, each and every line.

Do you write poems in a single sitting? Do you revise a lot?

I'm reluctant to write everything down at once. There were poems that I wrote in a single sitting. I don't think any more of them than I do of poems over which I labored. Not at all. [. . .] Naturally it's good when a poem comes all at once. When it doesn't cause any trouble and emerges like a chick from the egg. All this amazement about a poem that emerges in a single sitting just brings on a need to enlarge it, to push it further; other pieces come to you, other stanzas. If you keep it in the drawer until it's time to put a book together, it stays "all at once." But if someone (me) thinks of it, then stanzas get added, and it takes on new proportions. There are poems I wrote in a single sitting to which I added nothing. [. . .] But the mere fact of having had such a fortunate beginning — such a blessing — spurs you on to continue like that. That is, despite the fact that you write with difficulty, suddenly you've written without any strain.

When do you know that a poem is finished?

When I see that it's beautiful.

First of all, I don't believe that any poem in the world is ever finished. I've always had a feeling that a poem completes itself. When I say "a poem completes itself" — you accept it beside you, this bird — first of all you have a poem. It's important that I have a poem in hand. Then I announce that it's done, and I put it in my pocket. Later on, between its composition and its printing, nothing rests, it's with me in the drawer. They say that a poem ripens in the drawer. With me it isn't in the drawer, it's at the end of my pencil, it continues. That I've said it's finished — that's so I can get on with it. The principal's in hand, so I can trade in foreign currency. I continue quietly. If I'm not sure of a poem, the expansion won't go well. No poem is ever finished. All poems continue. The thread of a poem's life comes to an end with the date of its printing. And even then the account isn't settled. A poem has no border.

Is a poem finished with its publication?

When it's published I leave it for good. Without any longing, or fear that I won't see it again. I don't sit around congratulating myself for having written a given poem, and when it's printed its great forgetting begins.

Do you ever get the desire to go back to old poems and change them?

No. Never.

Do you ever miss rhymed poetry, or poetry that's more formal than what you write today?

No. And it's good that poetry doesn't rhyme. The poem's construction interests me, but rhyme is a kind of sleight of hand. As long as time passes and time approaches, we're obliged to use simple words. As much as possible, simple words about an infinite number of things. The less we understand the world, the simpler our words should be when we speak. I'm always envious of anyone who utters a simple phrase and you hear the power of the language, which is really a way of saying, "What do you want from me, I'm not covering myself up, I'm lying here with my legs spread open, I'm the language woman." A language has everything in it, man's most mysterious utterance, the revelation of his secret and mystery and much testimony about you, about yourself. The great witness to man is the language. And it has to be the truth, to get to the truth! When you don't find this, you feel cheated, and come away with nothing. [. . .]

You've said that one should use simple words as much as possible. But you yourself often twist words and invent new ones. These aren't simple words.

I listen with two ears, and each ear hears a different language. One ear hears Hebrew, the other Yiddish. Don't speak with me if you can help it. Yiddish is my mother tongue. And I've written that Hebrew is my mother tongue. When I say one should write with simple words, that's a wish, a desire. But it can't become a fact. I can't manage with simple words. Each word brings in its wake the world from which it emerged and in which it took shape. This yearning surrounds the language, it comes as though from the waves, like Jesus' boat on the Sea of Galilee. Suddenly the Russian word is fabulous. Like the honeycomb enveloped by bees. All this has an influence on my poems, and I can't help it. I don't want to leave that world behind. It brings me back to life.

There's one other thing I want to say, but with two words, not with one. To my great sorrow I need two simple words for this, not one. Each word belongs to a different language. One belongs to Hebrew, and one to Yiddish. Each is a simple word, but there has to be two of them. Not one. This is the secret of the failure. The secret of my difficulty. I dragged myself and that single word to this country, that word which brings with it the long train of a profound culture, and so it awakens endless associations.

All this because it meets a great rival in the other language. And so all sorts of formulations emerge, to clarify the use of this single word before the clarifying power of the other language. It may well be that the difficulty derives from the attempt to find the two words from the two languages and merge them into one. I've wanted to pour the two words into a single word.

Do political poems go through the same process you've described above?

No. It's not the same. Poems like that come easily. Without the stages we talked about. The materials are given in advance. In [one of my older political cal poems], I found myself in a certain emotional situation vis-à-vis the Arab–Jewish world. Between my personal situation and my situation as a Jew. And I was defeated. Not disappointed — defeated. Defeated as someone who had invested his entire world in something. And all of his faith. The idea of this land as a good country. I realize now that what I'd written of could not have been realized. I don't justify it, just as a person doesn't justify his suffering. Nonetheless, disappointment is too small a word. I experienced a total collapse of my world. You know, your house collapses, the roof caves in, and you live there still, perhaps in the same place, knowing that now it's more secure, more secure than the house you'd imagine should be there; you yourself have built the walls, and you live there. But the house doesn't give rise to poems. I was, at the time, a man who'd been utterly slaughtered within his world. Not then. I'm slaughtered now.

But every poem is a revolt against something. Every poem, even the most lyrical. A revolt against the existence in which we find ourselves. Against an accident that has happened. A revolt, a desire to throw off this situation. The intention being not to influence so much as to oppose, to protest.

Doesn't the desire to return to the success of an earlier poem constitute an obstacle to new writing?

No. There's a certain defect in me, or flaw, that makes me forget what I've written. Poems that made me happy when I read them, poems that I liked when they were printed, I somehow forget within a short time after they're published. I'd imagine that they themselves bring about this death in me, so that I'll be free to write new poems. They bring about a certain justice, in which there's a measure of malice, but it's good that they do what they do. Otherwise I'd spend all my life perfecting a single poem that I liked.

In your opinion, can poetry be edited in the way one edits prose?

No! No! And no again! Authentic prose can't be edited either. [. . .]

Has your poetry changed over the past few years, or is there something that you're trying to reach?

I don't see any line or point before me that I'm trying to reach. I'm completely blind and impervious to all that. I approach the poem blind. Entirely blind. I don't know what I want from a given poem, how I want it to be, or why I want it to be. What's the point, the pain, the burden, I would say, the unfinished burden that's weighing on me. I know, but I don't know how to make it articulate. Why do I write poems? Because I write poems. It's as though I were standing in front of a brick wall. I don't understand a thing.

You don't worry about repeating yourself?

Maybe. I haven't given it any thought. It's possible that I sin a good deal in repeating myself. Why do you people in your complacency always ask these stupid questions? Obviously one repeats oneself. How could one not? I love my wife. Do I have another one? A person can write about the same subject twenty thousand times. Do you love once? You love always. If you write a poem about a woman, is that the end of the matter of having once seen a beautiful woman? Are you angry now? Get angry a thousand times! It won't help you or me. I'm boring?! You're boring!!

In a single word I'd say: to write as I speak. It all fits in. Writing a poem is a way of life. The poem is a way of life. Everything that sticks to you from the clay, the mud, the earth — that's the poem. The process of making a poem is the poem. Others might tell you something else. The way of life is the way of the poem. The poem isn't what's printed on the paper. It always remains where the mixer gathers the eggs and the shells and the onion and the salt.

When a person arrives at the moment of writing, when he starts to weave the poem and the threads are stretched, he wants to put in all the thread, even more than is called for by the poem's context — he wants to fit everything in. When a person sits for a portrait, when he's painted by a painter, he wants him to fit in all that's in his soul, that the painter will know how to bring it all into the subject's face. Every person who writes poetry doesn't mean to describe anyone else but himself and the burdens he bears, to settle accounts. And this settling of accounts comes to expression in this painting and in the face of the person being painted. What weighs on a person isn't immediate. The immediate burden is the easiest one. The immediate isn't in fact such a burden — first of all because it's fresh, and can easily distract in all sorts of ways. The burden starts to become a burden when it starts to become the past and robs you of the feeling that you don't owe anyone anything. That you have no debts. All writing is a settling of accounts, whether or not one is conscious of them. But that's the foundation and essential truth. A settling of accounts. Between a person and what surrounds him, between himself and his past, himself and the future within, which is also the past and present inside him.

[PC]

Yonatan Ratosh

(1908–1981)

Though he was born in Warsaw (as Uriel Halperin), Yonatan Ratosh was raised
in an exclusively Hebrew-speaking environment, and Hebraicism lay at the
heart of his thought from the start. In time it would lead him to produce
what is easily one of the most intellectually distinctive and fascinating bodies
of work in all of modern Hebrew. Halperin arrived in Palestine with his Zionist
family at the age of thirteen. He very soon became involved with the right-
wing Jewish Revisionist movement fighting British Mandatory rule over—as
he saw it—all natives in Palestine; eventually he became the leader of what
was at first called the Young Hebrews and in time became known as the
Canaanites (the latter term was a pejorative that stuck, like the English
"metaphysical poets"). The Young Hebrews put forth a platform that involved
a radical critique of Zionism and called for a revolution of consciousness that
would replace deracinated exilic Judaism and its literature with a new secular
Hebrew culture and nation, one that was rooted in time and place. The
movement turned for inspiration to the prebiblical mythology of the Fertile
Crescent, seeing the Bible itself as the product of a diasporic (Babylonian)
religious sensibility, though proponents of Canaanism also recognized in the
biblical text a primal and potent kernel from which the new Hebrew culture
might grow: "Whoever is a Hebrew cannot be a Jew. [. . .] If only we might
brush the Jewish dust from our eyes and pierce the darkening Jewish fog,"

Ratosh wrote in a seminal 1944 counter-Zionist essay, "then the entire and tremendous world of the Hebrews of ancient days would fully assert its power within us and in our spirit" ("The Opening Discourse").

The political implications of the Canaanite movement were variable and could, in theory, have led from everything to the notion of a greater Hebrew nation reaching the Euphrates to a more circumscribed Hebrew state that would see all its citizens as equal (within the language), regardless of their ethnicity. The Canaanites were taken quite seriously in the mid-1940s and the early years of statehood. Massive immigration to Israel in the wake of the Holocaust nullified its relevance as a broader political movement, but the implications of Canaanism for Hebrew literature were of another order and, it has been argued, helped spur the development of Israeli literature as it would come to be known in the first quarter-century of statehood. Canaanite influence, for instance, can be felt in writers such as S. Yizhar, Amos Oz, and A. B. Yehoshua. The literary journals produced by the movement published the latter two and many other writers at the beginning of their careers, and they later gave a platform to Arab authors who were writing in Hebrew, including Anton Shammas. The movement also spurred a massive translation project, seeking to Hebraicize exemplary works of world literature.

Beyond politics and the culture wars, the most interesting aspect of the Canaanite movement may have been Ratosh the poet—with the writer's name itself being the product of the movement's ideology: though he never stated it outright, it would seem that Uriel Halperin derived his pen name— in the late 1930s, while in Paris!—from a Hebrew verb meaning "to sever, split open" (*leratesh*), which is exactly what he set out to do to the prevailing Hebrew-Jewish poetics of the 1930s and '40s. Employing on the one hand a powerfully cadenced archaism rooted in Near Eastern myth (he often invoked a variety of pagan gods and their consorts—El, Baal, etc.) and, later in his career, a "living" colloquial Hebrew, Ratosh developed an utterly singular body of work that met—not surprisingly, given the poet's politics and poetics—with initial resistance (or silence) in Hebrew, although the leading poets of the day immediately recognized his importance. It would take more than a decade after the appearance of his first book of poems (*Black Canopy,* in 1941) for his work to make its way into the Hebrew literary consciousness of the day.

The piece that follows was written as a talk for the radio in 1954.

ISRAELI OR JEWISH LITERATURE?

The accurate formulation of a question is half its solution, and it is entirely proper to ask if the formulation of the problem before us — Israeli or Jewish literature — is sufficiently precise.

And in fact, if we consider it, it isn't clear why that "or" has been placed between Israeli and Jewish literature. Do the two terms truly exclude one another? No, we would answer, with good reason, they do not. For in the end there is not and never has been a Jewish literature that was completely detached from a particular country or place. There was a Jewish literature in Germany, and it was different from Jewish literature in Italy. And each one of the two is unlike Jewish literature in Russia, and that is the general rule for the remaining Jewish literatures in their respective countries. Jewish literature worldwide is actually nothing but the sum total of the Jewish literatures in country after country.

A fuller formulation of the issue would yield the opposition: Jewish-Israeli literature / Jewish literature worldwide; but it soon becomes readily apparent to us that, on the face of it, the question itself is meaningless. In the State of Israel it is impossible for Jewish literature not to be Israeli; and so there is no obvious contradiction in its being part of the Jewish literature written elsewhere in the world. Why, then, should Jewish-Israeli literature be treated less seriously than Jewish literatures of other countries? Why that "or"?

Unless, that is, this "or" — which differentiates between the two, this same "or" that, on the face of it, seems superfluous — is felt to be essential. And this is the heart of the matter. Over the years, the question has been repeatedly raised and discussed, a clear indication of its continued relevancy.

It would appear, then, that the question's formulation is, in fact, insufficiently precise; as a result, the contrast between the two phenomena is blurred rather than sharpened.

We might better understand the difference between these two phenomena if we recall that Jewish literature exists and has existed — and not exclusively in the Hebrew tongue — throughout the ages. Sholem Aleichem, for example, did not write in Hebrew. Mendele wrote neither exclusively nor primarily in Hebrew. He wrote in Yiddish and, incidentally, in Russian. Likewise H. N. Bialik, Yehuda HaLevi, and the Rambam did not write exclusively in Hebrew. In our own times American-Jewish literature exists in Hebrew, in Yiddish, and in English. And Jewish literature exists in German and in Russian, and in its time also existed in Arabic. There is no question that for generation upon generation Hebrew was for Jews not only the Holy Tongue but also the language of culture, of thought and the sciences, as Latin was for the nations of Europe during the Middle Ages. But Jewish literature is not limited to Hebrew; it is not defined by it, nor is identical with it.

It may also be useful in broadening our understanding if we recall that Hebrew in its time was an elite and international language. For at certain periods during the Middle Ages Hebrew was among the languages of the general sciences, and it was not used by Jews alone — in medicine, for example, it was assumed that every doctor worthy of his name would have some knowledge of Hebrew, like Latin in our own times. And in sixteenth-century Hungary, for example, not only Jews but also Christians belonging to the nobility and the educated class were expected to know Hebrew no less than Latin and Greek. They even composed poems in Hebrew in order to broaden their knowledge of the language. Not only, then, is Jewish literature *not* confined to the Hebrew language, but — should we insist on being as precise as possible — literature in the Hebrew tongue is also not exclusively Jewish.

It may also be useful to recall that on the level of daily life there is nothing exceptional in this country when it comes to the world of Jewry.

There have been Jewish farmers, for example, in Argentina, and in various Russian provinces, no less so than here in Israel, and, it goes without saying, there have been military men. Nor are Jewish prime ministers and ministers unique to Israel; think of France, for example. What is unique to our own experience here doesn't pertain to any particular aspect of society, be it agriculture, or the military, or government. What is unique is the combination of all these things, the fact of our being natives. The fact that we see ourselves, that we feel ourselves as native sons, as inhabitants of a homeland, as a nation.

And if we consider Judaism as a unique sort of existence, different in kind from that of all the other nations of the world, and as an entity to which the rules of these nations do not apply — as, in other words, Judaism is accustomed to seeing itself — it will be difficult for us not to conclude that what is unique to Hebrew literature is not particularly Jewish.

Men involved in public affairs ask us to ignore, to blur this point. Politicians would like to reduce the opposition between the two terms. To see it almost as a formal matter restricted to one's identity card. Sociologists, public intellectuals, and critics see the direction in which things are moving and do not approve; they too ask us to resist it, [. . .] but they take note of the phenomenon itself.

And perhaps it comes down to this: not Israeli or Jewish literature — an imaginary polarity that turns out after brief consideration not to contain anything substantial — but Jewish literature or non-Jewish literature, Jewish literature or the literature of a nation.

It may be hard to determine where Jewish literature ends and a new literature begins — that of a nation. But this changes nothing when it comes to the facts themselves. In this same way it's difficult to determine at what point an Englishman who emigrated to Australia ceased being English and became Australian, or in which generation the descendants of immigrants to the United States become American. But it is a clear and universally acknowledged fact that numerous Englishmen emigrated to Australia and that only the Australian nation dwells there today — and we know that the Australians are not English, and that there exists in America a separate American nation.

I have tremendous respect for Jewish literature in all its languages. We are not trying to belittle its value; and we acknowledge its considerable achievements. All here in Israel have studied Jewish literature in Hebrew, but what we have learned is like the biological legacy of each individual. It's possible for a Polish-American, for example, to greatly resemble in terms of appearance and temperament some grandfather or distant uncle from overseas, who is himself the son of another, more ancient people. But from the national point of view he does not resemble that ancestor at all; he is altogether different. Nationality doesn't involve biological fact, but rather socioterritorial existence, which has its own value. And just like particular individuals, so too particular acquired literatures, drawn from other literatures, are present here within a different existential complex, one with its own laws and its own values, which are fundamentally different. Jewish literature, as has been said, may be important, and yet for us it isn't the principal thing. Every teacher of literature in every school in Israel knows this, has felt this day after day for years. Its very content, its very framework, its problems and solutions, are far from us; therefore, in practice, although it might be of paramount importance, Jewish literature remains foreign despite all the efforts of teachers and spiritual leaders. What is blossoming here is a new literature.

The schoolroom may in fact be at the root of many of the deficiencies that the teacher and educator attribute to their native-born students of literature: the narrowing of horizons, the superficiality, the Levantinization. For in the end, being Levantine is merely the fruit of the lack of correspondence and connection between the values of the acquired culture on the one hand and the development and experience of the student and his personal values on the other. The culture of France is extraordinary; but in the Levant, France produced Levantines. There is no reason that Levantines won't be produced here as well in the lap of Jewish culture, which may on its own terms be extraordinary; important as its values might be, they are viewed by all as foreign to our native sons, whether they approve of them or not.

As far as this generation is concerned, the principal problem in the context of this critique is perhaps with the definition of our culture. It is difficult not to see that only by building on the foundations of a proper definition of our independence will we be able to learn to benefit from literatures other than our own — without imitating them or blurring distinctions. And that, of course, also (and not insignificantly) includes Jewish literature from all around the world, and Jewish literature in the Hebrew tongue.

Jewish literature as it exists all over the world speaks in the name of continuity. Surely greater precision is in order: Jewish literature around the world has not developed naturally, or directly. It is made up — again — of disparate literatures. Each one the fruit of a different country, the product of conditions unique to itself. Each one existing separately. The lines of continuity have not been particularly durable, nor have they been all that consecutive. This continuity is at times almost like an external influence; more than conveying the real, it applies on an abstract and intellectual plane. Above all, this is continuity within time alone. It hovers within the world's time. With regard to place, for instance, it amounts to detachment. There is here a clear-cut instance of detachment, one that is also familiar and well known.

Jewish literature speaks in the name of the broadening of horizons: a Jewry that embraces the world. And here too it's best perhaps to be as precise as possible. Judaism has been acquainted with numerous countries and people; it has dwelled in them and been accepted by them; and it has had to struggle with all the problems that arose as a result of this. However, from a certain vantage point, that of the other, perhaps there is in this speaking of wide horizons also something narrow-minded: Jewish literature saw all of the above strictly from the point of view of the problems and needs of a Jewish way of life.

Be all that as it may, in as far as the literature of the nation written in Israel is concerned, it's entirely possible that this continuity and these broad horizons of Jewish literature have had a negative influence. The broadness of these horizons has meant for us, in effect, the constriction of the actual, proximal geographical horizon to the dimensions of the present-day State of Israel, and to the domain of exclusively Jewish settlement before the creation of the state. In effect, it has constricted the sphere of interest exclusively to the Jewish community, present, past, and even future, and has resulted in something of an ethnic approach, a narrowing of the horizon and of the mind, a sort of detachment from the country as a country, from its inhabitants as inhabitants of that country's land, and from its history as that country's chronicles.

The continuity of Jewish literature is by no means a continuity that can be identified with a specific place; within this place, this country, it assumes a large and weighty space of generation upon generation, of cities and land, existing beyond the boundaries of the knowledge and exploration of the spiritual approach. And for a literature of a country and a nation, nothing that is accomplished, neither yearning nor the building of castles in Spain, or on the banks of the Rhine and the Vistula, will be able to fill this space. The only literature that can possibly grow here, in the lap of Jewish literature — and within the framework and time of the Jewish world — will be thin and detached; it will be at best a provincial, but not a native literature.

And the choice is between such a literature and a rooted, native literature, the literature of a nation — one that will breach the defensive wall and, it's possible to say, widen the historical as well as the territorial horizon, and open the heart and eye to the continuity of time within place. In the end, such a literature will perhaps also embrace man for being man, and not for being Jewish — for belonging to a given ethnic community; it will embrace the world as the world, and not as an arena for Jewish wandering through the generations. From the wide, deep, and strong foundation of a native land, it will be possible to open one's eyes and heart to every expanse.

But for the sake of this future, for the reception and development of the nation's values and its dilemmas, emancipation is needed, release from the framework of Jewish literature and its values, its content, and its preoccupation with the tribulations of Judaism.

To put it more clearly still: the situation is like that of an old building, beneath which another newer, better, and more suitable building cannot be built without first removing the existing structure.

Or perhaps, in order to satisfy everyone: it's like a chick, which first must break through the shell, to crack it open and shake it off in order to come out into the light of the world. If not, it will suffocate within.

And like many great fundamental questions, perhaps this question too amounts to something fairly simple: There are two value systems here. The first involves a Jewish nation, a Zionist movement of revival, the Hebrew tongue, the Land of Israel.

A Jewish nation — living in the Diaspora, with its consolidation (if not its origin) in exile (Babylon). A Zionist movement of revival — founded far from Israel and called by the high-flown name of Jerusalem, the Holy City. The Hebrew tongue — which the majority of the Jewish nation does not know, and which was used as the language of the sacred and of culture (by, of course, the learned), and not as a living tongue. The Land of Israel — a term that, during its most significant era (the period of classical Hebrew) applied to the area of the Kingdom of Samaria and did not include the Negev or the coastal plain or Judea and Jerusalem; it is a very late rhetorical expression, which, to this very day, has no clear-cut meaning — and perhaps precisely because of this has spread and been accepted with such ease.

The second system of values is far simpler. It involves a Hebrew nation — native to its land; a Hebrew movement of revival — native to its land; a Hebrew language — the language of the nation; and the land of the Hebrews — as it has been throughout its history, its various periods, its tribulations. And these are the fundamental problems of our culture and our political situation.

The choice facing our literature is, essentially, the choice between these two systems — between the values of the Jewish Diaspora and the values of the Hebrew nation.

The name of our state, Israel, was chosen at the time precisely because of its vagueness, as a sort of slippery compromise that would avoid the need to decide between these two value-systems — between defining the state as the state of the Jews and defining it as a Hebrew state. Politics is politics; but at least when it comes to matters of the spirit, to literature, it may be best to call a spade a spade and to be as precise as possible.

A considerable number of distinctions are, it would seem, blurred in the use of the term "Israeli literature." For regardless of how we define things for the sake of discussion, the actual choice before us remains the same. And the problem is this: Hebrew or Jewish literature? Which will it be?

In life, in any case, we will have to provide an answer to this problem; we will have to choose between these two alternatives: Jewish or Hebrew.

Will the fact that the majority of the present-day inhabitants of the state arrived only a short while ago, or that they are foreign born, determine the solution to the problem?

Surprising as it might seem, common sense answers: Probably not.

The reasons are numerous. First and foremost — even today the relative majority among us consists, without a doubt, of children born or educated in Israel. And this is the only population that is growing and will continue to grow without cease — and regardless of any change in government and political policy (in contrast to other segments of the population arriving from all the countries belonging to the Jewish Diaspora). This segment of the population already constitutes the main body of the educated class in the country, in all the professions, across the board; and this segment is bound to keep on increasing from year to year. It is this very public that is likely to determine the features of the country in all spheres of life, and it is this public that will in the future produce our writers as well.

And it is this very public that will have to choose between the two solutions. Is there any doubt what their decision will be?

The only question is with what degree of awareness it will make its decision and, it follows, with what degree of completeness, of integrity, of innocence. In other words — the question is what the level of our Hebrew literature will be.

For the good of all, we can only hope that this level will swiftly rise and flourish.

[GL]

Natan Alterman

(1910–1970)

Natan Alterman was born in Warsaw and raised in Kishinev. He settled in Tel
Aviv when he was fifteen. His first book of poems, *Stars Outside,* published
when he was twenty-eight, catapulted him into the front rank of modernist
Hebrew poets, and he was long the dominant poet on the Hebrew literary
scene in pre-State Palestine. Very much a poet in the Russian mold that
Natan Zach and his peers would eventually attack, Alterman wrote a heavily
cadenced and sometimes hermetic verse that was characterized by brilliant
wit, a virtuoso metric, and not only an ear for the idiom of the day but one
that helped create that idiom. Alongside his more high-brow poems, he also
wrote popular verse that appeared in newspapers throughout his life and
served as a kind of running commentary on contemporary events, by turns
blunt, witty, and oracular. Early on, some of that political verse was banned
by the British. Alterman also published important translations of Shakespeare,
Molière, and Racine as well as a variety of Russian writers, and he composed
lyrics to popular songs.

Over the years, Alterman's political position shifted. He began as a
centrist Laborite but, after 1967, became a leading advocate of annexing
the Occupied Territories as part of so-called Greater Israel. His early avant-
garde reputation notwithstanding, he was long considered the literary

spokesman of the Jewish national movement, and he was, and still is, very much an "establishment poet." (Moshe Dayan, for example, was a major admirer and wrote introductions to several volumes of Alterman's work.) The essay that follows finds the poet in his symbolist mode at a self-assured twenty-three, taking on that seemingly timeless trope—the response by reader and poet alike to the incomprehensible in poetry.

On the Incomprehensible in Poetry

Darkness and gloom . . . I can't grasp hold of anything, not even half a thing! Why did he publish these words? Does anyone get any pleasure from them, or benefit? No, no . . . I'm not required to brood over this new hieroglyph. . . . To hell with difficult poetry!

Many readers, good readers, will I'm certain find in these sentiments some relief from the bitterness that has long accrued in their hearts. For it is evident, and commonly known, that readers never cease damning to hell the incomprehensible in poetry, though no less evident and commonly known is the fact of its obstinacy and refusal to go there. . . . Why? What power, what faith keeps it alive, common sense notwithstanding? What justifies its existence despite the rightness of the words of those who condemn it?

And here I envision the following:

The High Priest of Jerusalem has fallen asleep for a moment on the eve of the Day of Atonement. The great commotion of the preparations for the following day, the aura of sanctity, the prolonged expectation and the heavy responsibility incumbent upon him—all these have stretched taut and frayed his aging nerves without mercy. The High Priest, one might say, was very tired when he lay down on his bed, and so, bad dreams, which during the years would not have dared to disturb him, now grow insolent and stand in a long line next to his bed. Among them is one particularly dreadful dream, dreadful indeed. . . .

The High Holiday service has come to an end. The male scapegoat designated for sacrifice has been taken to the desert led by a venerable man.
There it will be brought to the top of a high cliff and pushed over, to atone
for all the sins of the House of Israel. So it has been every year. And so it
always was. This time, however, a courier appears and announces: The goat
is resisting. The goat is standing on the peak with its legs planted as though
in the stone, and no power could move it from there. It will not be thrown
over by any means! . . . Immediately the High Priest rushes to help. He
pushes with the pushers, pulls with the pullers. But in vain. His merit and
standing are of no avail, and the goat stands there. . . . Minutes pass, an hour
crawls by, and the goat takes not even a step. The sun is about to set. A great
dread falls upon the High Priest. . . . "My good goat" — he pleads before
him — "Please, my good goat. . . . Look, I'm petting you gently. I'm pros-
trating myself on the earth before you. I weep before you. . . . Go, please, to
Azazel. . . ." The sun keeps sinking. Now it has set. Then the High Priest lets
out a great, bitter cry of despair: "Why? Why were you so stubborn? What
power, what faith, kept you from falling?" He cried out and awoke, and
slowly came to understand that the goat hadn't submitted and did not fall
because it never existed, because it was only a dream!

May those who fail to understand this parable not think it a kind of modern literature. It's only meant to help me say that the High Priest, as I see it,
who struggles with the imaginary goat, resembles those who speak out
against incomprehensible poetry. But such poetry does not exist at all.
There is, in literature, no "comprehensible" and "incomprehensible." There
is only art and lack of art, and the number of obscure works that belong to
the artless part is not greater, in any event, than the number of transparent
works that have found for themselves a place in it. "Shake the paradox
well" — someone said — "and out of it the lie will fall, and nothing at all will
remain in your hand but the banal." If one may apply that saying to quite a
few incomprehensible poems, one can also alter it a little and say: "Shake the
accessible poem very well, and out of it the banal will fall, and in your hand
nothing at all will remain, apart from the lie." The aforementioned poems,
different as they are from one another in essence, together belong, therefore, to the artless type, composed of banality and lies. In accessible or com-

prehensible poems of this kind, lyricism is a chronicle of emotions, as an
epic is a chronicle of deeds; and in obscure poems of this kind, the lyricism
is a deliberate counterfeiting of emotion and vision, as the epic falsifies feeling for action and deeds.

That said, over this surface a living spirit blows, a power called artistic talent. For art is power, and more: it is a maker of miracles. By means of art the
author travels a very short, if dangerous, distance, between fabrication and
recreation, between exaggeration and exaltation, between boredom and
Stimmung (disposition), between the merely surprising and the new. Every
author's way of writing, like the specific nature of each individual, is *a fact.*
One might accept it, ponder it, and even try to alter it. However, by virtue
of that *talent,* by virtue of that art, this fact becomes *necessity,* and necessity
is always *truth,* subjective truth, which is the only truth. And here the miracle of art comes into play and turns this truth into *faith.* Truth and faith —
Hebrew prayer has bound these two together tightly [as part of the evening
service]; day after day Jews have repeated these two words in a single breath
["All this is truth and faith"], and this can serve as a symbol of literature. The
subjective, artistic truth of the author necessarily draws the reader's faith
after it. And faith, in this case, is that sensitive understanding, that echo of
life, which is repeated in the reader's heart, as a response to the artist's life
in the letters of the book.

Is it, then, correct that a certain, familiar type of *artistic* literature stands,
as it were, in the middle of the road and does not receive that same faith and
understanding?

Readers are certain: It is! And authors are then constrained to respond:
"Amen," and begin to interpret, to look for reasons, to justify the verdict
against them.

One of the more commonly held opinions is that which was expressed by
Avraham Shlonsky in one of his recent articles in *Turim:* Every human collective, every family, every group of friends, has, in addition to the general,
common language, a language of its own, particular to it alone. A few allusive
locutions, several symbols, and expressions connected to associations that
are not shared by the outsider, and to which the outsider cannot respond,
because he doesn't understand them. This is the special dictionary that is

acquired only through a life that is lived together, in a place, and time, and spirit. Let us imagine now an author who comes with his own inner world, with experiences, a style, a new manner of seeing and expression — one that is solely his. In a word: he comes with his own dictionary. Clearly before other people have gotten used to him, before they have been educated about him — they will not understand him, that is to say, the images, locutions, and words that he uses will arouse in them neither association nor response.

This opinion denies to art the value of strength, the element of hidden, unconscious influence. Indeed, the author gradually gathers his own circle of readers from his surroundings, enlarges it, and penetrates deeper and deeper into it. This, however, it seems to me, is more a process of popularization than of understanding. There is in it more agreement than love. Art, I believe, finds love and understanding at once, without any need for education or propaganda. True, this sudden love can come several centuries too late; but even then it will be pristine, like a newborn infant.

Here one might object and say: This shows that art has about it a certain timeliness, that a given generation wasn't prepared to accept the author, that he came before his day, and after a certain period of development, he found his reparation. Again, this is education, if not by the author himself, then by means of various factors that shape the reader's talent and ability to understand.

This view I reject as well, which would seem to bear no further reflection. Every artful writer is not only a person of his time, but a person *of all times*. Let us not confuse the areas of art with those of science and other forms of knowledge. A philosopher — yes, he might come before his time, be alien to it, or, on the contrary, suit *only* the framework of his own time and not fit into any other period or set of circumstances. Not so with the artist. The artist exists in the world as a living being, as a person, a heart. His words are not directed to the public but to the individual, to each individual, distinctly. To the depths of the isolated individual. Hence — just as it is impossible to drive a person out of a house that he has not entered, it is impossible to say to a writer: You are not suited *for your generation*.

From this matter of the relation between literature and time it is easy to pass on to a second observation: New works of literature, obscure works,

demand of the reader a Platonic attitude, demand of him that he set aside
the tale, the plot, the routine that is easy to swallow and digest. Who would
prefer these abstractions, especially *now*, in a generation that shows no
interest in poetry at all — a generation that is one of action and technology?!

Among all the things that were said about the relation between this generation and literature, many, granted, are correct and many are mistaken. I
can agree with some and disagree with others, but this statement about a
general lack of understanding, about the epidemic, God forbid, of the "generation of technology," is the only one that arouses in me no desire at all to
quarrel. Is it possible to express opposition to a joke, to a paradox? Indeed,
yes — technology. For in what other generation, in what other period has so
much use been made of technology to address people's emotional and spiritual needs?! Who could have imagined that a system of springs and steel needles and sheets of gutta-percha could inspire people with moods, make them
happy or sad, or even bring tears to their eyes? We call this a gramophone; we
call it — listening to music, and forget that it's technology. . . . And the cinema? The radio? The new theater with its revolving stages and its blazing
floodlights? And when, if ever, have so many people developed and refined
such an interest in the workings of the psyche? Has the human soul ever
drawn to such an extent the interest of all around it, beginning with school
and extending up through the courthouse, if not in this generation, the "generation of technology"? Even if we dismiss all this as not being particularly
important, is it possible to say that, with the penetration of the motor into
all realms of human life, man himself is becoming a robot? So long as they
don't put babies to sleep artificially, but sing them lullabies, as long as they
haven't invented a pump for the blood to replace the heart, there will be a
place for love songs.

Nevertheless it is true and cannot be denied — there were days when
poetry occupied a more important place in the human gestalt, far more
important than that which it occupies today; but let us not forget that in the
relationship between people and things, there is, apart from the true core, a
great deal of rind as well, the rind of fashion and snobbery. Poetry was then
in fashion. It was common and proper to fill albums with it, to quote it in letters, to learn it by heart and recite it, one hand pressed against the breast and

the other raised toward heaven. Young women used to read it aloud and dissolve in tears, and young men would, as I imagine it, listen with storm-tossed hearts and not admit, perish the thought, that in fact they were dying of boredom. This is what they called the *veneration* of the poet, and the poor venerated poet knew he was caught in a somewhat idiotic situation, but he had to agree to accept the verdict. That was the fashion, and that was sentimental snobbery. If that fashion today is gone, one should not thereby conclude that truth at its core has also been lost. The true relation to poetry, that which is planted in a person by his nature, does not pass away and does not change. If it now stands naked, without any official garb, it is seven times more precious to me, and I believe in it all the more — because it is entirely unnatural that human beings, en masse, should all love poetry and that each individual on his own should be prepared at all times to read a poem and respond to it, just as it is unnatural that every human being should know and love to sing, and that all should be willing to sing at any given moment and time.

It is clear, therefore, that neither the lack of early education nor the strangeness of poetry in general in this generation have created the attitude of the reader to literature that is called obscure. And here a new bomb is thrown before us: simplicity and the subject! Write about things that are close to us, about our lives, about our day-to-day experience, and then we'll feel literature as we feel ourselves. In short — tell us of suffering and we'll feel sorrow; give us good news and we will rejoice; give us life and we'll live it with you!

There is in these matters more justice than be can reckoned at first glance; but literature does not, and must not, fulfill that demand. It supplies, and must supply, far *more* than that. It does not tell of joy and sorrow, it does not *describe* life. . . . It *lives* life again, in primal, virginal, interior fashion, full of wonderment and surprise. In this sense, obscure literature is far more realistic than realistic literature itself.

And so, if someone says to a poet: Describe life to me, . . . the poet should answer: Why should I describe for you something that's always right in front of your eyes, that's always around you, and that never leaves you for even a moment? You can describe it as well as I can. . . . True, I can increase

your love for it, your love for life, or make you detest it by creating a particular situation or by scattering notions here and there; but to set out do so
intentionally is not my particular responsibility. That contribution can easily
be made by the fold of your educated friends in ordinary conversation, or by
the events — both good and bad — you experience, or by books of philosophy, religion, and sociology, which were written by learned men. But in no
way am I any wiser than you are, nor am I any richer. I cannot give you or
teach you a thing. I live my life just like you, and just as you sometimes feel
like laughing, or sighing, without any reason at all, or for a reason, so too I
sometimes want to write a poem. That's all. If the poem is understandable to
you, that's a sign that my way of writing is close to your spirit. If in you the
poem finds an echo — that's a sign that my laughter infected you. And that,
once again, is the whole of it. I do not belong to the school of the incomprehensible, just as you don't belong to the type of people without understanding. Perhaps you weren't capable of reading the poem at a given
moment (moments of a capacity to *read* are quite rare — no more frequent,
in fact, than of the capacity to *write*). And perhaps I failed in not making the
poem more salient, more penetrating. Sometimes, by means of a single
instance of a writer's brilliance, or a single moment of capacity, a moment
involving the reader's mood, a poem that was formerly incomprehensible
suddenly becomes as transparent as glass.

The obscure poet should not worry and be tormented because of the
reader's failure to respond. True response, which is not dependent on events
of the day, or the quotidian, will always be there, and it, *in particular,* is the
most assured, the most vital, and the most universal. Every true work of literature, be it accessible or obscure, is felt with true emotion only by a few,
singular individuals and only on rare occasion. Everyone understood
Pushkin, but his *poetry,* I'm certain, was absorbed and felt by only a few, no
more than those, for example, who had a feeling for the obscure Mallarmé.

Modern poetry, in as much as it is incomprehensible, has lost its popu-
larity. But it has lost nothing of its deep and rare relation to the individual.
What was lost, perhaps, will be restored — through education and over
time; but *true* understanding will not then be greater than it is today.

To many people, modern poetry seems like a fog, and it annoys, like thick and twisting smoke. But hasn't it always been, always and also now, that a person might go out into the street on an overcast day and instead of saying: What a thick fog this is . . . he'll say: How soft and deep this fog is! And instead of saying: This smoke burns my eyes . . . he'll say: Through this smoke one can look directly at the sun.

1933

[JG]

Lea Goldberg

(1911–1970)

Have you seen the rain? We are calm.
Three angels from an ancient story
are moving slowly between the trees and homes.

Nothing has changed. Only the rain
is carefully hitting the stone. The street is glassy.
We see how three angels are crossing
the street from an ancient story.

The flour is pure. The door is open.
The rain is quiet. The miracle has already happened.

The best introduction to Lea Goldberg's work is the work itself, and her poetry is certainly the best and necessary introduction to her prose. Noted for its lucidity and concision, its modesty and precise registration of emotion, Goldberg's poetry operates as what one fellow poet called "a system of echoes and mild reverberations." Her accomplishment is entirely within the subtle workings of the verse itself, rather than in any shocking confession or salient invention. It is a quiet poetry of surrender (with supreme attentiveness) to what is, and perhaps as a result has spoken, and continues to speak, to readers of diverse stripes over the years.

More than the other poets of her generation, Goldberg drew her influences—and she was a voracious reader—from the poetry of western

Europe. She felt particularly close to classical Italian poetry, and also translated Shakespeare, Petrarch, and Brecht and the prose of Tolstoy, Gorky, and
Chekhov. Throughout her career she was affiliated with Avraham Shlonsky's
circle of writers.

Born in Königsberg, Germany (then eastern Prussia, now Russia),
Goldberg attended the Hebrew Gymnasia in Kovno, Lithuania, and from
an early age declared her ambition to become a Hebrew writer (see the
first diary entry here, which was written *in Hebrew* when she was all of
fifteen). Goldberg completed her Ph.D. in Semitic languages at the University
of Bonn and emigrated to Palestine in 1935. Her first collection of poems
appeared that year.

The following selections from her recently published diaries cover a
range of periods in her life. After the initial glimpse we get of her as an
aspiring adolescent writer, the entries follow her through her twenties and
the publication of her first book and into her maturity. Among other things,
these excerpts highlight her intense relationship with Abraham Sonne
(Avraham Ben Yitzhaq, see p. 53)—about whom she would write a book,
Meeting with a Poet. In addition to being one of the most important poets
and translators of her day, Goldberg was also an extremely popular writer
for children and a founder of the Comparative Literature Department at
the Hebrew University. Goldberg's poetry developed steadily throughout
her life, and her final two volumes, which appeared in 1964 and then after
her death, are considered by many to be her finest.

FROM *THE DIARIES*

FRIDAY, 3 SEPTEMBER 1926

I sent my poems, that is, my translations of Blok, to the journal *HaOlam*, and
they have already been returned. They told me they don't publish translations. But I don't want to give up so quickly; I want to try my luck again. I will

send them two original poems. I don't believe they'll accept them, but still one must try the impossible. I don't know why I must be a writer, *of all things* a writer. I don't have ideal reasons for it. I have completely stopped worrying about humanity and trusting my writing (a very sad fact) because there is no faith in anything. And material reasons. . . . But the terrible condition of the Hebrew writer is no secret to me. His poverty and inability to get published are old stories. To write, but not in Hebrew — for me, that would be the same as not writing at all. And still I want to be a writer, and still I tie my future and my whole life to this desire, this is my sole objective, and if I don't reach it, if I have no talent, then it makes no difference to me what becomes of me. If I am not a writer, nothing will have any value for me. [. . .]

15 MAY 1937

[. . .] I copied out the poem "One Spring." I corrected "The Carcass" according to Ari's advice [Aryeh Navon]. He salvaged the poem. The poem is much better. But "still not it" — when will it be "it"?

G. used to say: One needs *the turmoil of the soul, emitting light* [Russian]. He never gave me anything of the sort. Not his fault. But he's right. A person who hasn't had such luck for at least a half year in his life cannot be a good writer. Ari, on Ya'aqov [Horowitz, a Hebrew writer, theater critic, and editor]: I don't believe that a writer stops being a writer because things are bad for him. He makes something great out of his suffering; ergo — me. Yes, but everything has its limit.

Usually I too believe there is nothing that can kill talent, or the necessity of being an artist. But not only the weak need *rest and respite* [Russian].

And am I really a weak person? I don't think so. Perhaps I am the only one who believes that. Just as I'm the only one who believes in my talent. Not "an unrecognized genius," but potentially much more than I've given so far. If I don't express "half my desire," the entire matter is worthless. Perhaps that's the reason for *turmoil emitting light,* like fresh air to breathe for half a year, a year. [. . .]

19 JUNE 1937 [ONBOARD THE SHIP TO ITALY]

Yesterday I was still thinking that the arrangement of things in the world isn't so bad: the spiritual emptiness created within and around me here on the ship is, after all, the best preparation for receiving new impressions, for the intensive life of the spirit in Italy.

22 AUGUST 1939

The greatest and only crime: spiritual laziness. And within that spiritual laziness, one doesn't even acknowledge it, making it seven times worse. My novel. I knew earlier it was no good. I felt the artificial glue of it long ago. And still, a few weeks ago I thought: I'll finish it and put it onto the market as it is. It will make for a fine commodity because in certain ways it's better than the other books. And it will have a role similar to that of the *Letters* [*Letters from an Imaginary Journey*]. Certainty of success, because it's "not bad." And that's me, who knows that everything that's "not bad" is very bad.

Today a clear decision: to rewrite. To omit every lying word. To omit all excessive "intellectualism," every unnecessary quotation. Without mercy. To throw away the most "successful" places, if they aren't the truth itself. It isn't easy. And if I don't succeed, I won't publish the book at all. I'll forfeit the praise and success.

Perlmutter [Avot Yeshurun] said important things:

I: I don't like both of my books.

He: Actually no one is asking you anymore if you like them or not. They have a life of their own.

It's true. And because of that, the responsibility is even greater. With children, at least, one can say: Go home and change your clothes. Here — everything lives life of its own accord. Even the typos.

4 JANUARY 1941

The poison of S. [Sonne] in my bones. For that reason, apparently, all conversation and words seem insipid and pointless. Quite simply — boring. I laugh, talk, play the part. But within, the certainty that I'm fooling myself and that none of this interests me in the least.

In contrast, I know my intellect doesn't reach that of S. and his wisdom, but I need a person like that by my side. Someone people fear a bit and respect (or adore — an adolescent word). The adolescent word is the only one.

And about the poems, no answer. Very painful. Still — perhaps a certain justice rests with the silent one. And yet I think the poems are excellent. I think this — when I don't doubt the entire enterprise. I also thought that one day I would have someone to write for. One person for whom I'd be willing to give up the entire audience. And that person hasn't expressed his opinion with even a single word. [. . .]

I would like to read a book that shocks me. Or (and much more) to converse with S. [Sonne].

9 JANUARY 1941

A telephone call [from Sonne]. A postponement until tomorrow. Foolish insult. Foolish excitement. An inability to concentrate on anything else. I work to forget myself. There's only one way to uproot it from the heart. Here again the diary of a high school girl. [. . .]

A desire to flee into illness. Fear of the day after. Fear of my inner emptiness. All the doubts at once. Too many superfluous things, and an absence of essence.

This spring I mark the end of my thirtieth year. The results are horrendously meager. I've done nothing. A few poems. I don't know how I'll relate to them in a few years. A "status" I do not value among a public I do not value. A diminishing group of friends. I'm beginning to believe that I won't live long. The desire to accomplish something — to write something that is very good, without taking into account whether or not it will please. And to live well for a short time. To experience one love in its fullness. I ask no more than that. But that, apparently, is too much and . . . childish.

10 JANUARY 1941

Again this morning anxiety before the telephone conversation. Later the meeting in the café. An extremely pleasant conversation, intelligent, brilliant.

Sadly, a confirmation of all my feelings. This man is as I saw him immediately. *The man* — for my feelings and needs.

At first: bitter jokes about Hebrew literature. The Bialik Prize. [. . .] He was, in fact, very warm to me.

At last, the anthology [edited by Shlonsky, and containing Goldberg's nine-part poem-sequence, "On the Flowering"]. A complete rejection of [Alexander] Penn [a popular Communist poet]. Too bad about Alterman. The extremely successful language-play. Evasion of the essence. Too embarrassed to tell him — from this the feeling of inner emptiness. Maybe resignation. Maybe even death. The influence of French poetry and the shame in admitting it. Something that arouses a sense of pity, even though all of this is most agreeable, even sometimes very good. One line in the [Alterman] poem "Father." The rest is naked, pietistic. Current events with terms coined after the rise of the Nazis, terms that in fact were introduced by them. A great deal of play. The height of naturalness in language. In [Alterman's] "Song," a classical intimacy. But mostly: *a useful art, tragic craftsmanship* [German]. In my opinion, a wonderful definition, cruel as it is.

On Rudi [Raphael Eliaz] with affection. On Bat-Miriam, as about her accomplishments, disregard.

On Avraham [Shlonsky] (after I asked), no admiration. Nothing made new. "Positive nihilism frightens me."

I waited, trembling, to hear about me. It was short. He said my poems are very beautiful. Especially number eight . . . the last line. "And that you dedicated them to me." . . . Apologetic laughter, perhaps also satisfaction. He said that in my poems, and only in them, is there the feeling of time, and that he can read nothing else now. He said, almost explicitly, that my poems are the best in the anthology.

On the face of it, absolutely enough. But I recall Misha Gorlin after he received compliments about his dissertation from his professor: "But I wanted him to cry!"

He will not cry.

After this I must gather my strength to face the day on my own. It is clear this man will never be more than a casual friend to me, a "close acquaintance," one who deigns from time to time to converse with me.

What I cannot forgive him is that he robbed me of all desire to meet with anyone else. Because, alongside him, everyone seems stupid. And strangest of all, not just mindless but also heartless. The privilege of meeting this man has also been a catastrophe.

Tomorrow we meet again. I have to, no matter what, even if they banish me from that idiotic "club." (If only they would!)

God Almighty, what a feeling of loneliness after all this! What terrible loneliness. As though everything has ended, forever, and still I have to go on living, somehow.

7 SEPTEMBER 1949

[. . .] I'm working a lot now on [translating] *War and Peace*. Working here is pleasant, also easier. I meet with people. Yesterday — Agnon. It was pleasant enough in his house, even though it's hard to see how bad his wife looks. In the large library of G. [Gershom] Scholem, in whose apartment he's living now, his manuscripts are stored in a cabinet that also serves as a writing-stand. He showed me the manuscript of *Shira* [his last novel], and for a long time he spoke about his fears regarding the publication of something as "frivolous" as this. He's afraid of the rabbis. Sometimes I get the impression that he would like to extract himself from the environment into which he has inserted himself, but he feels that it's too late.

His not particularly appreciative words about my prose pleased me (even as they pinched my heart, as does anything that involves critique when it's spoken directly to a person), because they proved that he took my work seriously, and what he said was, it would seem, also justified. That he offered to reveal to me some of the elementary secrets of syntax, to help me in my writing, seemed to me both extremely sympathetic and interesting, and I'll ask him to explain these things to me in detail. It will, I believe, give me a key to his writings, though I don't believe it will help me at all, as the syntax of Agnon is good only for Agnon.

Of course yesterday there was also the pretense of provincial innocence and so forth, and it was sometimes hard to determine the boundary between what was real and what involved the playing of a role, but there was something more open and direct than in all the previous times I saw him.

Tomorrow I meet S. [Sonne]. Something fills me with sorrow when I think of him. This afternoon I dreamed I met him, and he was wonderful, full of humor, forgiveness, and understanding. But I know that this is almost impossible now. By the joy with which he responds to the sound of my voice on the telephone, I fear he's been left entirely without people. What this person is doing to himself! [. . .]

10 JUNE 1950

On May 29, my birthday, Sonne died. Since then, nothing has mattered, apart from this fact.

17 July 1950

Depression, fear of life, a feeling of helplessness and inner emptiness — that's the state I'm in most of the time now.

After Sonne's death, it's hard for me to take an interest in anyone. There is an absence in everything, and one that cannot be filled. I'm not writing. I haven't written anything almost this entire year. Even the translation of Petrarch's poems seems to me pointless now. I'm very tired.

Thursday, 9 August 1950

I've finished Lawrence's letters. Today I read his poems. Some of them — the shorter ones — are beautiful. But generally, my god, what babble! The desire to be "spontaneous," at the expense of any form, has not benefited poetry. This outburst of feelings in short lines has led to a megalomaniacal exaggeration of every foolishness imaginable. If someone says: "Why do the Communists stick the hibiscus, of all flowers, into the lapels of their clothes?" — this is a question without much importance. But if a person writes:

> Why do the Communists
> stick the hibiscus
> of all flowers
> into the lapels of their clothes!

— it is as though someone considered the answer to this question an answer to the question of the world's existence.

In contrast, how much modesty, surrender, and care concerning what's important and unimportant is demanded of the poet by form, the strict and true form of a poem. All those fools, the writers of literary theory who do not know this.

23 July 1951

Today I translated a Petrarchan sestina — "L'aere gravato." On the whole, the translation seems to me very successful, aside from two places in need of correction. What's problematic for me is the use of the word "downpour" or "rain." On the level of sound, "downpour" is better, but perhaps "rain" fits the context better, all the more so as "rain" is the word in the Song of Songs. I'll need to decide. There's no one to advise me on this. There's no one to ask about anything I do.

Last night I dreamed of Sonne. I dreamed I was in Ramatayim, on the day of his burial. But he was alive, and I could go visit him in his room. He was sitting in a chair and was happy I'd come. I was happy he was alive, but I knew that none of this would last, that in a short while he would have to die. Afterward I walked by myself near a garden and I met him on the street, and he walked with me among the trees and was very friendly, and I told him how Sonne was alive (he was, as it were, himself and another person both), but I was full of remorse because his manuscripts and letters were in the hands of strangers, and I didn't know how to tell him this. I was afraid of his anger. He said to me, "But when he sees Picasso's death-drawing among his papers, he'll understand he has to die again, and it will be terrible." And he also said, "He returned here only for a short time, because he has to finish a few things in this world." Afterward he took my hand in his, and that's how we walked. His hand was warm and mine was cold. I said to him, "How warm your hand is." He laughed and took my hand in his other hand too. And I loved him very much. With that I woke — it was almost dawn. There are a few other details from the dream that I can't remember.

In the afternoon I walked by the military cemetery. The same two cypresses I loved last year. Mother calls them the two monks.

Tomorrow I begin lecturing.

17 JUNE 1952

Day by day, month by month, the moments when life is self-evident to me — in body, in consciousness, in feeling — have become increasingly rare.

Everything joins together into a thicket of things that seems to me like barbed wire, through which I cannot pass — not into the world and not into myself.

The political questions suffocate me more and more. The feeling that all writing is unnecessary and impossible is, sometimes, not only bad, but also quite comfortable. My inner heaviness has overpowered my attitude toward pen and paper as well. Spiritual laziness and despair live peacefully side by

side. I know this. And still I ask myself, if the same complicated and exhaust-
ing "internal work" that Tolstoy describes in his analysis of Pierre's mental
state [in *War and Peace*] might not be going on within me during this period,
without my knowledge. I don't know. Everything is horribly sealed off and
there are almost no intervals in which to breathe. [. . .]

22 JULY 1952

There was a meeting of the "Higher Council of Culture." I gave a (rather
superficial) lecture on translated literature. Later another more decent lecture was delivered. Afterwards the publishers began talking, with much
anger and bitterness, about technical difficulties, paper, etc., trying to prove
that nothing can be done now. That brought the tone down significantly. It
made what we had to say irrelevant, and indeed I believe that Dinabourg
[Ben-Zion Dinur, then the minister of education] called the meeting without a realistic agenda. The "doers" should have been consulted first, and
then, only afterwards, once decisions had been taken and there was something practical to discuss, should we have been invited to speak. I don't like
wasting time.

But that wasn't the worst. The worst was [poet, critic, and translator
Avraham Yitzhaq] Krib's outburst, directed at me, as "a typical representative of that stream" which wants "a translated nation." Against all those who
have no need for "roots" in Israel, those who know what the goyim did to us
and still kneel before them. What do we need these Balzacs and Stendhals
for! We don't need any Balzacs, they're good only for degenerate conversation in the cafés. That entire European culture is worthless, and L. G. [Lea
Goldberg] and her journal that holds memorial days fifty weeks a year for
one goy or another, live off their words . . . and the disaster of their translating all that vacuousness known as classical literature and so on and on.

All this was spoken with hatred, in a hysterical tone. [. . .] I was completely depressed. Not because the outburst was directed at me, but because
this cultural fascism is subscribed to by more than just this one maniac. And
it didn't matter that afterward everyone [. . .] tried to defend me, that they
asked me ("poor girl!") to lecture on literature in translation at this same
party; the worst was that they all tried to "understand his outcry," and I fear

that tomorrow or the day after they'll understand him so well that they'll stop understanding what I'm saying. What an awful development! On the one hand social realism, the Stalinistic line in literature, and on the other hand the "Blubo" [*Blut und Boden,* blood and land, the racist Nazi doctrine], along the lines of things I heard in Germany in 1933, about "roots" and the hatred of everything good and beautiful in the world. Where can we still flee to from this despair?

1 JULY 1954

That I have no possibility of showing my poems to someone whose opinion matters sometimes fills me with despair. And so, now I have no idea at all what value the things I've written have, and if they aren't in fact imitations of something or someone — and there's no one to turn to. I don't think poets have ever worked in such loneliness, such absolute solitude.

By and large, these are good days. I'm reading a lot of Dante, learning by heart and also reading well. Trying [word unclear] the *visitando* [to be on a visit, Italian], always finding new things. Again falling in love with Italian. Yesterday in the car from Jerusalem to Tel-Aviv I translated "Mai non ho visto piu belle cose" [I've never seen anything more beautiful]. [. . .]

JERUSALEM, 22 OCTOBER 1955
. . . LATER

I read all I wrote in my journal this last year. It's strange how I wrote of so few good things. Mostly illnesses and fatigue. And all this while my friends and acquaintances say: This is your peak. This year, a year of unprecedented ascent. And now I am a very famous woman "all the way from Tel to Aviv."

Still, perhaps after I calm down, I'll have the play [*Lady of the Castle*] translated (where will the money come from?) so it can be staged abroad. Perhaps. But I know that this wasn't a year of ascent at all, rather a year that showed the results of previous years. The book, the play — everything was written earlier. And now, as Avraham [Shlonsky] says, I am "reaping," but the harvest isn't giving me very much joy. That is, in certain moments, yes. But mostly I fear that "I'm finished." This too is a matter of mood and nothing more. One has to get on with things. But when will that be possible?

8 December 1956

This week should have given me more material for my journal writing than the previous ones. And still, while I'm talking, I'm not writing. More and more I'm inclined to deliver my impressions and thoughts out loud, and I have no need of writing. But even though I once wrote here "what do I care," and other such things, it's clear to me how dangerous this is and that perhaps I'm "going to waste." [. . .]

Yesterday and Thursday I was in Tel Aviv. I spent most of my time with Dahlia [Ravikovitch], and I was very happy about that.

Yesterday was the first meeting about the "Poets' Club." In attendance were A. Hillel, [Avner] Treinin, Dahlia [Ravikovitch], Dan [Pagis]. I don't know what will come of it, and I don't know if I was needed to found something whose agenda is to *kindle communal efforts* [Russian], but for some reason I have a feeling of responsibility for these young people, and sometimes I believe it might not be so bad. I particularly didn't like Treinin. Hillel has in him something of the good naiveté, which I hadn't thought was one of his traits at all. His faith in an "academic" analysis of "classical poetry," his desire to learn, and everything else he said almost convinced him that he wants to liberate himself from "the bonds of complete freedom" of his poetry but he doesn't know how. This could be interesting, and useful.

I myself hemmed and hawed and didn't know exactly what I wanted to say. I said I was willing to open the club with a discussion of modern poetry, and again I wasn't sure what I was referring to. Only at night, at home, did it become clear to me what I'd meant to say. I think I'll speak about what Tsila [Cohen] said about Gottfried Benn and the year 1951 (poetry that isn't syrupy, or florid, that doesn't resort to colors and "like" and so forth).

I wondered, am I so old-fashioned in my poetry? In this country, it's hard to know. Our development is different and we're very provincial. It isn't a question of not following fashion, but rather of "the spirit of the times" or something like that. I know that most of the young people like my poetry and consider me close to them in some way, also in their worldview. Still, I'm "a prewar poet" — as I once prophesied about myself.

The austerity of the new poetry, its seriousness, is also to my liking, so long as the poetry doesn't slip over into prose. That's the hardest thing. Who knows how that's done? It will be necessary to think about all this, and perhaps it will do me some good as well. The virility of poetry.

Yesterday I had a good work day. Only in the evening did I grow very weary, and I became deaf, as before the surgery. This morning I woke up not feeling well, afraid of the day and its cares. I sit down to write in this journal, which is like washing up: in order to enter the day in a more orderly fashion. I don't know if it will help.

I thought about [Shimon] Halkin and his constant lament about how the university robs him of all his writing time. Perhaps I've been too harsh in my words about him, perhaps he is right. Within the constant panic of preparing lectures, it's hard to write. How many people warned me of this!

I want to accomplish everything, and so I fear I'll do nothing properly. I think about Plato's words, that each person should do only one thing.

I read a bit in Chekhov's notebooks. Most of it — notes for stories whose details I don't remember ("Ariadne"). From these notebooks it's hard to judge what kind of person he was, and only one thing stands out really: his powers of observation and sense of humor.

17 APRIL 1957

[. . .] I can't say I'm sad or miserable, or that the negative account is the determining one. And yet, spiritually, I'm completely paralyzed. My reading in Greek (Protagoras) is slightly amusing, but I'm not doing very well. Instead of reading what I need for lectures, I flee into a biography of Oscar Wilde. In general, I'm evading every responsibility. Perhaps if I were given a full month of rest — that is, if I had really utilized my vacation — I'd now be doing everything with greater desire, or at least doing something. Now it's neither work nor vacation. Small cares. Regret and stasis. Also, there isn't any warmth in my attitude toward people. It's all lip service and strain. A slightly strange picture. I've even stopped enjoying the meetings with the poets. It all seems unimportant, or worse: pretentious.

I went back and read several sections of this journal. Why didn't I mention [Yehuda] Amichai then among the young poets? He's the most interesting one of them all. I've revised my opinion about Treinin. In the mean-

time I've read his poems and found some good things in them. [. . .] It's
true that on a personal level there's still something repulsive about him.

Reading in this journal has eased my mind a bit. I don't know why. The
truth of the matter is that from what I've written here it's clear I'm walking
in circles, returning to the same points, orbiting myself endlessly, and still —
some of the things I recorded here I'd forgotten entirely, and that astonished
me. The dream about the Yugoslavian spy was once again something entirely
new for me, and I was happy that I'd written it down.

[RTB]

Gabriel Preil

(1911–1993)

Gabriel Preil was long considered "the last Hebrew poet in New York" (even when he wasn't the only Hebrew poet in New York), and he cultivated his double life of exile with considerable grace, quietly living in English while maintaining an impeccable, flexible, and utterly nonvernacular Hebrew that, from his initial 1945 volume of poems on, nonetheless spoke to readers in Tel Aviv, Haifa, and Jerusalem. An old-world gentleman and a lifelong bachelor— one of his books is called *Courteous to Myself*—Preil was a master of all things minor, often writing in New York coffee shops and letting the world come to him as it would. His wistful and well-made poems are tiny monuments to modesty and anonymity.

Preil was born in Estonia and moved to New York when he was eleven. He wrote poems in both Yiddish and Hebrew early on, but soon turned to Hebrew exclusively for his poetry. On occasion, he also wrote prose in Yiddish and in English. American poetry had a pronounced influence on Preil's work; he was drawn in particular to Robert Frost and Carl Sandburg (both of whose poetry he sometimes translated). The romanticism of his exile notwithstanding, there was a price to pay: in a 1965 letter to poet Avraham Shlonsky, Preil noted that he felt himself "condemned to dangle over the void." Three years later—the link would seem to be obvious—Preil visited

Israel for the first time. His embrace of diasporic life notwithstanding, Preil's work throughout his career was well received there.

The essay that follows was written in Yiddish when Preil was in his fifties. It takes on a topic central to his work—the weather.

On Nature as a Source in the Poem

There are poets for whom the climate of a country or the season of a year determines the character of their creation. This often-acknowledged fact nonetheless constitutes part of poetry's mystery, and it undoubtedly plays a critical role in the composition of the effective poem.

If we accept the premise that everything that lives and breathes in the external world involves, in relation to the poet, an internal experience — and that a type of nameless striving streams into him and does not let him rest until it finds improvement through him — then we will be properly equipped to understand the degree to which weather is able to influence a poet.

Not all poets, obviously, are drawn to it — and especially not those whom one can identify as essentially ideological. They write what they write, which doesn't result directly from inspiration or *unconscious intention,* if one may put it that way; they want, first and foremost, to unload little thoughts here and there, even philosophical notions, and those external climatic conditions that rule arbitrarily on the *other* side of the window vanish almost entirely, like "last year's snow."

But the visual poets, those for whom natural appearances in all their aspects are not merely a proximate thing, but a principal and essential dimension of their poetic world, have a difficult time imagining any indifference concerning nature. These visual writers often see in the so-called aridity of their colleagues what amounts to an atrophying of poetic process. Clearly this is an exaggeration, and perhaps also a sign of limitation. A visionary writer needs to perceive and fathom the entire spectrum of creative possibility, regardless of whether that creation results from thought-, image-, or sound-based composition.

Understand, however, that this is the ideal. Poets who find that weather is a *necessary* precondition of their writing, create things through which breath passes: fall, or spring, for example, sings out from their lines unmediated, through the center of the writer's imagination. We find here that painterly inclination which is often accompanied by a pure, lyrical tone, or sober restraint. But the warmth or coolness of approach, of inclination, isn't in itself important here; what we notice is the strong pressure, the weight of nature — and nature alone — on such a poet. Without it, he would be left groping clumsily within his creation, unable to bring forth his singular word.

But there is more: almost inexplicably, the poet writes better poetry — and in other genres as well — in one of his favorite seasons. Or, to the contrary, sitting in the icy, snow-bound, storm-struck center of the city, for example, his fantasy might ardently burst into bloom with intimations of a distant inland sea. And there may prevail in the poet an ever-vigilant feeling for the natural image that is also spiritually nourished by contrast; it doesn't necessarily require a familiar sensory-manifestation to determine the formal composition of a poem.

Here is the place to add to that which we have previously suggested and note that, for these poets, ideological and metaphorical figuration can emerge from a consciousness centrally informed by the weather and the season; abstract concepts can embrace, if one might say this, an actuality that is resonant with metaphor, a sharper reality. In a good poem of this type, the initial train of thought in no way suffers; on the contrary, it is made complete with the breath and color of a landscape, as seen and felt by the poet.

[KH]

Noah Stern

(1912–1960)

"He didn't fit in. It wasn't just his inflexible manner and his difficulty in getting along with people," said Shelomo Grodzinsky, the critic who more than any other person is responsible for bringing the work of Noah Stern to light, as he tried to explain why Stern's work was virtually unknown until after his death by suicide at a mental hospital in 1960. At its best very fine, the poetry, Grodzinsky noted, was simply too far ahead of its time, having absorbed elements of English modernism long before the poet's Hebrew readership. During Stern's lifetime he published only a few poems in Hebrew literary journals; his pioneering translation of T. S. Eliot's *Waste Land* appeared in 1940.

Born and raised near Kovno (Lithuania), Stern moved to that city in order to attend high school (where Lea Goldberg was also a student). When he was seventeen, he moved to Canada and then the United States, completing his B.A. with honors at Harvard and earning a graduate scholarship at Columbia. His plans changed after a year in New York, and in 1935 he settled in Palestine, where he worked as a translator and high school teacher. He served for four (disturbing) years in the Jewish Brigade of the British Army, and after that returned to Palestine. In the mid-1950s, he took up residence on a kibbutz on the outskirts of Jerusalem, where his mental health rapidly deteriorated. In a bizarre incident—described in shadowy fashion, and as fiction, in his own journal—he tried to kill the kibbutz librarian, and was

eventually convicted of attempted manslaughter, for which he served five
years in prison.

PORTRAIT OF THE YOUNG POET

He loves himself,
the pain within,
and in another person —
pain's reflection:
his.
In the murderous
hot summer wind, he drills
of his own free will,
and in a fevered soul
descends,
emerging with — the poem.

His speech is not tucked in,
as though he were negating
a rule;
his mouth moves and doesn't move;
he will not notice if
the listener's listening,
but — the poem within him stirs
the song of a man he'll never know —
glowing so — and so sublime —
and oh so ironic.

He sends words
out to grope along the paths
of the imagination
of one who treads
out to the woods —
and then gets lost within its thickets.

The words, too, are lost
there — although the echo of an omen
returning from the forest
reaches him,
and the poem.

Between poem and poem,
between the village and the town,
he walks stealthily
and forgets, almost entirely,
the world.

And so he lives, who loved
solitude alone, and the hot summer wind,
who loves himself

the flame within,
and happiness in him
is wakened —
only by the poem.

[PC]

Zelda

(1914–1984)

A modest maverick, Zelda—as she signed her work—was a devout Orthodox
Jew who came from a prominent family of spiritual leaders associated with
the Chabad branch of Hasidism. She emigrated with her parents from the
Ukraine to Palestine when she was twelve and settled in Jerusalem. Her father
and grandfather died shortly thereafter, and Zelda (Schneersohn)—an only
child—was brought up by her mother and went on to a teachers' college,
where she began writing poetry. She eventually settled in a run-down part
of Jerusalem, where she taught elementary school. One of her students there
was Amos Klausner, who would eventually change his last name to Oz and
write about his teacher with great affection in *A Tale of Love and Darkness*.

In 1968, with her husband Haim's encouragement, Zelda published her
first book of poems, which was given a warm critical reception by the largely
secular Israeli literary world. She went on to publish another four volumes,
all after her husband's death in 1971. Though Zelda remained part of the
religious community to the very end, she had many secular friends and
possessed what seems to have been an exceptionally open and distinctive
spirit. Her poetry, which is marked by a casual alertness and consistent
freshness, is deeply rooted in the world of Jewish mysticism and traditional

sources but is in no way hampered by that grounding. "Words flew over Zelda," writes the Israeli essayist Azza Zvi, a close friend of the writer for many years and the addressee of the letter that follows, "and they're massed now in the lines of her poetry like birds on a beam or in the dark."

LETTER TO A YOUNG WRITER

Azka My Delight,

Sometimes you seem to take umbrage, as though you imagine I'd forgotten what it's like to be young with all the promise of things to come, the wonders and legends and torments of happiness, and yet you feel you're totally blind because how can you know what tomorrow will bring, whether you'll win or maybe, G-d forbid, lose everything. Or is it that you imagine I don't understand you or that I'm neglecting you because of my own troubles and concern for H. who is growing indescribably weaker — it's heart-breaking. I know I'm not easy to be with in this state of sleeplessness and anxiety, but please forgive me, dearest — you are one of the most precious people in the world to me.

Lately I've noticed that when a long time goes by "without getting any work done" as you put it, that is, without writing, I become irritable and depressed as though I'd let something I was supposed to do slip by, and then I feel bad about it.

It wasn't always like this: once I had a much more carefree attitude toward writing. I don't like feeling this way — I don't believe our importance should be measured by the number of poems we write, or the deeds we perform. It's enough that one thinks certain thoughts. Thoughts are extremely important, as are love and compassion and faith. When we start getting too particular about our time and our work there's already an air of death about it, of the "establishment" — a sense that if we don't do something right away it will never get done, till more than ever we become creatures of society, less and less of the sea and stars. But almost everyone is creative, and sometimes

I'm amazed at the way people from different spheres of life describe things with all the charm and force of poetry. And forgive me, dear friend, if I sometimes get upset when you criticize my poems. Your observations are enormously important to me, it's just that I need time to let them sink in.

Yours with much love,
Zelda

[BR]

S. Yizhar

(1916–2006)

S. Yizhar is the pen name of one of modern Hebrew's finest writers—a
novelist whose style was in fact so fine that it essentially defied translation
for the length of his writing career, though worthy English versions are at
long last beginning to appear. Like U. N. Gnessin, whose work he greatly
admired, Yizhar wrote sentences that proceed by a slow and painstaking
process of association that limns—in highly lyrical fashion—both the
contours of the natural landscape and the shapes of his characters' inner
lives. Yizhar Smilansky was born in the town of Rehovot to a family of
Russian-speaking immigrants who had arrived with the second wave of
Jewish immigration to Palestine after the turn of the century. He describes
his father—a farmer and writer—as someone who came with the Bible in
one hand and the works of Tolstoy in the other. His uncle, Moshe Smilansky,
was also a well-known writer. With the publication of his own first story in
1938, the younger Smilansky and his editor came up with the name he would
use in his writing for the rest of his career. "It's a small country," Yizhar has
said, explaining that he changed the name out of a sense of embarrassment.

Yizhar's breakthrough work was published in 1949, one year after the war
that erupted around the founding of the state. *Khirbet Khizeh* is one of the
very few works in the Israeli canon that treats with candor the Israeli-Jewish
approach to Palestinians living in the land at the time. Widely recognized as a

masterpiece of modern Hebrew prose, it has also provoked its share of
controversy: a 1978 broadcast of a made-for-TV film based on the novella was,
for instance, originally banned by the minister of education, and its essential
subject—the expulsion by the Israeli army of the native Arab population—is
one that continues to haunt the country.

In 1958 Yizhar published a colossal novel, *Days of Ziklag,* the 1,156
Hebrew pages of which recount in maniacal detail the conversations, exploits,
and "inner monologues" of a single detachment of Israeli soldiers during
a single week of the 1948 war. While Yizhar was awarded the Israel Prize
just after the publication of this book, at the age of forty-three, he also
endured a torrent of criticism, as audiences resisted the picture he paints
there of the national consciousness; in the wake of that criticism, Yizhar didn't
publish another work of adult fiction for thirty years. During that time he
continued to produce books for children and to write on politics, education,
and literature. Representing Ben-Gurion's Mapai, the forerunner of the Labor
Party, he served as a member of the Knesset from 1949 to 1967 and also
taught education and literature at various universities. In 1992 he began
publishing fiction again, and he went on to produce several more novels and
collections of stories before his death in 2006. The interview that follows took
place in 1994, not long after the publication of *Miqdamot* (Preliminaries), the
memoirlike novel with which he broke his silence.

The Need to Speak

In the final analysis every person speaks throughout his life about something
that he was born with. He doesn't choose it. He chooses only the theater's
setting, which presents itself, but the show takes place in any event. If that
particular element isn't the excuse or justification for speaking — there will
be another. An artist is born with this already in him. The need exists before
there exists a kind of environment or specific people within it. The need to
speak.

The need to speak exists before there's something to say?

Yes, it's something that has a form and music, a certain rhythm. There are forms that create pain and forms that neutralize pain. When the story is running along on its own it sets the pain free. If the givens of a certain reality or existence had not presented themselves, others would have been found. But the need to articulate them would still exist, because pain exists, and, in the place of this pain, that "something" opens, and becomes beautiful.

What is that "something"?

It can't be defined. Maybe it's that "something that leaves something," as Natan Zach put it in a poem. It's that special something of which the writing is merely the envoy, of which it speaks, and knows, the structure of the soul. And this structure of the soul involves a certain existence, like a color, orange, for instance — something that doesn't depend on the incarnations that will follow throughout one's life.

So, when I read certain writers, such as Proust, I feel that speech is the principal thing. The episode itself is simply an occasion to say something better; there is a pain that remains enfolded in you, and it's waiting for its occasion. Sometimes a person wastes the first part of his life in order to know what to say, because what he says is determined not by his nature but by his environment. A writer starts to speak when he knows the proper pitch of his voice and the musicality that will be within it. He has to work long and hard. To walk far. Sometimes, as with Proust, a large part of his life as a young man passes, and then suddenly, because of something, perhaps peripheral, perhaps incidental, suddenly he knows how he needs to speak. And when he knows, it flows. But this too is not infinite. Because every kind of pain speaks properly only up to a certain point, and then one needs to know to be silent. The greatest talent an author can have is to know when to lift up his pen at a certain point and say: Enough. There's always a certain temptation to go just a little further. [. . .]

What about your relation to the word?

The word, for me, is speech. And speech is exfoliation, articulation. To articulate for whom? For someone else? Who's listening? I don't know. Maybe for the listener within me, who reads what he writes, and maybe it goes much further. I don't see before me a certain someone (once I did, my cousin Yehiam [who was killed in a 1946 attack]). Speech is something closed that has to be opened. It can be opened poorly and it can be opened in order to add something, to make something. It isn't, by nature, beautiful or not beautiful. That depends on how it is said. It's also possible to speak without words. But I have words.

The word is what runs toward you. And words run toward me from all the various registers of the language. They come to me according to the need to speak. [. . .]

Do you have a sense of being intoxicated with words?

Sometimes very much so. It's a physical sensation. The danger is that I'll be drawn in after them and they'll turn into something too private, or a kind of fetish that isn't necessary for the development of the story and would only disturb its balance. It doesn't bother me that they might disturb a few readers, so long as they don't disturb the judge in me.

Freedom means to speak about what I want, despite what's expected of me, despite propriety and the rules involved. Sometimes there's the great joy of saying something, when it's said as it had to be said; and the freedom derives from the fact that I am the judge. And proper judgment is a melancholy judgment. It's never a matter of euphoria.

But are there moments of euphoria?

They are moments that pass through the melancholy judgment. Because in the end it's a sadness. Sometimes one forgets, and it seems that it has been overcome, but then, that joy is judged by the melancholy judgment. The beauty of the page is a matter of "nevertheless." It summons that sad judge and says to him: Look, be happy for once. These are the things that try to grasp hold of life.

What does a story start from?

One could say that it starts from a certain grasping onto a loop in life, but for me it starts with the proper sentence. When that happens, when the proper sentence comes to me, it's like an invitation. I extend a hand and dance with it. The story "Midnight Convoy" started from a description of a path and dust. A story waits for its first sentence. [. . .]

Do you see the language as a creator of reality, an expression of reality, or a description of reality?

It makes reality. It's like God, who spoke and the world came to be. He said "Let there be grass," and the earth brought forth grass. It makes reality and it also enables another person, a different person, who is not you, to see that it's beautiful. Beautiful not because it's pleasant, or sweet, and not because it doesn't hurt or annoy. But because it's properly made, organically, with the thing that wanted to be said. And was said well.

[PC]

Yehuda Amichai

(1924–2000)

Born in Würzburg, Germany, into an Orthodox home—his father ran a
wholesale needle-and-thread business, his grandfathers on both sides were
farmers—Yehuda Amichai learned to read and write Hebrew early on,
though he didn't begin to speak the language until 1936, when he settled
with his family in Jerusalem. He spent his formative years as a smuggler of
arms and a soldier, serving in the Jewish Brigade of the British army in World
War II, then fighting in Israel's 1948 war, the Sinai Campaign, and the Yom
Kippur War. He came to poetry relatively late, starting to write at the age of
twenty-five. He received his B.A. from the Hebrew University and, for most
of his career, made his living as a teacher of the Bible and Hebrew literature.

Amichai's first collection of poems, *Now and in Other Days,* was published
in 1955 and immediately changed the face of Hebrew poetry by introducing
the full range of a lithe, rich, yet ordinary vocabulary and syntax into the
matrix of verse. Though he denied ever having any desire to overthrow the
ways of his poetic fathers in the language—"poetry," he was given to saying,
"is both the most conservative and revolutionary of the arts"—the poems
he began writing in the late 1940s were cut from an entirely different cloth
than those of his literary forbears, Natan Alterman and Avraham Shlonsky in
particular, whose primary influences were Russian and modernist. Amichai's
verse stood out, however, even from that of his contemporaries, who had

deepened the literature's move into the actual landscape of the national myth but held on, nonetheless, to the idealizations and poetic lexicon of pre-State Zionism.

In practice Amichai had much more in common with younger writers— poets such as Natan Zach, Dahlia Ravikovitch, and David Avidan. Mixing dictional registers with aplomb, he wrote a love poem in the language of a rental agreement and a psalm for the building contractor who swindled him, and he sang the glory of God by the light of his open refrigerator door. Under the influence of the English poetry he had begun reading as a soldier and mingling a relaxed, Audenesque formalism with a highly poised free verse, he wrote hundreds of poems in a language that rode the rim of daily speech, gathering up elements of the complex present while echoing the past of the entire literature, religious and secular alike. For all his Israeliness on the one hand and his Europeanness on the other (in the English literary imagination he is grouped with the central European "poets of survival"— Herbert, Celan, Holub, and Popa), Amichai grounded his work in the placeless, borderless Hebrew of his childhood, and his poems often germinate in observations of its features. Amichai made a point of saying that his favorite poet was the great eleventh-century (exilic) Hebrew Andalusian Shmuel HaNagid, in whose secular, Scripture-based work he found confirmation for his faith in the fundamental power of the individual experience to include the experience of others and, in a way, to speak for an entire people.

Throughout Amichai's twelve volumes of poems, two novels, plays, and a collection of short stories, he spoke from the now-hard, now-softening middle of the flourishing language, through a private life that seemed for the better part of at least four decades to take shape in tandem with the life of the emerging state. His irony enabled him to survive the unavoidable distortions of the national story in the most unassuming of manners; and he saw his country's myths as just that, products of the imagination at the center of which actual people love, suffer, hope, grieve, forget, and remember. His struggle was as much to free himself from the past as to draw meaning and solace from his, and his people's, rootedness in it. He wrote about his city, Jerusalem, "the Venice of God," as well as anyone ever has. His greatest gift— and, according to Aristotle, "the mark of genius"—was for metaphor, that most magical bridger of difference.

How Do You Get to the Poem?

It's an emotional state, a state of emotional and even physiological concentration, a sense that something is suddenly and utterly dissolving in beauty, some kind of heat, a certain beauty. It all happens simultaneously, and whatever comes along, a particular tree, or face, or memory, it doesn't matter what, turns into one of the lines. Not always the first, and not necessarily the last. In this state of mind the poem is formed. Sometimes it forms itself all at once, but more often than not it's a matter of a single image, or scene, or several images, something external, a kind of external inwardness, I'd call it, a kind of short-circuit between what's external and what's within. And then, whatever enters into one's field of vision, or focus, makes its way into the poem. Sometimes I have a single image in mind, or I write something down on a piece of notepaper and, suddenly, after several years, its brother is born, its completion. I rely on my emotional Darwinism; I don't work on a poem. What should stay in my memory stays, and what's forgotten — even if it's a beautiful image or sentence, a well-turned phrase, even then — whatever's forgotten is forgotten. When something starts up, it activates memory with it, and also the present. Memory, let's say, is interpreted by contemporary phenomena. It might be a scent, or a voice, or something that happens, which it seems is somehow linked to what was then. It's a closing of the circle. Every poem is in essence a closing of the circle of things that were not bound before.

Let's assume for a moment that a poem is "about something," that it has a subject. Is that subject imprinted in it from the start?

No. Sometimes it has nothing at all to do with its surroundings. Let me give you an awful image, a meat grinder — the kind with which one used to grind meat by hand. Sometimes something would be left behind in the grinder, and you'd have to put in some dry bread so as to get the meat out. Sometimes a new situation brings out what's left behind of an old one that's still in the grinder — it drives it out. Now it's ready. Some of the poems about Jerusalem, about things that happened to me in Jerusalem — even during the War of Independence [in 1948] — suddenly came to me four years ago, while I was in New York. And nothing could be further from Jerusalem than New York, and from Israel in general. Apparently something there was shaken up and provoked it. It's really a kind of marvelous playfulness, a true pleasure, in which one can enjoy everything twice. The poem surprised me and brought something back to me within a true recollection. A poem is really the true recollection. More so than a picture album or anything else. It is, in the end, a kind of rumination. I've said it before: The cow enjoys grazing on fresh grass, but after a while it continues to chew, and chew, and then one sees its great pleasure. The poem allows us to chew over for a second time what we were, in another and different way, but perhaps with greater pleasure. The poem is the double-take of cinema. You pass by something, a tree you'd passed by yesterday, and the day before, and that same tree says to you: Just a moment.

I asked if the subject is born with the poem.

It might be that the subject precedes the poem. Usually there's a certain preparation, a readiness. When you reach that state, whatever comes to you from memory, as an event from outside, as an immediate occurrence, everything from a bus driver to a discarded rag you happen to notice and up to a Mozart quartet that you hear, all this comes into the poem. The things make the subject.

Does it ever happen that a poem leads you to write things you didn't mean to write initially?

Absolutely. That's the great pleasure. That's the gift. It's a matter of — like some kind of dream — something suddenly coming. Though in the dream you have no control over it; but here, you get down to work. Most of the poems involve a process of movement, even physical movement. Most of the poems come to me when I'm walking. I don't remember any poems that came to me while I was sitting with my books. I have almost no books in the room where I work. That would weigh on me. I prefer a certain disorder.

Most of the poems involve a process, of walking, in the simplest sense. I take the body, like a kind of engine that simply needs to be started, like a car that needs to be taken out for a spin in order to keep it in working order — its radio, its heater. I'm used to things coming to me while I'm walking. I have to walk. The movement has to be purposeless. I don't head out [like Isaac] in order to "meditate in the field at dusk" [Gen. 24:63], or so that [the poetry] will come to me. On the contrary, walking to the market, taking my daughter to ballet. I have to be going somewhere, somewhere that isn't poetic.

Is the mood that's revealed in the poem the one that you were aware of when you started to write?

Yes. It's not that I suddenly discover something new about my "emotional state," something I didn't know. Maybe after a few years that's the case. Sometimes, when a question about translation comes up, when a translator runs into a problem of some sort, in the passage to a different language, that sometimes exposes something about the person I was. It isn't exposed in my own language because it's mine, and sits in me. But no, I was always aware of things. Even in the thick of it, in the middle of the states I was in. I had a second sense, and knew it was this way and not that. Just as I have no sense of what's "early and late" in my own life, I live without a sense of what was when; it's not even a matter of memories — memories aren't memories, I live because I'm the child I was, and the lover I was, and the father I've been, and the son of parents who've passed away. My parents are present. Everything exists. Nothing dies for me. That's a Jewish quality — that "there is no earlier and later in Scripture" [Babylonian Talmud, *Pesahim* 6b]. David, the King of Israel, lives on; it isn't just a matter of faith in the messiah king, and so forth, so much as a sense that you simply have to reach out with your hand — and it's all there. You reach out in every direction, and take. It's all yours for the taking. It's all there for you. Umberto Saba, a wonderful poet, said once in an interview: "A poet is someone who is always wondering, 'What happened to the child I was?'" I am: within me is the continuation of the child I was. In fact, I'm still like I was then. Within a single space.

Do you consciously gather material for poetry?

No. Definitely not. So much so — and this too isn't right — that I take pains *not* to do that. I also don't keep a journal. Sometimes I write down an expression. I have notes in my pocket, and after a year or two I take out the pile of all the notes, and sometimes one sets something off and another doesn't. There's raw material there before you, and it's in fact the richest sort of material, and also the most direct. Sometimes you find something, and all at once it starts to leap. It's something between a lottery and a strategy. Life — not as a poet. That's the entire story. The wheels are constantly turning. Poetry is the least professional thing there is. In the best sense. It's the most wonderful sort of amateurism. You do what you love. For me it's important not to be a poet, but to write poems.

Your poetry is remarkably rich with images. How do the poem's images come to you?

This is the only advantage that a person who writes poetry has over one who doesn't — that he can make connections to other things. The metaphysics of it. The image is born of an instant, sometimes it happens so quickly that the vehicle precedes the tenor, so you sense that something is like a plant climbing a wall, and you don't yet know what that something is. You see it, and only later know what's like what.

How would you describe your relationship to the words at the time of writing?

There's something extraordinarily intimate about it. After all, the words are being used by everyone around you in the world outside, but at the same time they've become your words. Just as with a name. If a man calls his son by name, a common name, like David, until he calls his son by that name the name is general; but as soon as he names his son "David," suddenly "David" becomes something intimate. The same thing, exactly, happens with words. The words *table, bicycle, oven* at once take on an intimate aspect. Mine. When you say *hand, ear, foot* — for a doctor they're one thing; but when a person loves someone, then suddenly *hand, ear, foot* become something special. It would only be natural for a person in love to give every limb on the body of the beloved a new name, a name that he makes up. But the mere fact of his using the general terms for them makes the situation intimate. The poem has to create that sort of framework, in which general things become the property of an individual.

Did the fact that you came from a religious home deepen your sense of Hebrew?

Absolutely. Today it's called "enrichment." A child who grew up on a kibbutz in the landscape — that's enrichment as well. If someone asked me for a prescription for how to turn a child into a poet, I'd say: Have him grow up in a religious household. Not necessarily Jewish. Religious. It's a matter of concretion. Madness, but also concretion. Like confession. Playful, wonderful. That's really the first language, when you do things in which you connect your language to things that are entirely irrelevant, like God and prayer, and this is a real connection. Whatever a person gets in a natural way during his childhood involves a true richness, whether in language or emotion or faith. It's a geological layer that exists in me, although it's extremely compact, because it's so very early, therefore it's crystallized, and highly charged, and capable of breaking out. My first contact with Hebrew was, despite it all, with "the language of God," when I was three. Since our home was Zionist, we also learned the songs of the pioneers [in Palestine]. Among them all, "O foolish pioneer, / whatever are you doing there?" got stuck in my mind. I have a doubled relationship to the language, which is both a sacred language and the language of speech.

Does a poem emerge all at once?

Sometimes yes, mostly no.

Do you revise a lot?

With my first poems more of the poems came to me all at once, in particular the poems that were more formally "difficult" — sonnets and rhymed poems. For whatever reason a great many things came to me then all at once. Now it's less so. The process is much more beautiful. It's like fast food versus slow food. Now things are set over a low flame for a long time and then, all of a sudden, they're ready. It's a process of knowing when something is done. I don't work on a poem. It isn't a matter of my having an unfinished poem and deciding: "Tomorrow I'm going to sit with it." I've got lots of unfinished poems. It's like a painter, really. Painters sometimes leave themselves twenty unfinished paintings. You ask them why — after all, you're always complaining that they take up space. No, they can't do it. And then, all of sudden they finish several at once. I'm suspicious of myself — that I don't finish them on purpose. After all, when you finish them, you leave them behind. You separate from them.

If you have several unfinished poems, why aren't they combined into a single poem?

Sometimes I do have long poems that were assembled that way. Sometimes things link up in the most surprising ways — words, lines, and images move from poem to poem. That's the most marvelous sort of cooking there is. An image that leaps from one poem to another, and since there is no earlier and later, in fact all poems by all people comprise a single long poem. Even if it's not very long. The poetry of a single poet is one large mass. Even if he denies it and says, no, no way, each poem is born on its own — and this too is true — still, they all come together to form a single mass. Sometimes you move something, sometimes it moves on its own. Sometimes you come across something — what's that image doing in this poem? It doesn't belong there at all. Here, here's another. So I like to work on several poems at once. And sometimes the opposite happens. There's a long poem, and I see that the sections don't come together as they should. In a completely natural way, you feel that it's coming apart. And it turns into individual poems, or sections of other poems. And that's a large pleasure. The poem makes me focus on it, but it knows that it has neighbors and the like. That's how it has been recently. With my early work, each poem stood on its own.

When do you know the poem is finished?

It's a matter of experience. There aren't any rules. In the Bible it says: "And he saw that it was good." God made man; it's possible that he made a man that wasn't good, or a lion that wasn't good. There's a certain sense. I like to make jam. I have a sense of just when it's starting to jell, but hasn't gotten too thick. Most of the time, my instincts have been right.

Is a poem finished with its publication?

It's over even with its composition. And since I don't write on a typewriter, that helps me; again, it's a movement of the hand, just as before that there were feet, so there's writing and erasing and copying. That's part of the physical process.

Once you wrote in rhyme and form; do you miss that poetry?

On the contrary. When I started to write, the retreat from rhyme had already begun, and I had poems of both sorts. I took it, again, as a matter of there not being "early and late," or what was "worthy of being written," or what wasn't "worthy" now. I wrote whatever suited me. Just as I don't want to go back to being twenty years old — strange as that may sound coming from a man of sixty-two. I live what I need to live.

With you, as opposed to many other poets, there was a wealth of forms. You wrote sonnets, rhymed quatrains, etc., and in recent years the form has barely changed.

It's less pressing for me. It's a sort of beginner's flaw. The fixed forms helped me. It's a kind of stricture that sets one free. A person has to have a great deal of experience in order to write a poem without a fixed form and rhyme. But at the time, it seemed to me the greatest sort of freedom, because it came to me naturally. Sometimes even the artificial is natural. Today I wouldn't be capable of it. I stopped writing in rhyme because I didn't feel like it — it became unnatural. And if it isn't natural, why do it? Children are crazy about rhyme and rhythm. For them it's natural.

Do you ever get the desire to go back to early poems and change them?

No. Never. I'll read them when I read in public, but I never change them.

Doesn't the desire to return to the success of an earlier poem constitute an obstacle to new writing?

No, no. I'm not really concerned with that. After my first book of stories, *In This Terrible Wind,* which was written between 1956 and 1958, they told me, "Why don't you write another one?" But no. I have no desire to write prose today. Prose and poetry are carved from a single block: sometimes it finds expression in one way, and sometimes in another. My prose tried to describe the conditions in which my poems were born. The prose provides, as it were, the ambient elements and the setting; if the protagonist of my fiction had written poems, he'd have written poems like mine. It's a kind of background explanation.

In your opinion, can poetry be edited in the way one edits prose?

No. And I don't show my poems to anyone before they're published.

Have you ever written political poems?

Yes. Actual political poems. I think that a large part of my poems are political in the deepest sense of the word. My position is known. Whoever reads my poetry — that helps him keep from becoming a fascist. In *Ha'aretz* I published a poem in response to a poem by Uri Zvi Greenberg, who had written about the operation at Qibya [a 1953 raid across the Jordanian border in which Israeli troops, led by Ariel Sharon, in response to a previous attack by fedayeen and as an effort to "send a message," killed over sixty Palestinians in the village by that name and destroyed all of its homes]. He cursed me vehemently: "How can a man like that be a teacher in Israel?" The poem was published instead of an op-ed piece, and I achieved something in terms of the response that no article I might have written could ever have achieved.

Do political poems go through the same process that others do?

No. There's something different at work. Here it's as though I were acting, playing the part of myself. It goes much faster. When Stalin died, I wrote an elegiac sonnet. But it was a real poem.

What sort of influence do your surroundings and external events have on your writing?

Everything's stimulation for the poem, and everything goes into it. The poem, every poem of mine, is a summary of life, not only of the poem itself. It goes through life with me. It's a kind of black box that they find in airplanes. If it happens to be the last poem, then it's the last poem, and it contains the final summary, and not just something on the way to a further development. Others can comment about that later on. Every poem is the final word.

Don't you worry about repeating yourself?

I'm not bothered by that. It doesn't worry me, and I'm sure it happens. So there's a measure of repetition. So what? Just as I always have the same color eyes, and the same continuity, and the same genes, so with the things that were in me. So there's someone who likes it, and someone who doesn't. When I read other poets, I especially like the eccentric circles, where you always identify the writer, almost from his first poems. That continuity. I like Magritte more than Picasso, though I appreciate his genius greatly. I like artists who always do just one thing. Who have one thing to say, in large circles, even when their testimony grows distant from a central experience. It's still one thing. I like that in Agnon, for example.

Can you discern any changes that have taken place in your writing over the past few years?

Actually we've already spoken about that. The subjects are the same subjects. Love, death — even in the most recent book there's a poem about a friend who was killed beside me (during the war) in the sands near Ashdod. I don't know what brought it up. It's always in a single present for me. Really, life for me is one big present.

Today I write differently, but it's the same me that I was. I like my first poems in the same way that a man has no reservations about his first love, even if it was miserable, even if he'd fallen in love with a crook. The moment he has reservations, it means that he has reservations about his life, that he's living for effects. I don't deny my first poems, just as I don't deny my life. I can't hear "God Has Mercy on Kindergarten Children" anymore today, but I accept it, because that's how I wanted to write, and that's how I wrote. I don't deny myself as I was.

JERUSALEM, II DECEMBER 1986

[PC]

David Shahar

(1926–1997)

A fifth-generation Jerusalemite, David Shahar wrote about his city—or a few
specific streets within it—like no one else. Shahar's masterwork, his eight-
volume historical saga, *The Palace of the Shattered Vessels,* takes its title from
the qabbalistic term that describes the creation of the world, during which the
vessels that were to hold the light of the divine emanation were broken. The
sacred mission of man, who is born into a world of shards, is to bring about
"repair" by mending the cosmic catastrophe and restoring a wholeness that
would contain the original light. Elements of this mysticism run throughout
Shahar's sketches of the everyday life of the city, and critics have noted that
the modernist strategies of the author's dense and incantatory prose—
including the loosely associative flow of a fragmented consciousness and
narrative—constitute a fictional correlate to that religious model of restitu-
tion through composition, or re-creation. A similar quest for a return to
origins is the subject of "First Lesson," a short story in which Shahar sets
out to trace his writing back to its initiatory moment and what he calls
"the miracle"—the specific event or moment out of which all of his work
as a writer would unfold.

Thanks to the celebrated French translation of his historical saga, Shahar
became far more famous in France than in his own country—where he remained something of a writer's writer. Later in life Shahar divided his time

between Jerusalem and Paris; he had a very wide following there and was considered an "Israeli Proust." In addition to his *Palace of the Shattered Vessels,* Shahar published several other novels and volumes of stories.

First Lesson

In the beginning was the miracle, and the miracle was, and is, and will be to be marveled at always.

As for me, I have not stopped marveling to this day, to the writing of these very lines in the September of the year 1966 in the French village of Saint-Maur-des-Fossés in Josef's house right on the banks of the river Marne — I can see the tops of the trees on the other side of the river — and I am thirty-nine years old. And not only have I not stopped marveling, but the marveling increases from day to day, against all expectations and even, it might be said, against all ideas of decorum and good taste.

I well remember the first time in my life that I was smitten with the terror of the great miracle. It happened when I was a small child of about three years old. I do not know why I stayed up after my usual bedtime. In contrast to what was to happen later in my life, I remember the hour as a peaceful one in the house. The kerosene lamp burned on the table and its green china shade, in addition to the yellowish-whitish pool of light it shed on the table around the stem of the lamp and its base, diffused a dull green glow. My father sat poring over a textbook on bookkeeping and other books on accountancy in the English language (he had opened a commercial school and there were no books of this kind as yet available in Hebrew, except for two or three which failed to satisfy him). When I approached him he rose from his place, took me in his arms and went outside with me into the night.

This first meeting with the night sky filled me with an obscure terror. I saw the sky and suddenly it was black with tiny points of light in it. "Those are the stars," said my father, and added, "the host of Heaven." Somewhere a door creaked open and a stream of light poured out of the crack which opened in the blank dark wall, reaching the foot of the cypress tree that stood in our yard and wrapping its trunk in a mantle of day. Soft chill tongues of wind whispered between the branches, bringing with them from afar, from beyond the tombs of the Sanhedrin, a smell of damp earth and small humming, cricking, buzzing voices, the voices of night animals suddenly signaling and suddenly stopping, and the existence of the surrounding mountains — the mountains of Nebi Samwil and Sheikh Jarrah and Mount Scopus — was present and breath-stopping and heavy with the weight of an ancient-breathed quality, terrible in its dimensions, which were beyond the dimensions of man, and its eternities which were beyond the eternity of man, and in its indifference to the little men stirring on its back. The same quality of mountains and sky dimly perceived on my daytime ramblings along the mountain paths between the thistles and rocks (we lived then in the old Beth Israel quarter and our house was the last in the street; from it the track continued up to the tombs of the Sanhedrin, and from our window we saw the village of Nebi Samwil astride the hilltop) oppressed me now more strongly in the night world revealed to me. The mountains and the sky at night became more tangible in their distance, more oppressive in their tangible presence in the darkness.

I clung tightly to my father's neck, to the strong pleasant smell of his tobacco. "Come, Daddy, let's go back," I said to him, "let's go in." He looked at me and said, "Good, let's go inside." I saw in his eyes that he understood that the fear of the elements in the night had overcome its powers of attraction, and with his first surprise had come the understanding that I was not yet old enough to live in both the world of the day and the world of the night. As soon as we had returned to the shelter of the four walls and the soft light of the green lampshade, a heavy weariness fell on me, as if I had just returned from a long journey into an unknown land. After some time had passed — whether it was a matter of days, weeks, or months escapes me — I asked him to take me out again into the mountains and sky of the night. I think I was resentful. I felt a kind of anger, a kind of insult because he had hidden from me until now the other world of whose existence I knew nothing, and in which he continued to live after I had gone to bed to sleep.

The fear of the quality of the elements made tangible in the darkness, which disappeared completely with the love of the night world, came back to me a few years later in a strange form, almost opposed to the first form in which I had experienced it. The fear of the quality of the elements at night, which soon turned to longing (a longing which differed in kind from the longing for the alleys and streets of the town at night, of which we will speak when the time comes), gave way to a fear of the quality condensed into the stillness of a lighted room at night, but of this fear too the time has not yet come to speak.

I have described the first time I was smitten by the miracle. As for the last time, why it has just this moment occurred, with the writing of these very words. If I were a psychiatrist or a psychopathologist or a psychoanalyst or a neurologist or any other kind of diploma-ed soul doctor of our times, and if I were asked to give an expert opinion on the state of my own soul, I should be obliged to conclude that in the thirty-six years which have passed since then my condition has deteriorated steadily and that it is exceedingly doubtful whether any specialist treatment whatever could bring about a cure at the advanced and severe stage which it has now reached. For today there is nothing at all in the whole world that does not arouse my wonder and amazement, and the more I concentrate my attention on anything the more intense the wonder and amazement grow: these autumn colors in the garden and the sky outside, and the coal fire in the grate inside, and the house, and me myself sitting in it, and my writing hand, and the writing itself, and the drive to write. If I were living my life according to my true inclinations and the impulses of my heart, I would not be sitting and writing now but casting a line into the waters of the Marne by the side of that slender Frenchwoman with her hair blowing in the wind. All along the banks of the Marne there are Frenchmen fishing. Some fish standing, but most are sitting. Sitting and fishing and waiting patiently the livelong day with their eyes fixed on the float at the end of their lines, gazing dreamily at the little greenish-yellowish-brownish wavelets and the running water and the dancing specks of light, their thoughts drifting to and fro over the tops of the trees and the play of light among the leaves and the warbling of a distant bird, and their hearts longing for a sudden disturbance of the water and a delicate tug and the head of a hooked fish appearing on the end of the line. The fisherman and the fish. Past the fishermen go the sailors. Some row in rowboats and some are bold and skilled and sail in sailboats and some, who are rich and desire a maximum of comfort in their pleasures, drive far out in motorboats. Where the shore slopes down at the river's bend, at the section belonging to the village called La Varenne, stand the villas of the rich and of the singers who have made their fortunes by becoming public favorites, like Charles Trenet. This elegant fisherwoman is in all probability one of the mistresses of one of these rich men, which would of course not prevent me, if I were living my own life, from wooing her so that she would lie with me on the riverbanks after the sun had set and the fishermen and the rowers and the sailors had all gone away. The trouble is, I know in advance that in the act of lying with her, and even at the moment of climax, I will be haunted by longing and tormented by yearning, which is what happened to me last time with the aging Françoise in her flat on the Île de St. Louis opposite the cathedral of Notre Dame, and even before, with her predecessors. All of them fished for fish in their souls, but she did so consciously. It is the knowledge after the event that the body is the veil and the limit, and penetrating it does not lead to the essence beyond, and you can journey beyond it only in it and through it, and in order to get everything there is to get out of the journey itself, you must pay the price of yearning and longing in advance, and once this obligation has been fulfilled, the difficulties and obstacles on your way will be eased.

As for me, it seems that I must pay the price in writing, black on white. [. . .]

[DB]

Sami Michael

(b. 1926)

"I consider myself part of the Arabic language and Arabic life," said novelist
Sami Michael in Arabic, during a BBC broadcast from his Haifa home at the
height of the 2006 Lebanon War, "and at the same time part of Jewish-Israeli
life. And so I'm a kind of border—of peace and friendship—between the
two peoples. That border passes through me and through my work."

Born and raised in Baghdad, Saleh Menashe (as he was then known),
joined the Communist underground at fifteen. Two years later he began
writing (under the pen name Samir Marid) for opposition newspapers. When
a warrant was issued for his arrest in 1948, he fled to Iran, and a year later he
made his way to Israel, where he adopted the Hebrew name Sami Michael.
He continued to write in Arabic (as Marid) and worked as an editor at several
Arabic-language publications in the new state. He went on to study hydrology
and was employed as a water engineer with the Israel Hydrology Authority
for some twenty-five years. He stopped writing in Arabic in his early thirties,
eventually switching to Hebrew but publishing his first novel in that language—*Equal and More Equal*—only when he was forty-eight. Five others
have followed, among them the best-selling Baghdadi historical novel, *Victoria*,
and *Trumpet in the Wadi,* a Jewish-Arab love story set in Haifa. Michael has
also published several volumes of nonfiction and works for children. He has
been president of the Association for Civil Rights in Israel since 2001.

In the essay that follows, Michael walks back along the border between his two languages and recounts the ordeal of his crossing over from one to the other.

I'd Come Back from Work, Wash Off the Mud, and Sit Down at My Desk

As an immigrant to Israel I plummeted from the status of an Iraqi citizen with twenty-five hundred years of seniority into a world whose language, customs, and culture were all strange to me. That same decade the sky fell in when I discovered that communism wasn't the Garden of Eden but a tyranny that trampled human dignity. As an intellectual for whom language had been the most important tool in life, my faith in myself was shaken. Half of that decade I spent on a moshav and on a kibbutz whose members saw themselves as the elite of Israeli society. I had to find my place among young people whose capable teachers had designated them to be the leaders of the country.

I lived on the kibbutz as a hired hand, working as a technician in the hydrological service. The job was a gift from heaven for me. At times of emotional distress or existential crisis, I find comfort in manual labor. With pliers, hammer, or saw in hand, I'm called upon to fix a table, bureau, or rusty pipe instead of having to fix the world. The hydrological service was for me a kind of occupational therapy. On isolated paths and in treacherous floods, I found myself again. There I was exposed to the company of clear-thinking men who devoted themselves to a profession that demanded resourcefulness, a steadfast conscience, and natural intelligence. The work was carried out in open spaces empty of people, most often near the borders, which were also dangerous. It's commonly held that work in the heart of nature is romantic and tranquil. Hardly. Toxic insecticides, tension, heavy smoking, exposure to extreme cold and to dust throughout the summer — all these exact their price. The majority of the men in the service never reached the age of retirement. But they took pride in their work — despite the miserable salary, which lagged behind that of a construction worker.

I admired these tough men and valued the solidarity that blossomed in their company, though they were also capable of mercilessly crushing smooth-tongued types who were full of themselves. In the joy of doing I forgot my troubles, and I sought to express my admiration for this strain of man, which I had not encountered before. Prior to that, I had worked for many years among valiant colleagues of the moderate-to-extreme left. I had friends who were imprisoned and even executed. They withstood social ostracism and responded to these humiliations with scorn. That was courage of a different sort.

I learned Hebrew through listening and obsessive reading. When I sat down to write a novel in that acquired language, it was about this group of men into whose midst I had stumbled. I'd come back from work, wash off the mud or the dust of the day, take a short nap, then sit down at my desk by night. I didn't dare reveal to anyone my secret doings. I was still new at the hydrological service, and I understood at once the loathing my fellow workers had for people who put on airs. In great excitement, with torment and joy, the white pages began to fill up. I didn't have the means to buy a typewriter. The racing of my pen across the blinding whiteness of the empty page hypnotized me. I wrote, then, mainly for the sake of writing. I didn't dream of conquering the world, or even a remote village. Not for a minute. The pleasure I took in the act of writing was enough for me; or so I told myself. In the morning I'd pull on the patched boots of the hydrological service, wrap myself in my threadbare raincoat — an inheritance from the British Mandate Department of Agriculture — and sink my hands into the clear spring waters and the gushing floods.

I gave my manuscript the simple title *The River Rises*. A friend, the only one outside my family who knew about my secret writing, volunteered to type the manuscript in her free time on the service's typewriter. The office was in an old Turkish prison. In the basement, under the desk on which the typewriter stood, were the gallows with a pit in the floor and an iron door that opened upward to receive the corpse of the hanged. The room was large. We stored tools there and used it as a lab where we could check the water quality.

What does an immigrant who has entered the Hebrew language almost covertly do with a finished manuscript? I looked around for the most important venue of the day, and was directed to Am Oved, which was, I was told, a promising publishing house. This was forty-five years ago. The man who'd advised me had, perhaps, experienced disappointment.

"They'll send it back with no explanation."

"What kind of manners are those?" I wondered.

"In literature, there are no manners."

With some misgivings, I thought of all the sad and spurned people whose love letters go unanswered. Nonetheless, I went to the post office on the main street of Tiberias. A month passed, and I waited impatiently for the package's return. Instead of the heavy package, however, a thin envelope from the publisher arrived, startling me. Inside was a short letter signed by the poet Ezra Zussman asking me to come to 22 Mazeh Street in Tel Aviv for a talk. I appreciated the poet's gesture, particularly when I learned later that he had a heart ailment and troubled himself to come to the city from his home in, I believe, Nes Ziona.

He was a slender man and spoke in a quiet voice. His gracious manners impressed me. From his cautious words I understood that he wasn't disqualifying the manuscript out of hand. I remember his noting that, regrettably, writing about manual labor was no longer in fashion in Hebrew literature, not because the subject was uninteresting, but rather because most of the writers were educated men who taught at the university or frequented the big-city cafés. He believed my manuscript had potential. It goes without saying that my ego slowly deflated as the conversation wore on.

"And what's the bottom line?" I asked.

He looked at me with his wise eyes. "There is no bottom line. You're a writer. That is the essence of literature, that it has no bottom line. The manuscript you sent needs rewriting."

I thought back to the many months of nights spent at my desk after the days of hard labor, being jolted in a jeep across dusty roads and rocky ground. I thought of my protagonists who — unknowingly — were waiting to enter Hebrew literature. They had become very dear to me during the writing of the novel. And though the disillusionment and disappointment were not especially great, the words of this gentle-souled poet seemed to me like those spoken to a man who was being advised to take his beloved to a plastic surgeon. Throughout the long ride home, the manuscript rested on my knees. In those days no one revised a manuscript for a writer or reworked a novel's plot. Writers were writers, and editors dealt with copy. But ultimately, I remember the well-intentioned poet with affection. As I left, he added some words of encouragement: "Rewrite the book. It will be a success. Then you'll also be able to study at the university."

The first conclusion I came to — one that's still with me today — is that I should never, but never, allow a manuscript of mine to make its way to a publisher without first having shown it, repeatedly, to the harshest critic of all — myself, and that I would have to have the courage to give myself the most uncompromising advice and be prepared to toss out whatever was still unripe.

The second conclusion I reached was that I had to widen my horizons from within the walls of the academy. So I registered for studies at Haifa University, in the departments of Arabic literature and psychology. Four years later, I exited the university as I'd entered it, but with healthy and well-developed defenses against the blather of what's called the humanities, in which everything exists except the human. Still, I profited. During my studies I acquired habits of orderly thinking that are critical to the work of literary composition.

I can't say today where that manuscript has gone, as I don't usually save things. However, the old principle of physics, whereby matter is always preserved, applies to literary work as well. Forty years later, I wrote the novel *Water Touching Water*. Sadly, most of the men who had inspired the characters in that earlier manuscript had died. The poet Ezra Zussman had also passed away. Still, while writing *Water Touching Water* I told myself more than once that the imaginative connection between *The River Rises* and this new book comprised a kind of homage to a modest poet who had won me over with his charm.

[RTB]

Natan Zach

(b. 1930)

Natan Zach's poetry has been something of an Israeli secret over the years. While Zach lived in England for more than a decade and appeared regularly at poetry festivals around the world, very little of his highly musical work has been translated successfully into English, and so his poetry remains more of a rumor than a presence or influence in the international context. And that, it needs to be said, is unfortunate, for Zach is one of the finest poets of his generation and the person who has wrought the greatest change in the language of Hebrew poetry after the founding of the state. If Amichai represents the (traditional, if playful) Jerusalem face of that revolution, Zach is the quintessential (bohemian) Tel Avivian.

Like Amichai, Zach elevated spoken Hebrew to the level of poetry, sacrificing nothing in the way of precision and style and gaining everything in terms of content. His ear is calibrated to the subtleties of contemporary Hebrew, as it evolved between the 1950s and '70s. Though Zach is writing still, his finest work is found in his first several volumes, which are among the most important published in Hebrew over the past half-century.

Born in Berlin in 1930, Zach moved to Palestine with his family when he was six. The influence of European, and particularly German, poetry is evident in his work and also informs his prose. The essay printed here discusses the dangers of free verse, a mode at which Zach himself excels and with which he revolutionized the literature. The poem that follows the essay clarifes the provenance of his critique.

The Dangers of Free Verse

Almost week after week the dangers lurking in the writing of free verse are made apparent in the poems published in the literary supplements of the daily papers. Brecht speaks of "the great temptation of formlessness" that is bound up with the use of irregular rhythms in poetry. Here we'll concentrate primarily on another danger, one that also stands out in the new poetry being written in Israel today, and to which the following poem bears witness:

> The days' softness lazily
> slipping away caresses leaves by the side
> of the January pond. The hour
> of myrrh and balm —
> and a face vanished from me, to find its clearness otherwise
> and be immersed far
> from here and from the rain.

It would seem that we have before us a straightforward example of free verse, varying in line length and devoid of rhyme and metrical regularity. Nevertheless, we need only read the poem and listen for its caesuras in order to notice its basic three-beat metrical unit, which is repeated throughout the poem, without any conspicuous alteration. [. . .] If we then rearrange the poem, keeping in mind this recurring component, we get the following:

> The days' softness lazily
> slipping away caresses
> leaves by the side
> of the January pond.
> The hour of myrrh and balm —
> and a face vanished from me
> to find its clearness otherwise
> and be immersed far
> from here and from the rain.

The recurrent element here is not more-or-less identical metrical feet, but rather clusters of three stresses (which in Hebrew also contain the same number of words). The advantage of this sort of measure, in comparison, say, to more regular measures — such as those of Natan Alterman — is reflected in the naturalness of the reading: each word can be pronounced with its natural stress, without having to "wring" from it secondary stresses that belong to an underlying and mechanically produced metrical scheme. The position of the rising or stressed syllables is irregular, as is the number of descending or unstressed syllables; and there is no conspicuous friction between the natural and the metrical rhythms.

But that is as far as it goes — and from this point on we begin to note the resemblance between two rhythmic modes that, ostensibly, differ radically from one another. For the dreary effect, not unlike what we find with Alterman's fixed meters, is accomplished in the so-called free-verse example cited above by means of the repetition of a symmetrically identical unit — but without any compelling variation or conspicuous shaping of the melodic line, which is so vital to free verse and keeps it from sliding into prose. Monotony of this sort, moreover, cannot be alleviated by the hypnotic power of the fixed Altermanian scheme, which further strengthens the impression of uniformity created even by such a short lyric. Here too the measure is unable to contribute anything toward the meaningful framing of the solitary phrase, or to exploiting the significant intonations of its words. On the contrary, a richer line, in terms of its content, like "Days' softness lazily" is flattened beside part of a line whose content is thin: "of the January pond."

This poem and others like it represent a new "school" and one that's distinct from that of the Hebrew poets in their thirties and forties. In the new formal context, there appears as well a different technique for the introduction of metrical variation, of deviation from the schematic. In order to camouflage (but only to camouflage!) the symmetry and monotony of its lines, the writer divides them in such a way that the recurrent unit is swallowed within the visual field of irregularity and "freedom" (here too omission plays an important role). Except that no new tension is created between the line and its syntax, and so one need only read the poem aloud for the caesuras to disclose the poem's secret, its fashionable approach to "variation" notwithstanding.

The degree to which the desire to escape monotony has taken hold of us is made clear by the two final lines, which bring the poem to a close even as they introduce a slightly altered rhythm. The symmetrical unit disappears and the tempo slows. The change is refreshing.

The principal justification for free verse is the individual application it allows for, and in its being free *verse* — which is to say, *rhythm* — and not simply freedom from any metrical scheme, or a mere combination of irregular lines. However, precisely because of its individual character (with regard to the line, the poem, and the poet), free verse is extremely hard to employ. (Perhaps it is also difficult for the poet to release himself from an inevitable tendency toward the monotonous.) It is even harder to describe free verse, though it is certainly possible to sense its presence when one reads intuitively, just as one senses its absence. For wherever the same distinctiveness vanishes, wherever the poet is content to borrow the "free" mannerisms of others, and the measure is no longer based on the singular shaping of form — the marathon of the monotonous and the mechanistic is renewed, and "free verse" is exposed to the same danger of formlessness and featurelessness about which Brecht and many others have warned us. [. . .]

"The poet who writes 'free' verse," Auden declares in his *Selected Essays,* "is like Robinson Crusoe on his desert island: he must do all his cooking, laundry and darning for himself. In a few exceptional cases, this manly independence produces something original and impressive, but more often the result is squalor — dirty sheets on the unmade bed and empty bottles on the unswept floor."

And Ezra Pound seizes the bull by its horns: "I think one should write *vers libre* only when one 'must,' that is to say, only when the 'thing' builds up a rhythm more beautiful than that of set meters, or more real . . . a rhythm which discontents one with set iambic or set anapestic."

[GL]

To Put It Differently

Poetry chooses choice things, carefully selecting
select words, arranging,
fabulously, things arranged. To put it differently
is hard, if not out of the question.

Poetry's like a clay plate. It's broken easily   ·
under the weight of all those poems. In the hands
of the poet, it sings. In those of others, not only
doesn't it sing, it's out of the question.

[PC]

Dan Pagis

(1930–1986)

Dan Pagis was born in Bukovina (an eastern province of the Austro-Hungarian Empire, now Romania and the Ukraine) and raised, like Amichai and Zach, in a German-speaking environment. His mother died when he was four, and when his father departed for Palestine he left the boy with his grandparents, who raised him. In 1941 they were deported to a Nazi concentration camp in the Ukraine. His grandfather died there, but the poet-to-be escaped when he was fourteen and made his way to Palestine two years later. Within three years he was publishing poems in his newly acquired Hebrew. In addition to being one of the leading poets of his generation, Pagis was one of the world's foremost scholars of medieval Hebrew poetry, which he taught at the Hebrew University in Jerusalem for many years before his untimely death at the age of fifty-six. Apart from his eight volumes of poetry, he wrote several important works on medieval Hebrew poetry from Spain and Italy, and edited critical editions of medieval and modern writers.

Pagis is perhaps the quietest and most modest of all the major contemporary Hebrew poets, his poetry barely rising, it seems, above a whisper. Displacement is central to his work, and he is known in particular for his haunting Holocaust poems, "Written in Pencil in the Sealed Railway-Car" among them. His playfulness, sharp wit, and gift for irony are, however, apparent in the two poems translated below, both of which reflect Pagis's sense of the essential that is inconspicuous, and often surreptitious, in language and in life.

For a Literary Survey

You ask how I write. So long as it stays between us. I take a ripe onion, squeeze it, dip the pen in its juice, and write. It's an excellent sort of invisible ink: the onion juice has no color, like the tears to which it gives rise, and after it dries, it leaves no trace. The page once again seems as pure as it was. Only if you bring it close to the fire, and the flames flicker near it, will the writing be revealed, at first barely, a letter here, a letter there, and then as it should be — each and every sentence. There's just one thing. The secret source of the fire is known to no one, and who would suspect that anything was written on the pure white page?

Exercises in Practical Hebrew

"Are you well? Have you murdered and also taken possession?"
(an example of the interrogative statement in a book of grammar)

1

Shalom, shalom. Hebrew has a past and future,
but not a present, just a participle.
Now, let's look at the sentence.

2

A land that devours its inhabitants.
Those who love it devour
those who love it. Decline that in the future.

3

Lands flowing with milk and honey. That's declarative.
If you see them, say hello. That's the imperative.
And now the interrogative: What's new?

4

Pity me if I say it, pity me if I don't.
Tell us what is primary here, and what's subordinate to the
    condition.

5

Greetings and pleasantries.
Good morning, good evening, happy new year, congratulations.
Next time at your place. It's never too late.
Excuse me, is this the right place? Come back tomorrow.

6

A short composition. We went for a walk.
The cemetery is on the left.
The cemetery is on the right.
Where did we go wrong?
Thank you very much.

7

A snippet of conversation. Who do you belong to, child?
Father. The second wreath on the left.

8

Be precise: Don't say, It was worthless.
After all, you've already paid.
Say: For nothing.

9

Synonyms: Disgrace, abasement, dishonor, shame,
turpitude, contempt, contumely, scorn,
defamation, derision, slander, abuse,
pity the ears that hear all this,
denigration, condemnation, libel, censure,
mockery, cheapness, humiliation,
and you should be ashamed of yourself!

10

Spice up your speech with expressions.
Don't be sweet or you'll be swallowed.
A fish always stinks from the head.
Better a head to foxes than a tail to lions.
This is where the bone is buried.
You've come: know what you'll say.
Have you practiced what you've . . .
Are you well? Have you murdered and also taken possession?

11

And now one final drill to end with.
Two words through which you'll discern
the distinction between the terms:
Shalom, shalom.

[PC]

Shulamit Hareven

(1930–2003)

A self-described Levantine writer, Shulamit Hareven was born in Warsaw in 1930 and, at the age of ten, came to Palestine and what she would later write of as "the bright light pouring over the stone enclosures on the mountain." As a teenager she served in the Hagana underground, and she participated in the 1948 war as a medical orderly and later worked in transit camps with Jewish refugees from Arab countries. She published her first book (poetry) in 1962 and then, from the 1970s through the '90s, brought out a steady stream of novels, essays, stories, and works for children. A longtime political activist, she served as a spokesperson for Peace Now and worked ceaselessly for justice and coexistence in the region.

Hareven's best-known work, *Thirst: The Desert Trilogy* (1983–94), tells, in sparse and evocative prose, the story of the biblical exodus from the perspective of such insignificant characters as shepherds, warlords, and failed prophets. Hareven is sometimes referred to as "a linguistic patriot"—she was the first woman member of the Hebrew Language Academy—and language is consciously at the center of her concerns as a writer. The essay printed here treats the emotional, conceptual, aesthetic, and sometimes political limits of Hareven's world. In the process, she sheds light on Hebrew's "deep structure" and the ethical worldview out of which the language evolved.

THE LIMITS OF MY LANGUAGE
ARE THE LIMITS OF MY WORLD

The title of this essay, a quote from Wittgenstein, indicates its direction. Let me say right away that this will not be an essay in linguistics; I am not a linguist. I shall write as a craftswoman thinking about the tools of her craft; first, about language as a normative system; second, about the special nature of Hebrew as a normative system; and third, about what has happened to this system in our society over recent years and what possibilities are open to us in the future.

Language has two functions. One is to make communication between people possible. The other is the preservation of knowledge. Without language it would be impossible to prove any scientific truth or to learn from the experience of the past. All languages fulfill these two functions. And yet different languages have developed in such ways that each one represents the peculiar mind-set of those who speak it.

A child who learns a language — that is, learns to speak at about the age of one — is already learning subconsciously the system of thinking peculiar to his language, and also its mental categories. If we assume that the mental structures of a language in the process of its creation are not accidental, then they certainly are increasingly less so over the centuries, as succeeding generations are intellectually formed in that thought system and, indeed, contribute to its development. If this were not the case, we would be able to translate from one language into another with the utmost ease — which clearly doesn't happen. Many think that translation works only at a very low level of precision. Generally, we translate only one level of a language, the top of the pyramid, leaving very different levels concealed below.

Ancient languages are synchronic languages. Every moment in their present time comprehends all the past and all forms of thought that existed in the past. Hebrew, which is about four thousand years old, is undoubtedly a comprehensively synchronic language with characteristics unlike any other spoken language.

What do we mean when we speak of a normative system? As von Hum-

boldt put it, "Man lives in a world presented to him by his language," meaning that the characteristics of a language lay down the categories of thought.
I am told that Chinese has no verb "to be." Therefore it is impossible to
translate into Chinese not only *Hamlet,* but also the sentence "*Cogito, ergo
sum*" — I think therefore I am. It is not only that verb that is missing in
Chinese, but the parallel concept. Can we imagine Western culture or philosophy without the verb "to be"?

Western European languages are much concerned with time. They deal
with time in many different aspects, a factor that has certainly had its effect
on Western philosophy. But in the Hopi language, I am told, there are no
times or tenses, only completed actions, and those not yet completed. In
Hopi there is hardly any speculation about action in the future. In the
African Muntu language the words for "wet stone" and "dry stone" are
totally different, there being no single word in that language for the common
denominator — stone. What we have here is clearly a category of sensual
expression, not a synthesizing thought process. This has nothing to do with
the comparative richness or poverty of languages. The Inuit, for example,
lack abstractions, which are so important to the tradition of Western
thought. But they do have twenty words for different types of snow. These
are evidence of an exactness of sensual comprehension and an experience of
life of which we are ignorant. As for the fact that French lacks the simple
verb "to stand," what is one to make of that?

Wittgenstein was right when he said that the limits of our world are identical with the limits of our language, and, I would add, there is on an everyday level clear interaction between one's language and one's patterns of
thought.

It is not only vocabulary that orders a language's normative system. Other
features we often take for granted are influential and worth thinking about.
Syntax, for example, sets up a linguistic normative system and a cultural hierarchy. So does the sound pattern, and the relative weight a language gives to
noun, verb, and adjective in a sentence. For example, when Jorge Luis Borges
visited Israel, he complained to me about what he thought was a basic fail-
ing in the sound pattern of Spanish and of all Romance languages. What
worried him was the adverb. When one uses the adverb in English — for
example, *effectively, slowly* — the accent is on the action, the verb. In Spanish,

on the other hand, and in French, the emphasis is on the formal final phoneme: lente*ment,* effective*ment,* lenta*mente.* According to Borges, this stress pattern posits a false hierarchy that values form and formula over the action itself. The emphasis is formal rather than actual, a characteristic fairly true of Latin cultures. It is of course difficult to prove what is cause and what is effect. Does the formal preference take precedent to the culture's character, or does the kind of culture lead to a preference for a certain sound pattern? In biblical Hebrew many adverbs have no formal ending at all, like *maher* or *le'at,* not *bim'hirut* or *be-itiyut,* which is a latter-day preference, and we may conclude that in the Hebrew of the Bible it is the action that counts and not the formal marker.

Syntax also lays down hierarchies of value. Jacob Bronowski found that in all languages the order of words in a sentence corresponds to what is thought to be the natural order. At a certain age a child understands the sentence "The boy chases the cat," but not "The cat is chased by the boy." If the cat comes first (goes this logic), it has priority and initiates the action. One of the great advantages of Hebrew lies in its flexible syntax. In English you can say "The King went" but not "Went the King," except in very special usage. In Hebrew, if we rearrange the unit "The King fell on his sword" — "Fell the King on his sword," "On his sword fell the King," "Fell on his sword the King," "The King on his sword fell" — we find that all permutations are absolutely correct, allowing the writer to choose which hierarchy best suits his purpose. This syntactical flexibility is not accidental. One of the salient features of a Hebrew text is that the language never impedes the flow or the independence of thought. More of this later.

The value system of a language is also determined by the greater or lesser use of adjectives. Early Hebrew makes little use of them, in comparison with classical Greek, for example. The *Iliad* and the *Odyssey* give us "fleet-footed Achilles," "anger-browed Zeus," "the rosy-fingered dawn," "the sly Odysseus," and many more. But when we open the Bible to Genesis 1, we find: "In the beginning God created the heaven and the earth: And the earth was without form, and void, the darkness was on the face of the deep (in Hebrew this word is a simple noun, *tehom*): And the spirit of God moved upon the face of the waters. And God said, Let there be light. And there was light. And God saw the light, that it was good."

It has taken six sentences to reach the first adjective. In the style of Homeric poetry the passage might have looked something like this: "In the beginning the great God, he of the pelting hail, created the blue-eyed heaven and the fair-mounded earth." As Auerbach observed in *Mimesis,* there is not a single adjective in the whole binding of Isaac narrative, which gives the language immense power. In fact, every reader adds his own adjectives to the story — awesome, frightening, horrible, pathetic — but such expressions are not present in the text, and for a reason. Hebrew's distaste for adjectives is just one feature in a system defined by its conciseness, which is perhaps Hebrew's distinctive quality.

The laconic manner is characteristic of early Semitic languages in general. We have the possessive suffix form without the word "of" or the possessive pronoun — *shulhan* (table), *shulhani* (my table). We may conjugate the verb in past and future tenses, without employing the pronouns "I" or "you" or "he," by changing the suffix: *asiti ve asita halahti.* As a result, a three-word sentence in Hebrew becomes twelve words in French, enough to deter any translator. A Hebrew proverb of four words becomes sixteen words when translated into English: "Let not him who putteth on his armor boast himself as one who taketh it off." This gift of compression makes Hebrew a very algebraic language, a language of concrete concepts and codes that allow for intense abstraction. It is a language that, if taught correctly, can educate its speakers toward intellectual categories that are simultaneously concentrated, abstract, and flexible. Such linguistic achievements have certainly contributed to intellectual advance.

Here we touch on another dominant characteristic of Hebrew. The most ornate phrases began life as concrete terms. The modern cliché *betza keseph* (material greed) meant originally a coin cut in two, each part called *betza*. So *betza keseph lo lakahu,* "they took no gain of money" in Deborah's song, means more or less "They did not take half a coin, or the King's shilling; they were not mercenaries, but fought as volunteers." Similarly, the word *mal'ah* means simply "messenger," and not "angel," which in the Christian tradition conjures up an innocent blue-eyed child with wings. Finally, the word *nephesh,* commonly translated as "soul," originally meant "throat," so the expression *ba'u ma'im ad nephesh* (water has risen up to the soul/throat), meaning a desperate state of affairs, has its origin in the body.

Perhaps the most important feature of Hebrew has to do with value concepts. Every language is replete with such concepts, which are linked to a system of associations. In Polish there is a root form meaning "to conceal." Add
a prefix, and it becomes "to take out of hiding," "to uncover," and "to bring
up" (a child). This is no accident, but implies a whole pedagogic outlook. Add
another prefix, and the word means "to preserve." In Chinese, we are told,
"teacher" and "doctor" are represented by the same ideogram. This implies a
view of the teacher's function that involves curing the patient of his disease,
ignorance. Also, I am told, in China much of medicine is preventive, so doc-
tors in China spend much of their time teaching people rules. The Hebrew
word *le-hitbonen* (to observe), contains the concept *bina,* wisdom. The word
"illusion" contains the Latin *ludere,* "to play." Clearly, then, each language contains its own value system deriving from the special patterns of association
that help to construct it. Hebrew, a synchronic language, holds certain precise
ethical and philosophical value concepts that belong only to Hebrew and to
Judaism and that are really untranslatable. Such words cannot be learned simply as words, without their philosophical context. Some are whole teachings.
Thus the concept *teshuva* (repentance) is not what we think of today as repentance, or more commonly, becoming religious. In Judaism it covers a process
involving a complete change of personality — sometimes even a change of
name, work, and address. This significance is all but lost in its modem usage.
The word is still there, but, wrongly used, is bereft of its philosophy. Another
example is the term *malhut shama'im* (Kingdom of Heaven). In Judaism this is
a value concept signifying the acceptance of God as king, here, now and every
day; but we use this expression now with its Christian coloring of the kingdom to come in messianic times, which is a distortion of the Jewish vision of
the messianic period. Hebrew readers wrongly use the expression *dereh eretz*
(way of the world) as a synonym for manners or politeness, when this term
originally implied a whole ethical system of behavior. Then we misuse the
word *emuna* (faith, belief) when we say, "I believe it is late," thus jettisoning
the central Jewish concept of faith as trust in God. Perhaps the worst offense
of this kind is the political use of the Jewish value concept *z'hut avot* (merits
of the fathers). Traditionally this means the righteousness of our patriarchs,
which is thought to protect us, their sinning children. It never meant the
right of their children to settle in certain territories.

Such expressions, then, are like algebraic signs, or codes, for complete cultural concepts. If we lose their original meaning, or at least the knowledge that there is such a meaning, and use them to translate alien expressions, then we have erased one of the components of our culture. We end up speaking English or German in Hebrew words.

Why is Hebrew like this? Where did this concision and urge for laconism derive? How did the language become one of codes and associative headings? Perhaps the cause lies in Hebrew's very early move from an oral to a written language. Oral cultures have special ways of preserving knowledge, by aids to memory, for instance. Hebrew poetry and prophetic rhetoric do make use of devices such as parallelism and the alphabetical poem, but not of rhyme. Elsewhere the repeated adjective is a mnemonic device. Achilles is always fleet of foot, Zeus is always the thunderbolt hurler, and that is how we remember them.

In Hebrew, writing arrived very early, and the effect on the nature of the language was immense. What do you write down, especially if you have to carve in stone? Whatever is most worth preserving. And you do it concisely. Hebrew, remember, has very few vowels, especially in nonplene or unvocalized spelling. It is as if the writer was not concerned with the phoneticization of the word, its vocalization in speech, but did care about the root and the associations that grow out of that written root. We were always very text oriented. Hebrew writing was then meant not for reading pleasure, but for the notation of essentials. What is worth preserving are those concrete things that supply the need of the tribe's code of knowledge. As a written language Hebrew is basically a skeletal, short-hand structure, in which the main process takes place in thought. Such are the substantive features of Hebrew. Should we lose them, an entire culture is lost.

This is the language that we inherited and that has preserved our culture and ourselves for two millennia. During that period — in the Diaspora — the language has been a preserved language, without much development of vocabulary; with little adjustment to the changes taking place all around.

What happens to a language that serves as a cultural safe deposit alone? One might say that, like Latin, from the Renaissance onward, Hebrew became a language of men, used only outside the domestic scene. Women learned Torah less and were not expected to preserve the language and its values. The popular woman's Bible companion, *Tsena Ur'ena,* is full of Yiddish. The Sephardi woman prayed in Hebrew in the synagogue, but her private prayers at home were whispered in Ladino. The formal language of men was used essentially for purposes of rhetoric and dispute, two areas then foreign to women. Historically, one should add, the end of the teaching of rhetoric in European schools coincided with the demise of Latin as a school subject and the entry of girls into the classroom. So the connection is not accidental.

A preserved language also serves as a tribal code. When Sholem Aleichem's hero, Mottel, son of Peissy the Cantor, is caught by a policeman, a bystander whispers a phrase to him in Hebrew meaning "Free your hand from the Greek (that is, Gentile) and get thee hence, beloved," and the child understands. He would have understood not only in Sholem Aleichem's fictional *shtetl Kasrilevke,* but in Baghdad or Salonika. When Yaakov Sapir, an Ashkenazi Jew from Poland who lived in Safed, arrived in San'a, Yemen, in the middle of the last century, he had no problem talking to the Yemenite Jews. Hebrew was their common tongue. Professor Ze'ev Ben Haim, a senior [member of] the Academy of the Hebrew Language, states that in every generation, until about half a century ago, the majority of men in any Jewish community in the world could read and understand a Hebrew text.

Until about seventy years ago, Hebrew had all the structures necessary for communication, but lacked so many words that such communication was difficult. The effective date for the change of Hebrew into a language of everyday communication may be 1889, when Eliezer Ben-Yehuda and his associates founded the Clear Language Society for the Propagation of Unity and Amity in Israel. It is probably true that the generation born in Palestine sixty years ago was the first since the Dispersion whose parents spoke Hebrew as an everyday language. Also, for the first time in two millennia, there was no longer a division between the mother tongue spoken at home and the male language of study and ritual. This is no minor matter, for from a psychological point of view, Hebrew at that point stopped being only a language of learning and ideals and became a language of feeling. Let's not forget that this was a generation that grew up largely without grandparents, who stayed behind in the old country. We might put the question this way: Can such a laconic, reserved language be made to contain the myriad shades of a language of feeling, a gentle language of mothers and grandparents? One ought to remember that in Hebrew there were hardly any soft, playful words of a childish mode.

The simplest method of renewal was the coining of new words out of old words, structures, and emphases that had, before the Dispersion, served as means of communication. There are many curiosities here, including the coining of modern Hebrew words for common things such as "doll," "brush," and "tomato."

Only fifty years ago we used foreign words like "problema," "initsiativa," and "taxi," whereas today we use the Hebrew *b'aya, yozma, monit.* We had to invent the Hebrew equivalents of "involvement," "frustrations," "ambivalence," "pacemakers," "devaluation," and "linkage." So with many other words, including most of the military ranks, which are revivals of old Hebrew expressions and roots. For "rookie," however, meaning a new recruit, we have kept the Roman "tyro," in *tiron* — and the Hebrew *b'sis tironim* would be readily understood by the Roman Tenth Legion, who, presumably had their Basis Tyronum. Such innovations and coinages, some of them euphemisms, can almost be read as chapters in the history of our country; so closely do they document social processes. Words are indeed renewed at a quick pace. And renewal is perhaps only a minor problem, as it is guided by a competent authority — the Academy. More than 80 percent of our innovations are accepted by the general public. But when there is such a flood of new words to meet new needs, many of them turn out to be artificial and unnecessary improvisations. They are coined simply because they exist in English, and not even in good English, but in the jargon of bureaucracy and the social sciences. With such a wealth of neologisms, the miracle is not that some bad or silly words get through, but that there are so few of them.

The real problem is not words, but what Noam Chomsky calls the deep structure of the language, and the sentence, a structure that is part of the intellectual development of the group. If language is indeed a form of behavior, deep structure is the form of behavior of the language, and of whoever thinks in it. Single words are the variable factor in a language's basic formal system. Proof of this lies in stories written by computers. In a western written by a computer, the sheriff draws the girl out of his holster, shoots the outlaw with elephants and tundra, and the outlaw falls dead bleeding a pool of whiskey. Here the structures are logical, but the words are variable. About Hebrew, then, we should ask not what has happened to single words, but what has happened to the deep structures of the language these last fifty years? For while a language can bear the burden of unsuitable words, absorb them, and eventually eject them, it cannot suffer too many deep injuries to its very anatomy.

My answer is not a positive one. Bad things have happened to form and also to the transformation of concepts. I will try to explain some of these changes.

Hebrew is getting long winded, which is against its nature. Who uses the short form when a longer form of words can be found? So instead of *im* (if) we use the deplorable *be-mida ve* — not "if" you get to Tel Aviv, but "in the measure that, to the extent that," you get to Tel Aviv. Today, who would use a simple Hebrew phrase like that of Cain in Genesis, *gadol avoni mi-nso* — "My crime is greater than I can bear"? The King James Version translates this, erroneously, as "my punishment." We would say something like "The crime to which I readily admit in so many words is greater than my personal ability to cope with it adequately." Could anyone think this an improvement? Similarly, we make wise language look foolish, saying "Rise *up*" and "Descend *down*" when the verb alone indicates the movement. Then there is the matter of propriety. False propriety is one of the injuries we have inflicted on the language in the last fifty years; a kind of linguistic Victorianism has spread. The more permissive society becomes, the more prudish its language. A man does not have a mistress, but "his publicly known person." In the lonely-hearts columns we do not find a married man willing to pay cash for sex, but a nonfree man seeking intimate friendship and willing to offer financial support. One may imagine this nonfree type looking at his watch while engaged in intimate friendship, and discovering not an "obligation" to go home, but certain "constraints." This is the jargon of sexual bureaucracy. The word we use for "pimp," *sarsur,* is the same as that used until recently for any go-between, or business agent. In older sources a brothel madam was called *k'lonit,* an "ignominious woman," with all the moral stress of the word for ignominy, *kalon.* Ignominy must be treated sternly. "Agent," *sarsur,* however, is a neutral, anemic term. He will get away with a few months in prison.

When we sterilize language, we sterilize its values. When children were left to their fate in a terrorist attack at Ma'alot some years ago, it wasn't their "teachers" who abandoned them, but their "education agents." We have no "poor," only the "weaker strata," or lower echelons.

That is somehow less demanding, for the Torah commands us to succor the poor, but is silent about lower echelons. We have no "rich," but "the top 10 percent." We have no "luxury," but a "high standard of living"; no "apartments," but "dwelling solutions"; no "homes," but "housing." We must not ignore the emotional and practical significance of such changes.

There is an immense difference between a home and housing, as there is between luxury *motarot,* which in Hebrew signifies superfluous things, and a high standard of living, which is attractive. This illusory refinement is essentially crude. It sterilizes the language by creating distance between speech and the heart. No one dies today; they pass away. No one thinks, but is of an opinion. A woman doesn't conceive, but "enters into pregnancy," and apparently never gets out. Once pregnant, women give birth not to sons or daughters, but to age groups. If this goes on, we will have no hospitals in twenty years' time, but "temporary shelters for the unwell." Even today, they are called "medical centers," which are sometimes less hospitable than research oriented.

These false linguistic norms are the fault partly of our politicians and partly of social and behavioral scientists. Social scientists ruin many languages when they do such things as calling sleeping people "populations in a non-awake state."

Then there is the Hebrew of politicians. For linguistic features, single out the ambitious members of that breed. They love "parameters" and "constraints." They find themselves constantly "impeded" from doing things, and the minute they are appointed to high office they lose the ability to say "I hope," *ani m'kave,* preferring the stuffy formulation, *ani tiqwa,* "I am of the hope that. . . ." Add to this the psychological significance of the increase in the use of passive forms. We don't go to a reading but to a "being read to," *hakra'a.* Perhaps there is a connection between this and the fact that no one any longer fires shots. Instead, shots are fired. Measures are taken. One does not simply do something. Something is done to one. A whole nation is acted upon.

Another curious feature of our recent speech is its turn from feminine to masculine sound. Words with feminine endings are giving way to those with masculine endings. Meanwhile there is increasing confusion over the gender of words, and I confess that I do not know what this means. It may have something to do with the modern distaste for clearly defined sexual bipolarity.

Modern formulas of circumlocution abound. In the early years of the state people avoided the use of biblical or mishnaic formal phrases. They wanted to write what they felt, exactly, without recourse to ancient formulations. But recently phraseology and circumlocution have enjoyed a comeback — by the back door. These new forms are not the biblical kind, the use of which would at least show the writer's knowledge of the sources, but a modern type. Such expressions are both imprecise and betray the writer's laziness. For example, the whole scale of warnings and alerts has all but disappeared, to be replaced by the ubiquitous "blinking of a red light." We no longer speak angrily but "in high tones," erroneously from an acoustical point of view, as there is no connection between height of tone and power of sound. No one exploits an opportunity, but everybody hurries "to climb on the bandwagon." There is no majority, but "the lion's share." The worst thing about this imprecision and lack of imagination is that circumlocution multiplies and mixed metaphors feed on each other. This kind of language is certainly not worth preserving.

Every generation has its ignorant language. But what are we to make of the prevalent distaste for Jewish time, which for various philosophical reasons does not have a present tense for the verb "to be"? People apparently long for alien time structures and need a substitute for "is" to place before the adjective and even before the verb. Thus they do not say *ha'aretz yapha* (the land beautiful) but *ha'aretz hi yapha* — "the land she beautiful," where the "she" stands for the nonexistent "is."

Rabbi Adin Steinsaltz has already expounded on the subject of Jewish time with great authority. Suffice it to say that the lack of "is" in the present tense is no accident, but is part of the deep structure. Hebrew allows us a choice between saying "disappointment hard," *ha-ahzava kasha,* meaning "the disappointment is hard," and "hard disappointment," *kasha ha-ahzava,* meaning "hard is the disappointment." It all depends on the nuance, the

shade of our meaning. But to insert the pronoun "he" or "she" is totally foreign. Examples like this of a turn toward European linguistic forms are more
worrying than the misuse of individual words. As a result of this turn to alien
forms we end up spreading our bread "with" margarine, *im margarina,* which
in Hebrew means that we, together with the margarine, are spreading the
bread. Or we mistakenly work "with" (*im*), tools, giving equal status to man
and tool, which is alien to Jewish hierarchies of values, and also a breakdown
in functional thinking.

These are not just errors of language. They reveal our inability to adapt
ourselves to the real Hebrew structures, and they show our appetite for alien
forms. In this way we actually do injury to the deep structures of our language, or to its anatomy, and we are likely to pay dearly for this in the impov-
erishment of our culture.

Here I would like to return to the distinction I made earlier between the
two roles of language — that of preservation and that of communication. We
may well be entering a new oral age, for we now have the means to preserve
information possessed by no previous generation. We have audio- and video-
cassette libraries, computers, memory banks — everything is taped and
recorded. Immediate communication fills our space now more than the
function of preservation. Who writes a letter, when you can phone? The air
is full of sound — from transistors, cassettes, and TV sets. It is full of music
and songs and various forms of oral communication, often of a low common
denominator.

True, the technical possibility of transmitting such sounds has created
new borders. Our real neighbors are those we speak to on the phone, so
much so that we have a phone-call neighborhood at hand in our own house.
We know more about a foreign politician or entertainer than we do about
the man across the road. Such orality has rules and codes of its own, and its
influence on all languages is immense. Yet, together with this apparent
expansion of the limits of communication, an opposite process has
occurred. Our cultural and cultural-geographic borders have shrunk. We
have exchanged the long-term for a short-term, impoverished code. Once
upon a time the Jew from the *shtetl* could rely on a Hebrew reference to the
Song of Songs, and the ancient tribal code would be immediately understood
by a Jew in Baghdad; today an Israeli Jew cannot use his local slang or jingle

and be understood by an American Jew. The tribal code has shrunk and become short-term and expendable. It is not orality itself we should fear, but how we use it and how it could transform us.

What happens to Hebrew in the next thirty years will not be so different from what may happen to highly developed written cultures in general. Some of them are already reeling under the burden of the new Western orality. At some point we will have to decide whether Hebrew in the next thirty or three hundred years will serve merely as a channel of immediate and basic communication, as a language at the top of a pyramid, without any pyramid beneath it, a claustrophobic language not much different from Esperanto, or whether it will embody an entire non-Western culture that we know is worth preserving.

Since language shapes us more than we shape it, this decision will be essentially about our own identity. It seems more and more certain that this will be a matter of a conscious decision.

For the writer, that decision is an easy one. Writing in Hebrew means first and foremost that the writer is using tools — words, structures, and norms — that have been in existence for between four and five thousand years, many of which still serve us today. The good news is that in theory at least you can delve into any linguistic layer to make your meaning or nuance more precise — an immense richness of possibilities. Second Temple, mishnaic language or idiom would serve, for example, a more legalistic, rational style, the style of discourse and argument; this would include some use of Aramaic, the way an educated person would use Latin or Greek expressions in a Western language discourse. The use of First Temple, biblical idiom, or syntax, or even a single significant word, would denote a much more emotional stand. The choices are almost unlimited.

The bad news, though, is that this and other factors make Hebrew — good Hebrew — nearly untranslatable. A Second Temple Hebrew proverb says that anyone who translates a sentence literally is a cheat and a fraud. They must have had painful experiences with Aramaic and Greek.

The reason we authors consent to being translated, and quite often collaborate with the traitors — *tradittore traduttore* — is that although much gets lost in the translation, even more gets lost if you are not translated at all.

This brings us to the existential problems of writing in Hebrew. First,

Israel is a country of about five million inhabitants, in which more than half of all adults are immigrants and one-fifth are Israeli Arabs, not all of whom have internalized Hebrew to the extent of reading good literature. It is true that in book publication, in relative numbers, Israel is second in the world after Iceland — but the Icelanders have such long nights. The United States, incidentally, is number twenty or so, relative to the population. A runaway best-seller in Israel, however, would sell only about eighty to one hundred thousand copies, and that's very rare. Since readers of Hebrew outside Israel are not very numerous, we must be translated, or transplanted, into other languages, other cultures.

For some of us the wish to have one's work widely read generates a kind of impatience; one wants to be translated quickly and not create too many problems for the translator. The result, in many cases, is impoverished Hebrew.

The other danger to the original culture is secularization, which in Israel has taken the form of rejection, in many cases, of the Sources, so that not only much of the cultural idiom is lost, but also much of the deep structure. The result is that a great number of young people today simply do not understand the old cultural idiom, and not everyone is willing to look it up in the dictionary.

Finally, at the present stage of the conflict, it is easy to forget that Hebrew is a Semitic language, belonging wholly to this part of the world. We are exposed to American idiom much more than we are to Arabic. Peace with our neighbors will enable us to return to our common roots, vastly improving the parlance and style of both.

Writing in Hebrew, then, involves a great many decisions, most of which are unconscious. I would feel a bit claustrophobic in any other language, where I could not delve so deeply into time and nuance. In any other language I would miss the laconism, the almost plastic feeling of working in stone. And if the limits of my language are indeed the limits of my world, I cannot think of a world more open to exploration and discovery, more intriguing and satisfying, than Hebrew.

[MW]

Aharon Appelfeld

(b. 1932)

With "the playfully thoughtful air of a benign wizard," writes Philip Roth,
the novelist Aharon Appelfeld "would have no trouble passing for a magician
who entertains children at birthday parties by pulling doves out of a hat."
Roth finds it hard to square the image cut by his whimsical friend with the
wounded consciousness of the Holocaust survivor-author before him—"a
dispossessed and uprooted writer"—though he notes, hinting at the fictional
sleight-of-hand behind the work, that Appelfeld has "made of displacement
and disorientation a subject uniquely his own."

Born into an assimilated German-speaking family in Austro-Hungarian
Czernowitz, Bukovina, Appelfeld found his world destroyed at the age of
eight, when his mother was killed by the Nazis, and he and his father were
deported to a concentration camp in the Ukraine. Both escaped (separately—
they didn't meet again for another two decades), and after living as a
shepherd and hiding in the countryside for three years, the twelve-year-old
Appelfeld joined the Soviet army and worked as a junior cook in field kitchens
in the Ukraine. After the war he wandered through Romania, Bulgaria, and
Yugoslavia before coming to Italy, where he lived in a camp for displaced
persons before being sent to Palestine, which he reached in 1946. He worked
for a time on a kibbutz and studied Hebrew at night. When he eventually
enrolled at the university in Jerusalem, he knew more than seven languages—

including German, Ruthenian, Russian, Romanian, French, Yiddish, and
Hebrew—though he was rooted in none of them and had only one year
of formal schooling.

He soon began writing poetry and fiction in Hebrew, initially publishing
only short stories, but in time moving on to the novel. Now an internationally
acclaimed author whose books have been translated into over a dozen
languages, he is, he says, essentially "a Jewish writer . . . writing about Jewish
fate . . . for Jews." His fiction rarely touches on life in his adopted country and
city (Jerusalem), nor does it deal explicitly with the Holocaust and its violence.
"To be a Jewish writer," he says, "is a heavy obligation. My close family was
killed. My natural environment, my childhood, my sweetest memories were
killed. And so it's a kind of obligation that I feel . . . dealing with a civilization
that has been killed . . . to represent it in the most honorable way . . . not
to exaggerate, but to find the right proportion to represent it, in human
terms." And so it is that his work focuses on life all around that wound in
his consciousness —on people in whom, as Appelfeld himself has put it,
"fate was already hidden . . . like a mortal illness."

The reticence and dislocation in his prose notwithstanding, Appelfeld
identifies himself strongly with Jerusalem as the "center of Jewish history,"
and he has written most of his books there, and in public, always at cafés.
In a charming and disarming 2001 memoir of his writing life, *A Table for One*,
the magician-novelist comes down offstage and, while not quite explaining
his tricks, tells us how he came to them.

FROM *A TABLE FOR ONE*

2

Café Peter in the German Colony was my first regular café. I used to go
there for more than ten years, from 1953 till the mid-1960s. It was in its garden that I began my university studies and there that I completed them. The

dark, narrow little room that I rented in Rehavia was just a place to sleep; I ate my meals at Café Peter, read, prepared for the examinations — but mostly I wrote there. To be more accurate, it was where I struggled to find my voice.

The dream of becoming a writer had stayed with me since my discharge from the army. I said "dream," but it would be better to say "delusion" and even self-deception. In my parents' home in Czernowitz, I had finished first grade, but the war broke out at the end of that school year. In Israel, I studied for about two and a half years in the Youth Aliyah, and after that I did my army service. I completed my matriculation exams without any assistance: I bought used and stained textbooks for next to nothing, and got hold of a few notes from high school students. Algebra and trigonometry presented the biggest obstacles: I took the exam three times, and only passed on the third try.

That was my education — or rather my lack of education. It was with this meager equipment that I sought to become a writer. Though six years of war taught me many important life-lessons, you can't get far without any linguistic or cultural tools. My mother tongue was German. My grandparents spoke Yiddish. We lived among Ruthenian peasants and so we spoke Ruthenian. The government was Romanian, so we spoke Romanian. The intelligentsia often spoke French, so we spoke French. After the war I was with the Russians and I learned to speak Russian. Those languages that were not too deeply rooted in me rapidly faded in Israel; however, Hebrew had not yet taken root in my soul. To try to link my experience to the few Hebrew words at my disposal was too much of a stretch. But I'm rushing ahead.

Before I dreamed of being a writer, I had a different vision: being an Israeli, looking like an Israeli and behaving like one. All through the years in the Youth Aliyah and in the army I nurtured this illusion. It found expression, among other things, in jogging at night, working out, lifting weights, and various kinds of unpleasant physical exertions. But all this seemed to have no effect on my height, the way I walked, or the way I spoke. My shyness never disappeared, and I still spoke haltingly. Several of my friends in the Youth Aliyah did change — they did assimilate and when they were called up to the army they were accepted into elite units. But it was as if my body refused to change, and even my interior apparently insisted on remaining what it had been. Our desires, even the strongest ones, seldom dictate what we actually do.

What I couldn't bring about in life, I tried to do in writing. After failed attempts at poetry, I tried to write about my life in Israel. It was no less awful than the sentimental poems that I had been writing. Strange how what we want befuddles us; to what extent we are in fact hostage to our desires. It is only the fortunate few who, from the outset, recognize the path that fate has marked out for them.

As I said, Café Peter was a home to me; if truth be told, it was more than a home. All that I hazily remembered was revealed to me in the shape of living people who spoke in tones that reminded me of home and who, between one conversation and another, might let drop a word about the ghetto or the camp.

The people who frequented Café Peter in those years had come from Transylvania, Hungary, Bukovina, and Bulgaria; they spoke the languages of the Austro-Hungarian Empire, particularly German. Everything there — the taste of food, the manners, the tone of speech, the silence between the sentences — was just as it had been at home. The garden too — the huge atrium, the sideboards, and the chairs — all these were as if they had been reincarnated from "there" and had come here.

I don't remember who first brought me to Café Peter, but I do recall that no sooner was I through the doorway, than I knew that these people were my lost uncles and cousins; they had brought their language here with them — their attire, their little shops in the pastoral villages, and their splendid department stores from the towns from which they had been uprooted.

I had already been in Israel for some seven years, yet only now had I returned home. I was so enchanted by the place that whenever I had a spare hour I would rush over, and sit there spellbound. I understood everything that was said around the little tables, not only the words, but also what was implied, the hints and the silences. I immediately felt that these people, whose names I didn't know, were my real relatives. It was as if everything that had surrounded me up to now didn't touch my real essence. That essence was embodied by these émigrés, who spoke Hapsburg German, who had been uprooted from the land of their birth and now found themselves lost in their homeland. To assuage that loss, they would gather together, evoking and reminiscing about their homes and their fields.

One autumn night, I heard one of them confess that the years in the labor camp were a time when all reserves, body and soul, had been drawn upon, yet they were years of hope and immense belief. Since the Liberation, it was as if everything had been overturned: now it was hard to sleep at night, and torturous thoughts returned with piercing intensity — the body's betrayal. The restraint in his voice shocked me. Yet strange as it was, no one contradicted him. [. . .]

The 1940s and 1950s were years when lofty words abounded in Israel. Yet in this café, people spoke in the way we used to speak to one another, directly and without pathos. It was at Café Peter that I wrote the short story "Berta" in 1958. It portrays the change and the turning point that took place in me; not to write about the "new Jew" and not about the idyll of working the land in Israel, but about people who had been in places that I was in and ended up here. At Café Peter I learned how to listen to speech, to distinguish between what was spoken and what was unspoken; about what it was possible to speak of and about what was forbidden. At Café Peter, I became aware of myself and the people around me. [. . .]

4

Café Peter was my first school for writing. There I learned that simple words are the precise ones, and that daily life is our most true expression. During the 1950s, young authors wrote in very high-flown language, either imitating the ancient texts or inventing a convoluted style. I was also drawn to these lofty expressions. But whenever I sat next to my brothers, refugees like myself, I saw that life's mysteries should be clothed in facts. The simple and the factual lead to truth. An excess of words can be a serious obstacle. Another important lesson from my brother refugees is to see the essence and be sparing. What you don't have to say shouldn't be said.

Everyone at Café Peter carried a cruel country in his soul, a home that had been broken into, and people from whom they would never part. How does one go on living with this in dignity? They actually didn't discuss those "big" issues, but talked about practical matters. One of the useful unwritten rules was: A man should not talk about himself unless it carries some meaning for others. To speak about yourself just because something has happened to you is foolishness, or worse still, pure selfishness. For years I sat near them, and every day absorbed a tiny fragment of their soul. Maybe it would be more accurate to say that they were in me.

"How do you feel, Tina?" someone asked the woman in the wheelchair. Tina opened wide her large eyes and she said, "I feel good."

A question on one's appearance immediately draws close attention. People, even those who aren't particularly careful about how they look, are still sensitive about their appearance. They don't like to appear weak or sick. They have brought this fear with them from there, and it is betrayed in the hesitancy of the answer. I paid attention: a question about how one's night had been was usually met with positive descriptions: "good," "not bad." It wasn't that complaints were out of the question, but rather that they were few and usually well camouflaged. Pain is not something easily shared with other people.

Not everyone is as well educated as Tina. Arthur had a large general store in a village in the middle of the Transylvanian countryside, a kind of supermarket, long before "supermarkets" came into fashion. He was a tall man and broad — from his appearance, one could guess the dimensions of the store. Alongside this giant everyone looked skinny, short, and puny. His appearance was in sharp contrast to his character — reticent and shy, he would barely utter a word. But he was a master listener, and when he listened, his whole giant body listened. Such close attentiveness was not at all arrogant or mocking, as one might have expected. There was a kind of wonder in his attentiveness, as if everyone were his children or younger brothers to be encouraged.

Despite Arthur's height and his solidity, and despite what he had been through in life, he was full of naiveté. Served a sandwich decorated by vegetables, he could be delighted. He was very fond of children, though he wouldn't pick up a baby so as not to scare it. He would bend down to the stroller and make funny noises.

During the war he had escaped from a labor camp disguised as a chimney sweep, and that's how he managed to survive. Not a single member of his large family had survived. He was completely alone in Israel; his "family" were those people who surrounded him at Café Peter. He helped everyone, even the woman who owned the place. When they needed to move a table or an oven, he would do it with the alacrity of a young man.

It was at Café Peter that I learned the principles of my art. Later, at other cafés, I added knowledge and experience, but it was at Café Peter that my writing took shape and it was there that I wrote my first books. On several occasions I asked myself what place there could be for low-key literature like mine in a country that was entirely ideological, full of words and arguments and counterarguments; a country that spewed out words like a machine. [. . .] In such a country, is there a place for writing like mine?

It turns out that my fears were exaggerated. When my first book, *Smoke,* appeared in 1962, it was well received. Most praised it and there were also those who criticized it. I was happy for the good words, but in my heart I knew that there was still a long road ahead of me.

25

In the mid-1960s and up till the 1970s, I would spend my time in Café Atara, on Ben Yehuda Street, which was a well-known meeting place for writers, journalists, painters, and professors. Occasionally, I would also drop into the Café Rondo in the Independence Park, and to Café Nava on Jaffa Street, but my regular place was Café Atara.

At Café Atara, in the heart of Ben Yehuda Street, time pulsed at an accelerated pace. Here newspapers passed from hand to hand, every news item had its interpreters and explainers. This place was permeated with the here-and-now in the full sense of the phrase. After years at Café Peter, life here seemed to be effervescing. At first this sense of over-brimming bothered me, but I quickly got used to it. By now, I was no longer in need of "models." The faces, the languages, the gestures, and the silences that I had absorbed at Café Peter, at Café Pat, and at Café Rehavia, were already part of me. I had but to link them to memory; to knead it carefully and then to allow the story to flow.

Agnon was astonished: "You write in Café Atara — in the midst of all that racket and confusion, with everyone looking at you?" He himself was a fanatic about quiet at home, and everyone was warned not to disturb him. I never made a fuss about my writing. Everything I wrote was in cafés, mostly quiet cafés, but also in bustling, crowded cafés. It never bothers me when people talk. Many writers have tortured their families because the noise made it difficult for them to concentrate. True, literary writing isn't regular writing, but then, neither is it a disease requiring the hushed silence of those around it. I have a great deal of respect for an artist who doesn't impose his moods on those around him. Writing is a struggle, and it should be between you and yourself, without involving additional people.

A close friend made this comment to me: "You're moving from café to café like you did in the war — from hiding place to hiding place."

I didn't like his comment, but I knew that there was some truth in what he said. To this very day I don't feel so comfortable in a rigid orderly house, it makes me feel edgy. It is only among people that I feel free. I suppose that I've brought those feelings with me from the years of the war, among other bad habits from "there": smoking, cognac, and coffee. It took me years to wean myself off them.

"One doesn't always have to explain to someone what he's doing," I responded to my friend.

"Ah, perhaps I was being naïve, but I thought that a writer should be conscious about what he does."

"Too much consciousness isn't necessarily a blessing. The blind flow that rises from the lines is the main thing. Revising, editing — these are products of the consciousness. They may be necessary, but this doesn't mean to say that they always improve the writing that has emerged from the unconscious."

The long short story and the novel are the forms that I like. In fact, to write a novel, and sometimes even a novella, means living a double life for a year and a half or two. On one hand you lead a normal life, yet on the other, with the same intensity, you live another life in another place. For an author this situation is something that is not mysterious but rather completely mundane. For years I struggled to make a living, which wiped out the most productive hours of my day. I would battle my tiredness by sipping coffee or having cognac. Writing is a huge effort. But unfortunately, even at my age, I cannot say that I've discovered the secret of writing. In writing, you are tested each time anew. A page where the words are set down on it right and flows — this is almost a miracle. When I finished the novel *Badenheim 1939*, I wept from sheer tiredness.

It didn't end there. When a few chapters of this novella were published in a literary magazine, a reader pounced on me in the café. He claimed that I was blaming the victims with blindness and with foolishness, and someday in the future, I would have to answer for it. It was useless trying to explain my position to him. He stood by what he had said. Sometimes it seems to me that in a country so awash with ideology it's impossible to write literature. Life itself, in all its complexity, is not something we really ponder. Who are you? Are you with us or are you against us?

I hear this whenever I bring out a new book.

[AH]

David Avidan

(1934–1995)

Gifted, prolific, promiscuous, highly eccentric, and egomaniacal, David Avidan began publishing in the 1950s and immediately raised the hackles of Israel's generally conservative reading public, as he flamboyantly defied their expectations of poetry. The titles alone of some of his books are indicative of his oblique approach and inventiveness: *Lipless Faucets; Personal Problems; Something for Somebody; My Electronic Psychiatrist; Cryptograms from a Telestar;* and so on. Also a "painter, filmmaker, playwright, and publicist," as he himself put it, Avidan published some twenty volumes of verse. Personal idiosyncrasies notwithstanding, his early work—which was noted for its powerful, almost Audenesque musicality, and for its masterful blend of formal concerns and a contemporary idiom—became extremely popular, as did the poet himself. Interest in him diminished over the years, however, and by the early 1990s Avidan's mental condition had seriously deteriorated. When he died, at age sixty-one, still in Tel Aviv, he had been living in squalor for several years.

The passage below is taken from a note to *Something for Someone: Selected Poems, 1952–1964;* characteristically, it cuts against the grain of literary convention, dealing with what the poet sees as the essential purpose of poetry—not to "nourish" the reader, but to empty him.

FROM *SOMETHING FOR SOMEONE*

Whoever and whatever you might be, you are, in spite of everything, a product of Western culture. Whether you like it or not the notion has been planted within you that the greatest virtue of a religious scholar or an educated citizen is to be "full to the brim."

And so, a warning: the journey you are about to undertake with me, though not always in my continuous presence, involves neither a shopping spree nor any ordinary itinerary. These poems, whatever else they might be, are in no way "food for the soul." They are not meant to "fill you up," but rather [. . .] to "empty you out." The only thing you might stand to gain over the course of this journey, if you don't spoil your chances with your own two-lobed brain, is an almost unproven, concealed (incidentally, to its benefit) feeling of advantage, which will suddenly permeate you. At the journey's end (that is, during one of the inevitable breaks between the end and the renewed onset) perhaps you will feel that you know more about words than you ever knew before. Words know far more about you than you know — or will ever know — about them. But if you have within you the slightest itch for existence-awareness, then it is worth your while to at least attempt — in the few and diminishing years that remain for you — to reduce the gap.

No, just not "full to the brim," for then you will be irrevocably lost to me and to yourself. On the contrary: at the end of this journey I would like to see you lighter, more mobile, swifter, more open, more excited, more autonomous.

Think long and hard about your autonomy. The sovereign reader is an irreplaceable asset to any culture. A writer can perhaps be more than an autonomous reader — even, at times, much more, but he can never occupy the same rung as a sovereign reader.

Rabbi Ori said: "David was able to compose the Book of Psalms, and what can I do? I can recite psalms."

This marvelous and precise confession constitutes proof that man can truly grow taller by bowing. From the depths of sorrow, yearning, and admiration there floats up a balanced feeling of gain. Had King David heard how Rabbi Ori envied him, it would have behooved him to envy Rabbi Ori in turn, not only in light of the Rabbi's manner, but also on account of his envy's cause.

So don't be tempted at any stage of your journey with me to put yourself in my place — at least no more than I try, if I do at all, to put myself in your place.

Try to look at what passes by your eyes (and not before your eyes) as a broken-line-of-light — one that pierces an agonized, yet bemused longing for a redemptive and lost haven of certainty within the vast darkness enveloping us both. But even so, think of me as a stranger. I am not you and you are not me, since I am neither able nor allowed to accompany you, just as you are not allowed or able to accompany me.

In this matter I am somewhat fortified by the words of Rabbi Menahem Mendel of Kotzek: "If I am I because I am I, and you are you because you are you, then I am I and you are you. On the other hand, if I am I because you are you, and you are you because I am I, then I am not I and you are not you."

Let us both ignore a certain schematic quality inherent in such wit, as in an overly symmetrical structure. Even relative truths, when articulated with such sharpness, can and must remind us of our respective sovereignties.

[GL]

Ya'aqov Shabtai

(1934–1981)

Widely regarded as the greatest Hebrew novelist of his generation, Ya'aqov
Shabtai produced just one novel, several plays, a children's book, and a
collection of short stories before his death, at age forty-seven, of heart
failure. The loss for Hebrew literature was catastrophic. Shabtai's utterly
singular prose wound snakelike through the psyches of his protagonists as
it sketched an unidealized portrait of a still vibrant but crumbling culture—
not only of Tel Aviv, his city, but of Israeli society as a whole. The 1977 novel
on which his reputation is based, *Past Continuous,* is in fact a single paragraph
(in the original Hebrew) that runs for some 282 pages and seems driven, in
retrospect, by the knowledge that its author had little time left (he'd suffered
his first heart attack in 1971, after which he devoted himself exclusively to
his writing). This vortex of a book paints a portrait of the Zionist matrix
falling apart—"paradise exploding," one fellow-novelist called it—"a lofty
dream gone haywire," and its impact is unlike anything else in the language.
Electric, dense, and held together by principles of association rather than
any conventional plot, it is one of the most original creations of Hebrew
fiction after the founding of the state, and it jolted the medium into a
new era.

A version of the novel that Shabtai was working on at the time of his
death was co-edited by his widow and a leading scholar of Hebrew literature

and published in 1984 as *Past Perfect*. While clearly unfinished, and flawed, it nonetheless contains numerous passages of tremendous power and vividness.

The interview with Shabtai that follows was the only one he ever granted and took place just a few weeks before he died.

ONE OR TWO THINGS I'D LIKE TO WRITE

I just can't go down the street where my parents lived. And if I could, I'd give all the money in the world if their house would just evaporate and vanish — that it would simply disappear before my eyes. My memory's sufficiently alive to see what was there before. And sometimes that involves extremely powerful and painful experiences. I think of myself as a refugee from Tel Aviv. Like a man exiled in his own country. And that's a difficult feeling. It doesn't derive from other people, or all sorts of political change. It comes from daily experience of the place, from the sights themselves. And like all experience of longing, it's painful, but also nourishing. And in a certain manner not unpleasant.

On the whole, my immediate memory, in relation to my childhood, is exceptional. Despite the fact that when I look back at my childhood, objectively, as it were, and accurately, there are many painful things there. A great deal of pressure, a lot of anger, nerves, tension, and just plain physical hardship. I remember that we had an icebox, and that the wash was done in tubs. My mother would sit for days on end and do the wash over the tubs, over the kerosene stove, over small fires. Even, I remember, in small basins. We had nothing. But somehow, and a little insanely, my overall and ideal memory is exceptional. All I have to do is want it, and all these people instantly descend from the heavens and stand here before me. My grandmother and my father and mother, this instant — and I had a lot of trouble with them, it wasn't at all easy, especially with my father — all I have to do is want something and they come down from the sky. And I expect this, and wait for it day after day. They just come down from the sky and stand here before me.

I wanted *Past Continuous* to tell everything. And I don't mean big stories. Really, I'm talking about the smallest things. A certain yawn someone yawned, a certain sentence that got stuck in my head way back when. A man's face, a near or distant relative, someone from the town. A piece of clothing, a shape, a gesture, something that happened. The tiniest, most inconsequential thing. I wanted in one way or another to capture all that in the book.

I made huge lists, and only very gradually as I worked did I realize that it was utterly impossible to surround all these things and capture them. And I also came to see that this was, in fact, beside the point. That it was possible — and in fact there was no other way to do this except — to make a certain selection, and include just a part of that list. *Past Continuous,* at least as I see it, is written as a network, or enormous mosaic, of miniature stories. And when I say story, I mean the tiniest particle: a certain movement, a sentence. Each of these, for me, constitutes a story.

I don't see myself as a naïve writer. I think of each work as an enormous mound of material that has to be organized in a certain manner, otherwise that's all it will be, a heap of material that doesn't mean a thing. Scribbling. A work turns into a work, a creation becomes a creation, the moment its materials are organized according to certain aesthetic criteria, but also, it goes without saying, according to criteria of meaning. There's an entire dimension of aesthetic treatment involved — word choice, and the like — and this too requires a certain knowledge and forethought. I don't believe that it's possible to write without intuition; but I also don't believe that it's possible, or desirable, to write only out of stupidity and blindness. There has to be a certain balance between intuition, or, let's say, emotion, and thought or understanding. In the end, there are moments — many, many moments — in the course of one's work when thought is useless. It stands there off to the side, utterly helpless, unable to decide what to do. Sometimes it's like trying to split a storm in two. Or trying to split a storm that doesn't exist in two. In other words, it's like trying to distinguish between two things that are almost identical. The difference between them is more than subtle. At this point, only intuition can tell you how to act. Or else one just shuts one's eyes, leaps in, and slices. [. . .]

The form — how did you build the external form of the book?

The form as a whole, the twisted and winding shape of the sentences, is something that developed in the course of the writing. It was clear to me from the start, from the moment I began writing, that I was going to use long rather than short sentences. Several things went into that. Some of it was, clearly, capricious — a kind of rebellion against the sort of writing that was common here [in Israel] — writing that used short and seemingly "winnowed" sentences, and created a certain effect of cleanness and style. I simply rebelled against all that. It provoked a certain resistance in me.

It has been said that the book is really one long complex sentence. There's a certain principle that I tried to establish. It developed, and then I saw that this is how it was, or would be, in any case, and so I tried to stabilize it. In some places, perhaps, I succeeded, and in others I failed. A sentence, let's say, that begins with one character and ends with another. Or begins at one time, or location, and ends in another. A labyrinthine sort of sentence.

The principle was: I wanted to write a book that propelled itself in the telling, one whose story was told in the writing. Whose movement would be inward. As though it were driven on by its own power. I don't know how else to describe it, because I don't know how to define it conceptually. Certainly not in theoretical terms, or in terms of literary theory.

During the course of the writing there developed a certain concept that was entirely private, and which I don't think has any validity: that writing should have in it an element of the chronicle (as in the word "chronic"). It should be very flat, and in a certain sense also monotonous. I've called this the music of prose. Naturally that's nonsense; who knows what the music of prose is? Why should this in particular be the music of prose, and not the prose of another book? There is no such thing. But this was the private name I had for it.

I hope that the structure of the book expresses something about the relation between it and the inner content or understanding of the book. That the inner nature of the book manifests itself outwardly in the book's structure, in the movement of the sentence, and of the words.

What's the connection between what we received in the end and reality? What link is there between the materials after they were written, after we have Past Continuous, *and the material that went into it? How does that work with you?*

The truth is that I didn't write this book from a sociological perspective, and it didn't begin as a book about society. The social or period dimension is actually a by-product of the materials of the reality that fed the writing.

The intention at the start wasn't to write a book that would reflect a period, or that would somehow bear witness to it or its zeitgeist. Any reflection of the period that appears in the book is, as far as I'm concerned, merely a by-product. The network of connections isn't always so calculated from the start. Sometimes it's a matter of something that happens in the course of the work. Things are remembered, things line up, and one thing turns it into something else and feeds another thing that it's linked to.

There was a desire to tell the stories, and in doing so to tell the story of Tel Aviv. I remember the city from a very particular period, in the middle of a process that was, as I saw it, critical — namely, the awful change that the city experienced and that left me, as someone who was born in Tel Aviv, feeling like a refugee there. It's that simple: as a man who felt like a stranger in his own home. And not just me; I feel myself and all those who were around me were turned into refugees in their own city. That the city had changed drastically, and was for me, in a sense, destroyed. It doesn't matter — I love it, but it has gone through a process of metamorphosis, which I've found extremely depressing.

Look, this is a book that, in the end, leaves me, as a reader, with an extremely uneasy feeling. As though you'd gone several steps further, consciously or unconsciously, to the point where things begin to fall apart. That says something very powerful about existence in this place.

At root, it's really a matter of separation. Not of falling apart, but of separating. [. . .]

And disintegrating?

Also disintegrating. But disintegration is another form of separation. And I mean separation. Not just putting distance between people who were once together, in the family, who have gradually grown more distant. I mean the destruction of the body, of health, and of course the thing that most involves separation, in the extreme sense, is death, which is the ultimate separation.

What causes this is life itself, which, seen as a whole, is a process of separation. At any rate, this is the dominant feeling I've had.

What I saw in Tel Aviv, or in a certain sense in my Tel Aviv story, was an expression of that same sense. What concerns me as someone who lives in this country is a certain process of turning one's back. And I don't, for the moment, mean turning one's back on socialism, but on several fundamental assumptions, or principles, that nourished this country and in fact helped with, or made possible, its establishment in the first place, and its development. I'm not talking about anything political or party-based, but about the necessity of labor, of humanistic values, of truth-telling, of striving for the truth. And I'm also thinking of — and I think this was a concept — the tremendous appreciation of idealism, of the high-mindedness of the so-called bleeding hearts. In the final analysis this country was founded by idealists and on the strength of idealists, and in a certain respect *for* idealists. This never kept people in the past from building houses or establishing an army, or defending themselves, or attacking and doing whatever was necessary. I confess that this turning of the back arouses a kind of revulsion in me, and depresses me greatly.

As someone who lives in this country, I'm alarmed by the process of brutalization, of vulgarization, of the anti-enlightenment hatred for culture that is increasingly prevalent in the state. So much so that it's become part and parcel of its bon ton. I find it frightening. And these, I think, are the things that most threaten the future of the country. It's not a matter of my not liking it, in a private sense. I don't like it, of course; but I think that it's something that could bring about the destruction of the state.

I don't like literature that serves as an illustration of something. I want a literary work to be autonomous, to exist by virtue of its own vitality. I'm not saying that there can't be political work; but I don't like it when the work becomes a kind of political propaganda. I don't rule that out in principle; I'm speaking now about my own work and what I like. And as with many things I love, it happens that I'll suddenly come across something that contradicts it completely. I'll say that I like a certain kind of book, and then suddenly I come across a book that stands for precisely the opposite of these principles, and I'll love it deeply.

Something experiential lies at the heart of every literary work. And experiential doesn't necessarily mean emotional. One says "experiential" and everyone immediately assumes that it refers to some traumatic event. But it often happens that there might be an intellectual or conceptual disturbance or excitement. And that can enter the literary or poetic or any other kind of work with power.

I'm totally opposed to any sort of romantic treatment of literary creation.

In the end, it's just something that people do. And there's no such thing as a person sitting down to work on something for months or years and being in a constant state of ecstasy or inspiration. Making any sort of ultimate demands on writers involves a kind of stupidity or lack of understanding. Though it's also possible that works of real worth have been made in this way. Stranger things have happened, and who am I to come along and say they can't, only to find that in fact someone has already had a gun put on the table before him and created something extraordinary? In my own work I prefer that things be kept very flat and that meaning be found at the bottom. I don't like it when the work ends up resembling a wolf with a sort of hump of whipped cream at the top. I don't like it when there are all sorts of symbols and things of that nature. That's why I also don't think that the story in this sense is anything allegorical. People ask me what something or other symbolizes. I try hard to keep things from being symbolic, to make things themselves, first of all. So that they'll be charged.

What are you aiming for?

If there's a work whose meat is good, so that you can sink your teeth into it, and that's also charged — by all means, that would make me very happy. I don't like works that are only lean. I'm not interested in eating dry sticks. I really don't like work in which the surface is everything and there is no flesh at all — work which has skin, and beneath it layers of bones made of all sorts of ideas and symbols and allegories, and god knows what — all sorts of exotic finery — but work that is missing just one thing: life. [. . .]

There's something extremely solitary about this work.

Yes, absolutely. Like a long-distance runner. Especially in prose. Like someone running a marathon.

There's a certain connection between the hope that people will read you and the act of writing in this intense and very dense manner over great distances, as in prose.

I can only speak for myself. And even then, barely, and cautiously. I confess that while I'm writing, none of these things matter to me. I'm not concerned with what they'll write or won't write, how many people will read me, and if they do, *how* they'll read me. I'm engrossed in a competition with myself. Apart from that, I'm not really concerned with anything else. I also don't believe that a person can sit for two or three years and write a work of prose, which is a kind of hard labor, and all the while be thinking of whether or not he'll be read. As though he could derive any satisfaction from that — if a great many or only a few people will read him. If that's the satisfaction you're getting, you're better off not getting into this in the first place. After all, how big a readership is there, anyway? I confess, none of this really concerns me.

You say that the competition is with yourself.

Faulkner once said in an interview I read that a writer's problem is to compete with himself. And to carry that out to the limit. Regardless of what the critics might say. That comes later.

What is a story built from?

You need a certain measure of talent, and of course the drive or desire to tell the story. To narrate something, to express something. But once that's in place — the talent and the desire to tell the story — then you need a truly endless supply of stubbornness. At least in prose.

Isn't that desire?

I don't think it can be desire. What sort of desire would have you sit day after day, hour after hour, without end, turning words upside down and having them face now in this direction and now in another as you ask yourself whether it's better to use the word *fear* or *fright* or *anxiety,* and in this way to waste your days. I think it simply requires a great deal of patience, endless patience, and an enormous amount of stubbornness.

One of the qualities that's important for a writer of prose to have, as I see it, is a certain measure of obtuse stubbornness. A little like a horse. He has to be part mule, part ox. I'm not saying the work is completely devoid of any experiential dimension or involvement. It brings with it its own kind of experience and involvement. There are also different phases of the work. Each time there's a phase of discovery in which something different emerges. And there are little pleasures along the way. To find the right way to put something, or just the right word. You work and work and work, and suddenly there it is — the right sentence. That's a pleasure, absolutely.

This book really isn't so much a treatment of anything as it is — in a certain sense — a way of life.

An editor once told me that people sit around in cafés and form all sorts of rebellious literary groups, and so forth — and that prose writers aren't usually part of them. But there are poets and painters. Writers of prose aren't usually among the café-sitters or the creators of revolutionary movements.

This isn't something I've looked into, but they just don't have the time for it. There's simply not enough time for it.

How do you let go? When is something finished, and how do you know?

I don't know. There's simply a moment when you reach a certain exhaustion. You hit the wall. I don't believe that there's anyone who's ever written a book and thinks that he's completely exhausted his material or brought it to its ultimate realization. After all, there's always a certain distance between you and the perfection of the work. And there's a continual process of trying to perfect it, to exhaust a subject, to refine it further and further. I'd imagine that everyone who writes and does any sort of creative work has a similar feeling. I find it hard to believe that someone one day suddenly says, that's it, it's perfect — let's publish it. It's always more a matter of getting to a certain point at which a person says: true, it isn't perfect, but that's as far as I can take it. Sometimes that's for financial reasons, sometimes simply because you've run out of strength — it's impossible to actually see the lines any longer, or the words and the characters that are running around before you. You simply get tired of it all and can't stand it any longer. And sometimes it can be for a very simple reason, that you want to move on and write a different book. With prose writers that's a real problem. Sometimes you find yourself in the first year of a book and suddenly you have an idea for a new book, and you have to hold yourself back for another two years until you've worked out a certain desire.

In the end, I think it's a matter of arriving at a state of exhaustion. It's coming out of your ears. And then — that's it.

You send off Past Continuous *and it hits the market, and then what happens? Does it sometimes come back to you? Suddenly it's autonomous and living its own life.*

There's something marvelous about prose, as opposed to the theater. In the theater one does, granted, receive immediate feedback, but with prose the premiere is ongoing. For as long as the book lives. Suddenly after three years someone comes along and says: Listen, I read the book. That's of course if the book hasn't completely disappeared, something that happens to most books — which simply disappear and die.

Past Continuous was also unusual in that it had about it a certain strangeness. I was very curious to see if readers would know what to do with it.

Why do you think there was something different about it?

Because of the kind of writing there, which is difficult. The dense pages, the absence of paragraphs, and the like. All that created a certain difficulty for the reader. At any rate, I imagine that all writers are eager to hear how their readers respond, since, at the end of the day, they become the true proprietors of the work. Of course one anticipates hearing from people. If, that is, anyone reads it at all. And if someone has read it, whether or not it gave rise to any sort of response. Joy, sorrow — whatever. Or revulsion. But something.

Suddenly there's this creature, with a life of its own. Obviously I know that it is somehow the work of my hands; but in another sense, it's autonomous. And it makes its way in the world on its own, and attaches itself to people. And now one has other things to do.

I admit that much of the feedback I've had, and the criticism, reflects an understanding of precisely what I was aiming for in that book. But there was much that came as a total surprise to me. I took all that in, listening as one would to talk about something completely different from what one had done. And sometimes I found myself wondering for a moment and not really able to connect what was said to what I'd written. At any rate, they found things in it that I'd never considered or thought about.

There are writers who have written many books, and that can definitely give rise to a certain envy and also admiration. That abundance, for instance, with writers like Agnon and others, isn't negligible, though I don't think it's the main thing. But it is something, and that can leave one envious.

I don't know how things will develop. I don't feel the need to write a great deal, and don't feel I'm capable of writing a great deal. There are one or two things that I'd really like to write. And I very much hope that will work out. But these are long-range plans, and they involve something completely different from *Past Continuous* and what I'm working on now. I'm not expressing any wish here; I'm simply saying that if I have any particular and personal desire, that's what it is. In the area of work.

There are other desires, which involve the opposite of work. Because I'd also like to take a rest from writing, and for a long time. It leaves you utterly exhausted, and sucks the life out of you. I'm hopeful — I don't know how to say any more than that.

[PC]

Harold Schimmel

(b. 1935)

Harold Schimmel is a birdlike arranger, a draftsman-poet for whom memory is as physical as seeing, and seeing as complex and luxurious as a meal in all its stages. Like Callimachus, one of his Alexandrian models, he avoids the "carriage roads" in his writing, preferring the risks of the "narrow course." Also Alexandrian is the manner in which his poems highlight the poetry's construction and delight in the pressures of their constraints.

Schimmel's oeuvre, easily among the most innovative in contemporary Hebrew, is characterized by this trademark combination of precision and polymorphous pleasure taken in flux, as his writing glides between cultures, eras, and individual histories. His work moves the reader from contemporary Jerusalem to Boston's Back Bay, from an idyllic Manhattan to pre-State Palestine, and—as in the excerpt from the aphoristic essay that follows— the updated timescapes of the early Arabic ode, or qasida. Ostensibly a meditation on that elusive pre-Islamic form, *Qasida* is in fact an ars poetica that sketches a detailed and tactile poetics of vision and recollection: "a concept of form for the complex poem . . . polyphonic, shifting, fickle."

Schimmel, whom Robert Creeley has called "an impeccable master of his art and as interesting a poet as one can find in any language," was born in the United States and settled in Jerusalem in 1962. After publishing poems in English in British and American journals in the 1950s and '60s, he began writing in Hebrew. He has published extensively in that language since. Schimmel is the author of six collections of poems and has also translated the poetry of Avot Yeshurun, Yehuda Amichai, and Esther Raab.

FROM *QASIDA*

An apology for poetry, every so often one feels the same desire to set it down, not because poetry needs it (this much is clear) but because we do. . . . As for the engagement itself, one always asks what for, a mental soundtrack accompanying the entire mechanism of self and person. Virtually endless seeing, listening in a ceaseless flow, a touching that includes that of finger to finger on a single hand, the cycle of seasons one smells (the new moon of the month of Tammuz, the height of the line from still-green to yellowing and finally straw), tastes in the mouth, not always with food. What am I leaving out. These are everyone's endowment. But we who note, who write, who gather, lovers of the paper itself, require from time to time an accounting.

—H. S.

1. The apparatus of poetry itself, which is to say *a poem* as a formal mode without center, a *qasida.* A concept of form for the complex poem, *the style of the qasida,* polyphonic, shifting, fickle.

2. True thought is construed through the form of the poem around the question of an "I." A storm of ideas, the heart's vision. Like a centipede, multiple voices. Deep depressions, hesitations, boasts, bold ascents on the basis of successful reconstruction of thought's figures. What else could justify the means if the end isn't relevant to poetry.

3. We identify not only the place in our having been there, but a chainlike series of associations follows with what we did, people we met, and even unvoiced thought-fragments of things that crossed our minds while we were there.

    To this entire mechanism we'll grant the name *nasib* (the turning), and the place itself we'll refer to as the *atlal.* I turned my heart to give it direction (*nasabti et libi*), because this was the primary factor in the alteration of everything.

4. *The Solidity of the Past.* Because what happened once can't be re-trieved. This is perhaps the principal meaning of "what was, will be," which is to say, "it will be," in as much as it still is, so it will go on being. And not "history repeats itself," a fairly boring formulation.

5. *Re-joining.* And from there, the extension, the continuity of imagi-nation's proliferation. A qasida as a handbook of poetry, and hence the Arabic meaning of the term, "poem."

   Does it designate the form itself or a sketch of a notion of form.

6. A *desert* as a model of a world made concrete in erasure. "In-the-footsteps-of and falling behind." Erasure enforcing a trace of a kind. What once was, is no longer.

   Mere chicanery. But the whole purpose of the movement was its after-image, an abiding impression as specter of what once was sim-ple being.

7. Remembrance as re-collection. Therefore the detailing of parts through a system of differences. Re-membrance as a joining of limbs anew.

   Therefore, interludes of sensuality. Re-placement.

13. I'm speaking here about a "code" of innocence, like childhood's code. A code of sexuality. I'm inventing a pattern called "poetry," which I choose to call (for now, for a while) *qasida.*

18. Not as in Joyce, where certain sights recall for someone "the pur-pose of the journey," but that in the qasida the sight removes all possible purpose — for an extension of the journey with meaning.

19. So in the qasida, recollection is what's already been learned, already experienced. But an active memory, as in Cavafy, the imperative, "Body, Remember."

28. The existence of the poet-speaker. The kingdom of flora and fauna, domesticated animals, women. The women linked as way-side stations on a journey.

   Eruptions into the landscape of invasive weathers.

32. One always enters the past through a door (traces, signs) whose hinges are a present, a situation's links.

36. Al-Jahat's comment that poetic content (*"al-ma'ani"*) is scattered all along the road. The business of poetry is simply to choose from that content, arrange it, and give it order.

37. The search for the actuality of experience in overtones and hints of meaning, ramification, and tone. But isn't that a definition of poetry.

38. The *nasib*. A (contemporary) camp of one (singular consciousness) on a site (read: *atlal*) of the encampment that is no longer.
    Which is to say, it contradicts absence with bolstered presence. Presence, like a total absence of moon auguring the crescent of the new lunar month. Like a full moon, whose implication (after-the-fact) is diminution.

60. Thoroughly absorbed in the living moment of the poet-hero's evanescence. And thus engaged in reading traces of himself.
    Like a cat twisting back at the defecation content of a hole it just dug.

61. I'm not involved in any sort of "search for." I find. It's a matter of simply bending down and lifting up what's there.

62. *Guide for the Perplexed.* Never anything without "something else."

63. A present longing for a future and a future drawn back to a past. This is all of man. Touching the last solid thing in order to regain a place to work from.

64. A sign is not a sign until it is "readable." It first of all has to be discerned. This is the beginning of the *atlal*.

70. A simple retreat from the flow of experience. Stubborn refusal of longing-in-motion. If you are not somewhat prepared to cease flowing, you will not gain access to the insinuating polyphony which is the exclusive right of your world of meaning.

71. The consciousness of the poet-hero passes (unceasingly) from a muteness that is natural to it (the cipher of his heart's leaning) toward a readiness of speech, equally his.

82. Absence and presence as the wink of an eye, but intertwined.
    He's capable of stopping and seeing what's there before him
    only with the assistance of *what was there.*

83. The lines live a life of their own. Never slack or bland. But taut,
    alert.

84. And with this one awakens a sense of expanse, a quality of space,
    of congruence.

85. The motion of a cult dance in a private enactment. Movement
    by movement like tracks left in sand. All is noted, and loved in
    its own right.

86. You said qasida. To lay out a great number of diverse and strange
    things on a flat surface. Fluidity, yes. Intensity, of course. And
    fluctuating.

105. Qasida. The entire range of speech's art, from the reflective
    to the emphatic.

108. Thoughts began with the word, that's where the whole
    sequence began as well. But what turns them into a sequence.

124. I write all this not about an actual qasida but create a concept for
    my own designs, to employ it consciously in an improper manner,
    the term "qasida."

125. What of the genre (the qasida's) overlaps with or even represents
    poetry in general. Is this like looking for hereditary resemblance
    between a child and the rest of his family.

136. Because landscape is like reading words on a page. You can't absorb
    them all at once. You have to start from a specific place
    like Hockney-the-photographer from his unmistakable shoes
    with socks of different color. Is each separate Polaroid photograph
    a "view."

153. The bedouin trackers as the qasida's interpreters of trace. Reading
    evidence as a form of sight within and before the world. And so
    with the dung of animals. Its hardness, its concentrated blackness,
    its condensed quality, constitute a declaration like the bare oaks
    indicating a season.

154. Sight, say, as promiscuity, as penetration.

158. An imperative printed on a t-shirt, "Think Qasida." Which is nothing other than "read the world."

210. *Theory of poetry.* All the reader is capable of managing on his own, let him. But who is this "reader." The self-imposed delusion of a poet. An abstract notion toward which (among other things) one now extends a hand.

212. Method. Take hold of the original idea in its form, the smallest, most miserable thing in all its poverty.

   Now let it (ugliness notwithstanding) proliferate.

236. *Syntax.* A positing of parts of speech like rivers, mountains, lakes.

241. *Atlal.* If everything behaves as "significancies" for marks of a former site, you're already embarked on the qasida's journey.

254. Stopping-points along the way, yes. But remember, the journey isn't that of a pilgrim.

255. What is the smallest unit one can still measure. The basic items in the refurbishing of the world. Via these dry bones.

1993

[PC]

Dahlia Ravikovitch

(1936–2005)

Dahlia Ravikovitch's poems give voice to an essential vulnerability and sense of hurt, or injustice, against which the only defense is the strength of the poet's ductile prosody. Especially in her early work—she published her first book in 1959—that voice is tempered by traditional forms and rhyme, and by what Irving Howe described as a severe and costly wit. Idiosyncratic allusion to Scripture, along with the prospects of escape to a fantasy world of her own creation, also work to reduce the often intolerable burden of the sensibility evident in these quietly disturbing poems. In her later work the voice is more exposed—as it addresses questions of intimacy on both the private and public planes. Over the years the political dimension of the work became increasingly pronounced. She has long been considered one of the foremost poets of her generation.

Born in Ramat Gan, Ravikovitch went with her mother to live on a kibbutz when she was six, after her father was killed by a drunk driver. At thirteen she moved to a foster home in Haifa. She began publishing while still quite young; the poet Avraham Shlonsky championed her work, including it in a journal he edited. After studying at the Hebrew University in Jerusalem, she lived most of her adult life in Tel Aviv, where she was active in the Israeli peace movement. In addition to her ten volumes of poetry, she published short stories, children's books, and translations of poems by Yeats, Eliot, and Poe. She also translated *Mary Poppins*.

SURELY YOU REMEMBER

After they all go home
I remain alone with the poems,
some poems of mine,
some of others.
Poems that others have written I love best of all.
I remain in the silence
and the choking in my throat relaxes.
I remain.
Sometimes I wish they would all go home.
Writing poems may be a pleasant thing to do.
You sit in your room and the walls grow taller.
Colors grow bolder.
A blue kerchief turns into the depth of a well.
You wish everyone would leave.
You don't know what's the matter with you.
Perhaps you'll think of a thing or two.
Then it will all pass, and you'll be pure crystal.
And then love.
Narcissus was so much in love with himself.
Only a fool doesn't see
that he loved the river, too.
You sit alone.
Your heart pains you, but it's not going to break.
The faded dramatis personae are erased one by one.
Then the flaws.
Then a sun sets at midnight.
You remember the dark flowers too.
You wish you were dead or alive or anyone else.

Isn't there even one country you love?
One word?
Surely you remember.
Only a fool lets the sun set at its own pleasure.
It always sets off too early westward for the islands.
Sun and moon, winter and summer will come to you.
Infinite treasure.

THE HOPE OF THE POET

What's up with you,
O young poets,
that you write so much about poetry
and the art of the poem
and the uses of raw material,
God forbid
writer's block
should descend upon you
and wreak havoc.

For lo, a remedy is at hand
to banish all grief:
to repose at the breakfast table
with its slightly faded oilcloth,
mooning at the windowpane
till the noon hour draws nigh.
And should slumber seize you, banish it not,
nor set at naught the taste of honey and butter.
Thou shalt not multiply poems and poesies,
nay, thou shalt do no work at all
and should thy heart find ease,
conceal it for many days
lest any eye behold.
For why such a hurry, my dear,
to take the slippery poem by the horns

or goad it between the ribs
the way a lone Bedouin lad shall lead
his tarrying ass?

After all, any good that may come of this
in the best of all possible worlds,
even after appeals to the mayor's office,
is a gravesite just for you,
in the Writers' Section
of the cemetery on Trumpeldor Street,
a sixty-meter dash
from Bialik's Tomb.

[CB/CK]

A. B. Yehoshua

(b. 1936)

Like Amos Oz and David Grossman, A. B. Yehoshua lives a kind of double
life as a writer of fiction and a spokesman for, or color(ful) commentator
on, the State of Israel. He gets as much attention for the often controversial
pronouncements he makes in the latter role as he does for the books that
have built him his bully pulpit. That is, perhaps, as it should be, for he has
spoken bluntly and with considerable frequency. Tonal considerations aside,
Yehoshua has made a compelling case for the necessity of the writer's
involvement in public affairs, particularly in Israel: noting the parallel and
related developments of the modern renaissance of the Jewish people
(Zionism) on the one hand and the revival of Hebrew as a modern language
on the other, he concludes that it is only natural that writers, as citizens who
are intimately involved with these developments, be asked to comment on
the shape that revival is taking and the effects it is having. Moreover, given
the writer's unique perspective in this sociolinguistic force field, it is, says
Yehoshua, the writer's moral duty to speak out. And speak he has—on
everything from the presence of Arabs and other non-Jews within the Jewish
state ("If you want your full identity," he said to novelist Anton Shammas,
"[and] to live in a state with an original Palestinian culture . . . get up, take
your belongings, and move one hundred meters East"), to peace and the
nature of American Judaism (which he has called "masturbation," as opposed
to the "real thing" of Jewish life in Israel).

In the essay that follows, Yehoshua discusses the tension between the
writer's responsibility to his work as *literature*, with all the intimacy and
psychological nuance that entails, and the moral demands that attend to
holding forth on issues that go beyond the literary. (Elsewhere Yehoshua
laments the fact that younger writers have—with a few exceptions—gone
the way of a postmodernist apathy and no longer involve themselves in the
weighty and sometimes debilitating affairs of the day.)

Yehoshua was born and raised in Jerusalem to a Sephardic family that
had lived there for five generations. He studied literature and philosophy,
then began publishing his fiction some nine years after the founding of
the state. With the appearance of his first stories in the late 1950s, he
immediately established himself as one of the leading writers of his
generation. His powerful early works—"Facing the Forests," "Three Days
and a Child," "The Continuing Silence of the Poet," which some would argue
constitute his most important contribution to Hebrew literary culture—apply
a kind of modernist abstraction (derived from Kafka and, to an extent, Agnon)
to Israeli society. Yehoshua abandoned that starker style in his late thirties,
when he began writing novels and turned in a more polyphonic Faulknerian
direction, emphasizing what he sees as the democratic impulse behind
Faulkner's technique. It is these midcareer and later works that have brought
him international recognition. He has published numerous novels as well as
several collections of stories and essays. His books have been translated into
many languages.

The Nonliterary Reality of the Writer in Israel

The nonliterary reality of the writer in Israel has in recent years become more
palpable than his literary reality. We find him attending assemblies and demon-

strations, signing petitions, speaking at symposia, writing for the papers, giving speeches and lectures, and wandering from schools to army bases. [. . .] Suddenly it's become clear that the primary battleground of authors, among themselves, is no longer that of books and literature, and no longer treats aesthetic problems or controversies between literary schools; instead, the focus now is on politics and policy, social problems, and ethical issues in public life. The argument over the future of the occupied territories, for example, has become the locus of much broader-ranging and deeper debates — concerning the very understanding of Jewish history, the essence of Zionism, and so on.

The critics and literary functionaries of the 1950s — who inveighed, at the time, against certain writers, especially those of the "Generation of the State," for shutting themselves up in ivory towers and cutting themselves off from reality — today would be only too pleased to take a few authors and send them back to their ivory towers, and also to put some bolts on the outside doors, so they wouldn't be able to leave.

Let the writer write, let him compose poems, stories, plays, abstract and eccentric as they might be — but, above all, let him stop shouting. . . .

Even those who seem to be silent, whose voice isn't heard, who have sworn off all nonliterary activity, whether for lack of faith in the utility of public debate, or out of fear of the public or violating their aesthetic sense; those who've sat at their desks, it appears, in order to write and only to write — they too now find the news seeping into the pages of their poetry or prose, while the transistor radio stands always in front of them, and they take in its chatter, or perhaps talk back to it. With them as well we find precious psychological resources — energy that should be devoted to literature alone — being siphoned off and sucked away into nonliterary matters.

In Hanoch Levin's latest play, *Schitz,* there's an accurate description of the presence of the state in our lives:

> Already, under the bridal canopy I saw
> I wasn't my husband's only bride.
> Beside him, digging her fingernails into his arm
> stood the state as well.
> And when we walked — she walked with us.
> She kept us company day and night,
> climbing into bed with us,
> sitting with us while we ate,

coming at us from every angle,
and drifting in from the earth and sky —
through the radio, the paper, and films,
and infiltrating the water pipes,
the cracks in the wall, the shutters' slats.
She blocked out the sun and the stars from our sight,
penetrating our eyes, our ears, our noses,
and even the pores of our skin.

I'm not saying that works of literature haven't been written over the past two years, but for one reason or another, they haven't been the focus of our lives. Their significance has been diminished.

Does the writer have to justify himself on this account? Does he need to explain why, of late, his reality has been so nonliterary? Certainly, he must. The writer should be able to account for every moment that he doesn't devote to creation itself, for every moment that he isn't writing, even for daring to live. Sleeping, eating, raising children — all that is vanity. An inner voice (and sometimes one from outside) pursues him constantly and says: There's only one thing worth your while — write, write! write! If possible, write beautifully and well. But the main thing is — never desist from writing.

How, then, can the writer justify his actions? He can say that in recent years Israeli reality has become so literary, that the mere fact of contact with it — without the composition of a single line — is in itself the embodiment of literature: insane fantasy has become political reality; neurotic personal anxiety is inscribed in political platforms; dramatic personal conflicts are heard as headlines on the hourly news; comedies and absurd burlesques have become scandals that are handled in court. The myriad subtle psychological currents that feed literature and constitute its legitimate domain have broken forcefully into our external reality.

The writer can say: What do you want? Israeli politics is so wholly literary, capricious, arbitrary, and emotional that dealing with it is itself a literary act. But that, of course, is a dubious explanation. For we've all learned that there is no literary or nonliterary reality; all reality, even pastoral relaxation along the banks of a lake in the summer, is dramatic reality — depending on what one does with it.

Perhaps the deepest and most compelling justification would be that which connects the nonliterary reality of the writer with the urgent need for prophecy, which has awakened recently in the State of Israel. The position of the prophet has been greatly enhanced, especially after the crushing failure of so many experts — Orientalists, military commentators, professors of political science, economists. Suddenly it has become quite clear that these people have failed to identify the true nature of our reality. Now that they're trying to be more cautious, and "softening" their learned prognostications with qualifiers such as "it seems," "perhaps," "it's possible that," "in a certain sense," "the various options," and so on and on — one turns away in disgust.

The public feels that it's standing at the edge of an abyss, and the sweet illusion that this abyss will somehow fill up on its own and that one fine day we'll continue comfortably on our way — this illusion has been shattered. It has become increasingly clear that either we'll fall into that abyss or else we'll leap across it, even though we may have to stand beside it for a long time (and that, too, is unpleasant). In situations like this, one is left feeling that the true questions don't concern the depth or width of the abyss, or even the trajectory of our leap; the public wants something more tangible, more general, some sort of vision that can help it leap across the abyss with real force. It wants basic answers in response to basic questions: How did we come to this abyss, and what extends beyond it? And in seeking the answer, it begins to yearn for prophets and prophecy. After all, this is the nation of the prophets. The public demands a proper vision, and it's prepared to accept a variety of versions. It's prepared to listen to prophets of wrath and rebuke, and to prophets of greatness and comfort. It will accept the cruelest reproaches. I sometimes wonder about this public of ours. What happened to it after the Yom Kippur War? It sat there quietly, listening to the cruel things being said about it. It didn't agree with what was said, but it was willing to listen, and took a kind of masochistic pleasure in it. Of course, from time to time it needs to balance the wrathful vision with a vision of megalomaniacal greatness, such as, for instance, the one that claims that the day will come when all the Gentiles will bow before us. This type of prophecy appears on the prophetic program as well, and the audience won't forgo it. One way or another, it knows that the prophecy found in the Bible is only a fraction of the prophecies that were pronounced. . . . The classification of true prophets and false ones is made by subsequent generations. At the present stage, we're willing to hear them all. . . .

Given that there is such a feeling abroad, a call that emerges from the public — "Come and prophesy to my people" — the author seizes up and asks himself: Why not me? Within every author, or at least within some authors — and this isn't necessarily a Jewish phenomenon — lies a frustrated prophet. The moment has come, the author says to himself, the time is ripe. He's suspicious of journalists of various stripes and reserve generals, the pundits and Orientalists, who've suddenly managed to switch professions and become prophets; and so he rushes to make his way into the picture as well, since, after all, he has several talents that are decidedly relevant: linguistic dexterity; a rather developed ability to deploy imagery; a certain capacity for abstraction (not too great — a prophet mustn't be an abstract philosopher, lest he soon lose his audience); minor personal neuroses, which produce the strangeness that always suits prophecy; a wild imagination, which sometimes suits Israeli reality; a degree of disdain for the public — a willingness to provoke for provocation's sake, regardless of "what people will say"; and here and there a distinctly ethical sensitivity, which has always been an integral component of the prophet's character.

And so the author, too, has worked his way into the "prophetic process" that is sweeping the State of Israel today. He says: Reality compels me. But that is only part of the truth. Reality compels him — that's true. But he brings himself to it. Now he's there, deeply entangled in political and social life, and he rents out his pen for matters that are decidedly not literary, and in doing so endangers his powers of creativity. The author harbors no illusion that his extraliterary activity might somehow improve his literary work. To a certain degree, he'll try to defend the arena of pure creativity, so it won't be overly neglected. When people present him with hard-core cases, by way of example, as a warning — "See what will happen to you?!" — he gingerly counters with other examples: reputable figures, such as Dostoevsky, Brenner, or Alterman. But then, of course, they tell him: How could you even contemplate making the comparison? . . .

Such, at any rate, is the advance with eyes wide open toward the neglect of creativity. Some writers, however, cannot refrain from responding to the great call. Paraphrasing the poet's words, they reply: "And I, with my fat and with my blood, will feed the fire." And so the author enters the public arena and becomes deeply involved. Beyond his personal opinions, his great or small understanding, his intuition, and his dubious name, he can, it seems to me, bring with him from the field of his art certain things that are missing in public life today. Let me try to outline four abilities that are distinctly his:

1. The author can bring with him a sense of linguistic responsibility, which is absent today. I say "linguistic responsibility," not fancy words and a rich vocabulary, proper grammar, or polished Hebrew. The writer can fight the "erosion of language." We are prey to a process of corruption in the language, to deception. This isn't a matter of grammatical corruption. Even people who speak splendid Hebrew corrupt the language. Full-scale battles are being waged in Israel in the arena of language. Far more common than gunfire is the incessant hurling of words, from every direction: among ourselves, between us and our enemies, between us and the world. There is tremendous violence in language, and I do not think that it needs to be muted. If language is a weapon, it must be violent, and there is no need to obscure that violence. It is, however, certainly possible to demand a bit more responsibility in the use of language, and this is something the writer can bring from the realm of literature. He can show how the language is used to deceive, what it conceals, what it blurs, how it misses the mark, and how it strikes in vain; how the concepts that the language uses become increasingly murky. He can try to make them clear, he can restore vitality to worn out words and wear down the meaningless ones. He can ask for a measure of logic in language and for minimal consistency within it.

2. The author can bring with him from the field of his "profession" the moral sense of the individual instance.

In all literary writing, there exists — explicitly or implicitly — an ethical attitude. The importance of the moral sense in the private, individual instance is emphasized here, since there is no better method of moral evasion than the effort to place every ethical problem in a broader context, in order to blunt the specific outcry against a specific outrage. The state, like every state, has a particular talent for silencing outcries by means of historical description and impressive diagrams or statistics that demonstrate the rate of economic growth. The writer can bring the discussion back, again and again, to the individual, in order to protest against injustice, to combat the effort to obscure it.

In August 1971, some twenty writers, all with extremely divergent political views, went to the prime minister to protest government policy with regard to Iqrit and Bir'am [two Arab villages in Israel whose residents have — since 1948 — been promised the right to return to their land but have not been allowed to do so]. Torrents of opprobrium and abuse were rained down on them after the meeting. Leading the chorus of scorn were, of course, several journalists. The same journalists who regard themselves as experts in just about everything in the world, whose sermons and "wisdom" we're exposed to day after day in the papers, were the first to condemn the writers who attended that meeting: What special right do writers have to interfere in the matter? What expertise do they have that enables them to judge it? In what way are they better than the carpenters or farmers?

Certainly, in a democratic state, everyone is entitled to regard himself as an expert on all its matters. Writers or professors have no right to expect preferential treatment to carpenters or tailors, but neither is their right any less than that of the carpenters and tailors. And if other groups of professionals, for example, wanted to go to the prime minister and present her with an argument about Iqrit and Bir'am, she would have received them with no less love, for they certainly represent a broader public than do the writers. But the fact is that the carpenters and tailors do not go to talk to prime ministers about problems of morality that don't affect them personally.

The writers went to the prime minister, and in a long and drawn-out meeting they tried to present an argument about one limited matter, about that specific injustice. They did not come for theoretical discussion about moral issues in general. But there was, of course, a conspicuous desire on the part of [Prime Minister] Golda Meir (who was extremely cordial) to talk about "more pleasant" topics — the vision of the Jewish people, the education of youth, and other things not particularly pressing. And we said to her: No, we want to talk about the injustice of Iqrit and Bir'am. Everyone spoke, almost imploringly. But in vain. The failure of that meeting is well known, and it deterred authors from intervening in other cases, which is a more grievous failure than the failure in the matter of Iqrit and Bir'am. Afterward it turned out that the heart that was indifferent to the problems of the Arab citizens was also indifferent to the problems of Jewish citizens, because it was the same heart.

We like it when famous writers all over the world come to our defense. [. . .] And we get very angry when artists and writers are silent when injustice is done to us. If the intervention of gentile writers outside the country has any significance for us, then the moral intervention of writers here in this country is significant as well.

3. With his ability to express opposition to the monochromaticism that dominates the presentation of spiritual reality in the country, the author can bring with him to public life in Israel a sense of reality's complexity.

Two profound spiritual processes are at work in Israeli society today. Both have deep roots in our culture and tradition and therefore pose a threat to society: an intensifying process of hatred, and an intensifying process of self-aggrandizement. On the one hand, a process of cutting ourselves off from ourselves, an expression of total despair with the Jewish people; and on the other hand — detachment from the world. These two opposing processes amount to different responses that derive from a single source; identical factors comprise the spiritual mechanism that drives them. Since both these processes have deep-seated foundations in our culture, and since neither involves assault by an evil spirit or a spirit of foolishness, we must be wary of them seven times over.

The writer, who by nature deals with complex situations — and who always is wary of black and white, and everywhere looks for shades of gray — can combat the simplistic thought that lies behind these two phenomena: self-hatred and self-aggrandizement.

Present reality can lend superficial legitimacy to self-hatred, until it takes hold of actual things in our character, which is our fate. Loathing of talk and fancy rhetoric about the connection between the Jewish people and the Land of Israel, while 80 percent of the Jewish people live in the Diaspora and have no desire to come here; bombastic speeches about our being a light unto the nations, a chosen people, a unique entity — things that we find crammed into every schoolbook — and, in contrast to them, corruption, injustice, mediocrity, all at a frightening distance from these terrible pretensions; self-righteousness, use of historical suffering as the coin of the realm — all of these are real things, upon which a process of self-hatred can seize and thus intensify its course.

On the other hand, the processes of self-aggrandizement and isolationism also seize upon entirely real phenomena in our lives. Preservation in itself isn't what's important here, for there are nations more ancient than we that have survived to this day. Self-preservation through loyalty to a spiritual essence; a unique sense of solidarity that still pulses within us; the ability to hold up under difficult situations; that true, inner strength that is found among many of us; the ability to rise up from the dust, to renew ourselves within ourselves after repeated blows; the self-criticism, the true democratic power inherent in us — all of these things can certainly encourage the feeling that the community living here has unique qualities and is different, more wonderful than any other.

And the writer, in the face of these two processes, without denying the true things that nourish both, must restore a sense of proportion; he must demonstrate the dark and contrary side of every phenomenon, provide a sense of reality, stop the drift to the margins, restore us to the world and to ourselves. We are not a rotten society. A rotten society would not have withstood the last [1973] war as we did. And on the other hand, we are neither required nor do we pretend to be a model society in order to justify our existence.

4. The author can bring with him the feeling of freedom from his "profession" and direct it toward political reality. Over the past two years the feeling of freedom in this country has been seriously impaired — perhaps not only in our country, but in the whole world. This is one of the reasons for the depression that afflicts us. Objectively speaking, the comforters are right who try to show us with signs and wonders that in our history, and even our short history here in Israel, we have known periods far more grievous. The situations we faced twenty, thirty, and forty years ago were far more dangerous. Such deep depression, however, didn't descend upon us in these graver situations because we always had the feeling (which may well have derived from an illusion) that our fate was in our hands, that we were free to lead ourselves. Apart from the political disagreements of the past two years we have also been overwhelmed by a sense of fatalism — the familiar Jewish fate.

If the sense of loyalty to Jewish destiny had been what drove the first

Zionists, the State of Israel would never have arisen. If ever a thing was contrary to the sense of Jewish fate, it was Zionism. Jews rose up and said: No, there is no invincible, unalterable Jewish fate. For if there were such a Jewish fate, we'd have continued living in the place where that fate had established us. Zionism was a concept that defied the notion of fate and replaced it with a concept of freedom, of self-liberation, of the belief that one should be free to act on one's own — a concept that in some cases was ingenuous, even naïve, impertinent. Precisely this feeling of freedom is what we are losing.

Freedom is the basic feeling in the work of a writer. Freedom is a necessary condition for creation. The author must make certain that his readers, too, enjoy freedom, because if the reader isn't free, he won't be able to absorb the work, and it, in turn, will have no existence. The author can help restore the depleted sense of freedom. In the end — freedom was the primary goal here. The Land of Israel, the state — these were only means to achieve the Jew's freedom, but suddenly they've become ends in themselves. Here, indeed, was the dividing line between Zionism and Jewish life in the Diaspora. And for that reason Hebrew literature was so deeply bound to the Zionist movement: to free the Jew, to free him from restraints, and primarily from his own restraints.

But within the concept of freedom there is also the freedom to choose not to fight for freedom. This, too, must be guaranteed. You have the freedom to give up your freedom. Whoever doesn't want to be here is free to leave. It makes no sense to create a feeling of entrapment. There are people who think that by promoting a feeling of there being "no alternative," and of being hemmed in, it is possible to block those who harbor transgressive thoughts. It will not help. Nothing can stop those who want to escape or give up. The sense of fate will only oppress sevenfold those whose decision to remain derives from their responsibility and their freedom.

What does the Israeli writer get back from the reality in which he is immersed up to his neck? What does he get that might be of use in his writing? Ostensibly, a great deal. In fact, a pack of troubles. Which is to say, it cannot be denied that "the big themes" lie around us in enormous heaps.

"Material" is not lacking. The Swedes, the Danes, and the Swiss doubtless
envy us enormously as they chew on their pencils: Ah, if only I lived in Israel,
how good things would be for me. Israelis have real dramas. . . .

First of all — there is death. Death is a classic subject for literature, an
authentic subject. And death is sown all around us. One cannot deny the literary possibilities. It's easy for us to make our heroes die a death that
appears credible when we get tired of them, or when we don't know what to
do with them. We just send them out on reserve duty, or we start the plot
half a year before a war, bringing them along a sure path to the bitter end.
The Danes or the Swedes have to come up with intricate and clever ways to
kill their heroes. We have it relatively easy. That's an advantage. It casts even
the most evil protagonists in a softer, finer, and more melancholy light, as in
the case of Charkhes in Levin's play *Schitz*. Suddenly, when he dies in battle,
a halo or kind of tragic glow descends over that super-jerk. Even superficial
characters, when death descends on them, suddenly grow in stature. All that
makes characterization easy, to put it cynically.

But in fact there are a great many pitfalls here. This dramatic, tempestu-
ous reality is a mirage. It's easy to be seduced by it, hard to conquer it. It's
liable to toss us out, to catch us up in external events so that we miss the
inner feeling. At least 50 percent of the works of Hebrew prose that I've read
are connected with war. Sometimes you see how people, who had never
thought of writing, are lured into it by the dramatic nature of the subjects
that surround us. The subjects give rise to works, but few of them are any
good. What, then, remains of this reality for us? There remains solidarity —
solidarity as an operative and fundamental asset of Israeli reality, its problems, pains, and upheavals notwithstanding. Solidarity even with your
fiercest opponents. Solidarity that's capable of lending wings to true talent.

Not long ago Virginia Woolf's *Mrs. Dalloway* was published in Hebrew,
and once again attention was turned to that marvelous writer. When one
looks at the story of her life, the fact of her suicide stands out. Woolf was
born in 1882 and committed suicide by drowning herself in 1941. There is
nothing more dreadful than a person's suicide. Who knew of their terrible
suffering? Who can judge them? The suicide of a writer might be even more
horrible: all of a sudden such failure of faith in creativity. That, indeed, is
extremely depressing. But I found myself wondering: suicide in England in

1941? England — "at her finest hour." The battle for her liberty, almost for her very existence, in a war of the few against the many, in darkened Europe, at the most critical point in all her history — to commit suicide at that time? The "plight of England" was important to Woolf. What happened in England mattered to her greatly. England didn't just provide the setting or scenery for her characters. England was their inner essence. Virginia Woolf dealt with its society, its various strata, and their political associations. At an hour of such importance for England, she took her own life. In other words, English solidarity did not blunt her feeling of personal isolation.

For some reason it seems to me, and perhaps any comparison is groundless, that among us this would not be possible. Solidarity's power is greater here. We're gripped by our history. But I might be wrong.

MAY 1975

[JG]

Yoel Hoffmann

(b. 1937)

Stylist, trickster, and sage, Yoel Hoffmann is, critics around the world and in
Israel have agreed, contemporary Hebrew's most startling and innovative writer
of fiction. His work might also be described as fiction for lovers of poetry, and
poetry for lovers of fiction. Hoffmann's detached and idiosyncratic prose—at
once distinctly Jewish and Zen-like—follows out the contours of his characters'
patterns of thought, letting the odd angles of their intersection determine the
shape of his narrative. His books are built up from short poemlike fragments, as
though the world were being seen through a tremendous kaleidoscope. All that
is perceived, and all that is remembered—whether it involves the fractured
consciousness of a Holocaust survivor or a child's amazed inside-out view of the
world (without the backwash of grown-up sentiment)—is rendered with
remarkable sweep, musicality, and delicacy. The results are, as one leading
American journal has put it, "beautiful, humane, priceless."

Hoffmann was born in Hungary and came to Palestine at the age of one
with his Austrian-Jewish parents who were fleeing the Nazis. (His Hebrew is
laced with German, Yiddish, and other foreign lexical items—as though it had
first been heard through non-native ears.) His mother died while he was still
young, and Hoffmann spent several years living with other relatives and in a
children's home before his father remarried. He published his first fiction at

the age of fifty-one, having previously devoted himself to study and teaching. He earned his doctorate in the philosophy of religion in Japan, after a two-year stay at a Zen monastery there, and for many years taught Japanese poetry, Buddhism, and philosophy at Haifa University. In addition to his nine volumes of fiction (most of which have been translated into English), Hoffmann is the co-author of a now-classic English volume called *The Sound of the One Hand,* which contains answers to the traditional Zen koans and commentary, as well as a volume of Japanese "death poems." *Curriculum Vitae* was published in Hebrew in 2007.

FROM *CURRICULUM VITAE*

14

I dream that the manuscript has been lost. We (my wife Nurit and I) are looking for it, but not finding it.

The light bulbs don't go on, and in the other rooms people are sleeping. Who are these people?

And what will happen now to the characters in the manuscript? Some (those who really were) are buried beneath the ground. But where will the others go?

And there are, too, the characters who haven't yet come into the story; and also those who haven't yet been imagined. And who am *I* in this darkness?

I want (precisely because of this uncertainty) to introduce here the Roman emperor Nero. Did they have underwear in those days?

The balcony he sat on while Rome burned was (I know) a Bauhaus balcony like those in Tel Aviv. His mother shouted to him from within the room, but he closed the sliding doors and lowered (how? from outside?) the shutters. Outside (which is to say, in the street) horses and donkeys were fleeing the fire.

Most likely he sang the choral part from Beethoven's Ninth Symphony, and his testicles (on which there were lice) were squashed against the seat of the chair.

In 1960, we were married, my first wife, Yolanda, and I, at the offices of the rabbinate in Ramat Gan. My father leaned to the side, but Ursula, my step-mother, stood like a Japanese wrestler in the middle of the circle.

All sorts of German émigrés (on one side) and émigrés from Romania and Poland (on the other side) were eating, at 29 Rabbi Kook Street, from the cake that Ursula baked, and afterward we traveled (Yolanda and I) to the convalescent home at Kibbutz Nahsholim.

I remember that storks stood in the fish ponds. Yolanda leaned against the window and said: Storks. Amazingly, she'd uttered this word on our hon-eymoon (hers and mine). Most likely she was thinking of children.

83

It's possible to write only by means of nonwriting. When things come from the opposite direction.

My aunt Edith rises out of the ground and returns to her bed in the nurs-ing home. Ursula, my stepmother, is walking backward. All sorts of wilted flowers bring their petals toward themselves.

All we need is yogurt and a spoon. We'll already know what to do with the spoon. We'll lead it toward the right place (which is to say, the yogurt) and from there toward the mouth. But the mouth isn't fathomed. Likewise the word that stands for it (mouth) is strange in the extreme.

Or take, for example, the hand that's holding the spoon with the five tragic fingers. There's no logic whatsoever in there being five. Like five widows who've gathered because their husbands have died, and they allow themselves this gesture through the air in order to keep from losing their minds.

There is no limit to the beauty of things that are sad. Like old clay vases or a wagon's shaft in a junkyard. Every year the plum trees flower anew, and peo-ple whose names are Shtiasni or Dahaan open doors and close them.

All these things fill the heart with great joy. The beauty of death and the violet colors accompanying it. Announcements that make nothing dawn on one, and the dawn itself rising from nowhere like a birthday present 365 days a year.

84

We came small to this book and now we're big. And we've learned to lie.

For instance, we've seen Professor Pinto at the café in Lisbon, but we haven't seen his dentist, and now we're sending him to the dentist.

We saw a beautiful woman at the ceramic tile shop but we haven't slept with her, and now we're taking her to the hotel next to the ancient Alfama quarter and removing her dress and bra and panties and kneeling on the floor and kissing the soles of her feet and between the toes and her knees and the hair between her legs and her belly and doing to her what all the priests dream of doing on sheets across which small flowers are printed beneath the forty-watt bulb.

We can perform a de-Hoffmannization of ourselves. In order to become someone else. A fucking expert on stamps sitting in his apartment in Stockholm, and all day saying, *Yoh, Yoh.* . . .

87

If you want to tell a story, you'll have to deny the Holocaust.

Imagine for a moment a story that someone is writing in Berlin, about Kurt and Brigitta. Something about an office and difficulties with what they call relationships, and the subletter they call Yo'akhim, and so on.

Now, unless you introduce red air and red earth into this story, Brigitta and Kurt and Yo'akhim will only be thin lines drawn with a pencil. A shoelace. A dead centipede. A beetle's case. Dust. Nothing.

Only the blood of the dead can give them life. Therefore Brigitta (even if the story takes place in 1992) is red and Kurt is red, and the air is red, and they need (in the true story) to speak within this air as one speaks in water. For instance, if Kurt says, What did you do yesterday, bubbles of blood will emerge from his mouth.

Just as the religious strengthen things by means of the letters *beit-samekh-dalet* (short for "with the help of God"), so they need the red. Their red common market. Their red sky. Let them say: *Guten Blut Morgen* [Good Blood Morning].

It's strange that throughout Europe people strip off their clothes and walk around naked here and there at different times and in different places and not everywhere all at once (as the Jews did).

[PC]

Amos Oz

(b. 1939)

Amos Oz was born in Jerusalem and raised in an intensely intellectual refugee
environment. His father was a librarian and scholar, and one of his uncles—
the historian and critic Yosef Klausner—was a leading figure in Revisionist
circles. His mother took her own life when he was twelve. The precocious and
rebellious Amos was, by then, already on his way to becoming a Labor Zionist,
and at age fifteen he joined a kibbutz. Early in what would become a thirty-
two-year stay at Kibbutz Hulda, just south of the Jerusalem–Tel Aviv highway,
the adolescent Klausner changed his name to Oz (meaning "strength"). He
left Hulda only in 1986, when he moved to the small desert town of Arad,
because of his son's asthma.

Perhaps Israel's best-known writer today, Oz is the author of some
twenty novels as well as several volumes of cultural and political commentary,
for which, in a way, he is equally famous. Because of these, and the many
articles he has published in prominent papers and journals in Europe and
America, Oz is often seen by the world as a fearless prophet and his nation's
conscience—a role he did in fact play as a younger man: he was among the
first and most eloquent of Israeli intellectuals to speak out about the dangers
of occupation after the 1967 war. Both Oz and the political situation have,
however, changed over time, and it is clear today that he has all along been

a classic representative of the centrist-liberal Labor Zionism of his adolescence. It was precisely that centrist position that early on allowed him to speak out so clearly. Today, critics on the right find him unpatriotic, while on the left he is regarded as someone who—as the liberal sensibility was once defined—always comes down firmly on both sides of a question.

Oz first gained fame with the 1968 publication of his hugely popular novel *My Michael,* which established him at the age of twenty-eight as one of the leading writers of his generation. No stranger to public discourse—he'd grown up surrounded by politics and had already published two other collections of fiction—he responded loudly and articulately to the social turmoil that was then erupting after the Six-Day War. The novel itself, while ostensibly a psychological portrait of a depressed and disillusioned woman in her mid-thirties, has also been seen as a critique of masculine Israeli society—from which politics are rarely distant. Throughout the novel, its heroine fantasizes about being ravished by Arab men. With his fiction and his commentary, then, the handsome young author strode into the lion's den.

Each of Oz's novels has taken up a different tack. For Oz is, as he has said of himself, less the conscience of his country than its "tribe's conjurer": "I bring up evil spirits and record the traumas, the fantasies, the lunacies of Israeli Jews, native and those from Central Europe. I deal with their ambitions and the powder-box of self-denial and self-hatred." Those words were uttered in the late 1970s, but they have held true through the arc of Oz's long career.

His recent memoir, *A Tale of Love and Darkness,* is among the best-selling literary works in Israeli history. Like much of his writing, it blends the public and intimate—in this case weaving the story of his own modest immigrant family with the larger story of the state and its growth. The excerpt below tells of Oz's relationship with modern Hebrew's greatest writer of fiction, S. Y. Agnon, who lived across the street from his Uncle Yosef.

FROM *A TALE OF LOVE AND DARKNESS*

The Agnons' house was set in a garden surrounded by cypresses, but to be on the safe side it was built with its back to the street, as though hiding its face in the garden. All you could see from the street were four or five slit windows. You entered through a gate concealed among the cypresses, walked along a paved path by the side of the house, climbed four or five steps, rang the bell at the white door, and waited for the door to be opened and for you to be invited to turn to your right and to climb the half-dark steps to Mr. Agnon's study, from which you reached a large paved rooftop terrace that looked out onto the Judaean desert and the hills of Moab, or else to turn left, to the small, rather cramped living room whose windows looked into the empty garden.

There was never full daylight in the Agnons' house, it was always in a kind of twilight with a faint smell of coffee and pastries, perhaps because we visited just before the end of the Sabbath, toward evening, and they would not switch on the electric light until three stars at least had appeared at the window. Or perhaps the electric light was on, but it was that yellow, miserly Jerusalem electricity, or Mr. Agnon was trying to economize, or there was a power failure and the only light came from a paraffin lamp. I can still remember the half-darkness, in fact I can almost touch it; the grilles on the windows seemed to imprison and accentuate it. The reason for it is hard to tell now, and it may have been hard to tell even then. Whatever the reason, whenever Mr. Agnon stood up to pull out a book from the shelves that looked like a crowded congregation of worshippers dressed in shabby dark clothes, his form did not cast one shadow but two or three or even more. That is the way his image was engraved on my childhood memory, and that is the way I remember him today: a man swaying in the half-light, with three or four separate shadows around him as he walked, in front of him, to his right, behind him, above him, or beneath his feet. [. . .]

My mother used to say about Agnon:

"That man sees and understands a lot."

And once she said:

"He may not be such a good man, but at least he knows bad from good, and he also knows we don't have much choice."

She used to read and reread the stories in the collection *At the Handles of the Lock* almost every winter. Perhaps she found an echo there of her own sadness and loneliness. I too sometimes reread the words of Tirzah Mazal, née Minz, at the beginning of "In the Prime of Her Life":

> In the prime of her life my mother died. Some one and thirty years of age my mother was at her death. Few and evil were the days of the years of her life. All the day she sat at home, and she never went out of the house. . . . Silent stood our house in its sorrow; its doors opened not to a stranger. Upon her bed my mother lay, and her words were few.

The words are almost the same as those that Agnon wrote to me about my mother: "She stood upon the doorstep, and her words were few."

As for me, when many years later I wrote an essay called "Who Has Come?" about the opening of Agnon's "In the Prime of Her Life," I dwelled on the apparently tautological sentence "All the day she sat at home, and she never went out of the house."

My mother did not sit at home all the day. She went out of the house a fair amount. But the days of the years of her life, too, were few and evil.

"The years of her life?" Sometimes I hear in these words the duality of my mother's life, and that of Lea, the mother of Tirzah, and that of Tirzah Mazal, née Minz. As if they too cast more than one shadow on the wall.

Some years later, when the General Assembly of Kibbutz Hulda sent me to the university to study literature, because the kibbutz school needed a literature teacher, I summoned up my courage and rang Mr. Agnon's doorbell one day (or in Agnon's language: "I took my heart and went to him").

"But Agnon is not at home," Mrs. Agnon said politely but angrily, the way she answered the throngs of brigands and highwaymen who came to rob her husband of his precious time. Mistress Agnon was not exactly lying to me: Mr. Agnon was indeed not at home, he was out at the back of the house, in the garden, whence he suddenly emerged, wearing slippers and a sleeveless pullover, greeted me, and then asked suspiciously, But who are you, sir? I gave my name and those of my parents, at which, as we stood in the doorway of his house (Mrs. Agnon having disappeared indoors without a word), Mr. Agnon remembered what wagging tongues had said in Jerusalem some years before, and placing his hand on my shoulder he said to me, "Aren't you the child who, having been left an orphan by his poor mother and distanced himself from his father, went off to live the life of the kibbutz? Are you not he who in his youth was reprimanded by his parents in this very house, because he used to pick the raisins off the cake?" (I did not remember this, nor did I believe him about the raisin picking, but I chose not to contradict him.) Mr. Agnon invited me in and questioned me for a while about my doings in the kibbutz, my studies (And what are they reading of mine in the university these days? And which of my books do you prefer?), and also inquired whom I had married and where my wife's family came from, and when I told him that on her father's side she was descended from the seventeenth-century Talmudist and qabbalist Isaiah Horowitz, his eyes lit up and he told me two or three tales, by which time his patience was exhausted and it was evident that he was looking for a way of getting rid of me, but I summoned up my courage, even though I was sitting there on tiptoe, precisely as my mother had done before me, and told him what my problem was.

I had come because Professor Gershom Shaked had given his first-year students in Hebrew literature the task of comparing the stories set in Jaffa by Brenner and by Agnon, and I had read the stories and also everything I could find in the library about their friendship in Jaffa in the days of the Second Aliyah, and I was amazed that two such different men could have become friends. Yosef Haim Brenner was a bitter, moody, thickset, sloppy, irascible Russian Jew, a Dostoevskian soul constantly oscillating between enthusiasm and depression, between compassion and rage, a figure who at that time was already installed at the center of modern Hebrew literature and at the heart of the pioneering movement, while Agnon was then (only) a shy young Galician, several years Brenner's junior and still almost a literary virgin, a pioneer turned clerk, a refined, discriminating Talmud student, a natty dresser and a careful, precise writer, a thin, dreamy, yet sarcastic young man: what on earth could have drawn them so close to each other in the Jaffa of the days of the Second Aliyah, before the outbreak of the First World War, that they were almost like a pair of lovers? Today I think that I can guess something of the answer, but that day in Agnon's house, innocent as I was, I explained to my host the task I had been set, and innocently inquired if he would tell me the secret of his closeness to Brenner.

Mr. Agnon screwed up his eyes and looked at me, or rather scrutinized me, for a while with a sidelong glance, with pleasure, and a slight smile, the sort of smile — I later understood — that a butterfly catcher might smile on spotting a cute little butterfly. When he had finished eyeing me, he said:

"Between Yosef Haim, may God avenge his death, and me in those days there was a closeness founded on a shared love."

I pricked up my ears, in the belief that I was about to be told a secret to end all secrets, that I was about to learn of some spicy, concealed love story on which I could publish a sensational article and make myself a household name overnight in the world of Hebrew literary research.

"And who was that shared love?" I asked with youthful innocence and a pounding heart.

"That is a strict secret," Mr. Agnon smiled, not to me but to himself, and almost winked to himself as he smiled, "yes, a strict secret, that I shall reveal to you only if you give me your word never to tell another living soul."

I was so excited that I lost my voice, fool that I was, and could only mouth a promise.

"Well then, strictly between ourselves I can tell you that when we were living in Jaffa in those days, Yosef Haim and I were both madly in love with Samuel Yosef Agnon."

Yes, indeed: Agnonic irony, a self-mocking irony that bit its owner at the same time as it bit his simple visitor, who had come to tug at his host's sleeve. And yet there was also a grain of truth hidden here, a vague hint of the secret of the attraction of a very physical, passionate man to a thin, spoiled youth, and also of the refined Galician youth to the venerated, fiery man who might take him under his fatherly wing, or offer him an elder brother's shoulder.

Yet it was actually not a shared love but a shared hatred that unites Agnon's stories to Brenner's. Everything that was false, rhetorical, or swollen by self-importance in the world of the Second Aliyah (the wave of immigration that ended with World War I), everything mendacious or self-glorifying in the Zionist reality, all the cozy, sanctimonious, bourgeois self-indulgence in Jewish life at that time, was loathed in equal measure by Agnon as by Brenner. Brenner in his writing smashed them with the hammer of his wrath, while Agnon pricked the lies and pretenses with his sharp irony and released the fetid hot air that inflated them.

Nonetheless, in Brenner's Jaffa as in Agnon's, among the throngs of shams and prattlers there shine dimly the occasional figures of a few simple men of truth.

Agnon himself was an observant Jew who kept the Sabbath and wore a skullcap; he was, literally, a God-fearing man: in Hebrew, "fear" and "faith" are synonyms. There are corners in Agnon's stories where, in an indirect, cleverly camouflaged way, the fear of God is portrayed as a terrible dread of God: Agnon believes in God and fears him, but he does not love him. "I am an easygoing sort of a man," says Daniel Bach in *A Guest for the Night,* "and I do not believe that the Almighty desires the good of his creatures." This is a paradoxical, tragic, and even desperate theological position that Agnon never expressed discursively but allowed to be voiced by secondary characters in his works and to be implied by what befalls his heroes. When I wrote a book on Agnon, *The Silence of Heaven: Agnon's Fear of God,* exploring this theme, dozens of religious Jews, most of them from the ultra-Orthodox sector, including youngsters and women and even religious teachers and functionaries, wrote personal letters to me. Some of these letters were veritable confessions. They told me, in their various ways, that they could see in their own souls what I had seen in Agnon. But what I had seen in Agnon's writings I had also glimpsed, for a moment or two, in Mr. Agnon himself, in that sardonic cynicism of his that verged almost on desperate, jesting nihilism. "The Lord will no doubt have mercy on me," he said once, with reference to one of his constant complaints about the bus service, "and if the Lord does not have mercy on me, maybe the Neighborhood Council will, but I fear that the bus cooperative is stronger than both."

I made the pilgrimage to Talpiot two or three more times during the two years I studied at the university in Jerusalem. My first stories were being published then in the weekend supplement of *Davar* and in the quarterly *Keshet,* and I planned to leave them with Mr. Agnon to hear what he thought of them; but Mr. Agnon apologized, saying, "I regret that I do not feel up to reading these days," and asked me to bring them back another day. Another day, then, I returned, empty-handed but carrying on my belly, like an embarrassing pregnancy, the number of *Keshet* containing my story. In the end I lacked the courage to give birth there, I was afraid of making a nuisance of myself, and I left his house as I had arrived, with a big belly. Or a bulging sweater. It was only some years later, when the stories were collected in a book (*Where the Jackals Howl* in 1965), that I summoned up the courage to send it to him. For three days and three nights I danced around the kibbutz, drunk with joy, silently singing and roaring aloud with happiness, inwardly roaring and weeping, after receiving Mr. Agnon's nice letter, in which he wrote, *inter alia,* ". . . and when we meet, I shall tell you *viva voce* more than I have written here. During Passover I shall read the rest of the stories, God willing, because I enjoy stories like yours where the heroes appear in the full reality of their being."

Once, when I was at the university, an article appeared in a foreign journal by one of the leading lights in comparative literature (perhaps it was by the Swiss Emil Steiger?), who gave it as his opinion that the three most important Central European writers of the first half of the twentieth century were Thomas Mann, Robert Musil, and S. Y. Agnon. The article was written several years before Agnon won the Nobel Prize, and I was so excited that I stole the journal from the reading room (there were no photocopiers at the university in those days) and hurried with it to Talpiot to give Agnon the pleasure of reading it. And he was indeed pleased, so much so that he wolfed down the whole article as he stood on the doorstep of his house, in a single breath, before so much as asking me in; after reading it, rereading it, and perhaps even licking his lips, he gave me that look he sometimes gave me and asked innocently: "Do you also think Thomas Mann is such an important writer?"

One night, years later, I missed the last bus back from Rehovot to the kibbutz at Hulda and had to take a taxi. All day long the radio had been talking about the Nobel Prize that had been shared between Agnon and the poet Nelly Sachs, and the taxi driver asked me if I'd ever heard of a writer called, what was it, Egnon. "Think about it," he said in amazement. "We've never heard of him before, and suddenly he gets us into the world finals. Problem is, he ends up tying with some woman."

For several years I endeavored to free myself from Agnon's shadow. I struggled to distance my writing from his influence, his dense, ornamented, sometimes Philistine language, his measured rhythms, a certain midrashic self-satisfaction, a beat of Yiddish tunes, juicy ripples of Hasidic tales. I had to liberate myself from the influence of his sarcasm and wit, his baroque symbolism, his enigmatic labyrinthine games, his double meanings, and his complicated, erudite literary games.

Despite all my efforts to free myself from him, what I have learned from Agnon no doubt still resonates in my writing.

What is it, in fact, that I learned from him?

Perhaps this. To cast more than one shadow. Not to pick the raisins from the cake. To rein in and polish pain. And one other thing, that my grandmother used to say in a sharper way than I have found it expressed by Agnon. "If you have no more tears left to weep, then don't weep. Laugh."

[NDL]

Aharon Shabtai

(b. 1939)

The enfant terrible of contemporary Israeli poetry, Aharon Shabtai is not
only one of the most visible, inventive, and disturbing writers in the country,
he is also, as American poet C. K. Williams has put it, "one of the most exciting
poets writing anywhere, and certainly the most audacious." Over the course
of a career that began in the mid-1960s with the publication of the objectivist-
realist *Teachers' Room,* Shabtai has been a protean poet who reinvented
himself every few volumes (he has seventeen to date), as the circumstances
before and around him altered.

The height of Shabtai's objectivism was reached with two book-length
poems from the mid-1970s, *Kibbutz* and *The Domestic Poem,* which took
laconic inventory of the poet's surroundings. Ten years later, in *Love,* Shabtai
(who is the younger brother of Ya'aqov, the novelist) erupted in a dithyrambic
dismantlement of that domestic-objectivist self, as the violent return of a
repressed passion led to a transformative moment of self-recognition and
the most sexually explicit and ribald work in the history of modern Hebrew
poetry. After the election of Benjamin Netanyahu as prime minister of Israel
in 1996, and in the wake of the curfews, lynchings, sieges, bus bombs, road-
side ambushes, and extrajudicial executions of the second Intifada, Shabtai
risked what he called poetic suicide: seeking the recovery of the moral
perspective in poetry—in the face of a public discourse that, as he saw it,

created numbness and de-moralization—he began addressing the events of the day directly and in immediate fashion. The results were, astonishingly, printed in the country's daily paper of record—*Ha'aretz*—every few week-ends (the equivalent of their being featured on a regular basis in the *New York Times Book Review*). Angry letters to the editor and threats of canceled subscriptions followed (though the paper's editors were not swayed), and today Shabtai is, it's safe to say, one of the more notorious and even reviled figures in the mainstream world of Israeli literary culture, even as respect for his work increases exponentially abroad.

Behind all of Shabtai's changes—from the early avant-garde objectivist poems through his mid-1980s midrashic paean to right-wing leader Menahem Begin and onto his smut-ridden sonnets of the 1990s and the jeremiads of the past ten years—there lies a deep and abiding sense of ethos, of right relation to and within the fabric of words and work and the world. Shabtai is Israel's preeminent translator of Greek drama and has rendered into Hebrew virtually its entire corpus as well as large selections of Pindar, Hesiod, and the lyric poets. Drawing in profound fashion on that Greek literature he has lived with for many years, he has followed out the Hesiodic directive, which sees the poet's role in the simplest of terms: to praise and to scorn.

The Good Poem, the Good Poet: Some Notes for a Talk

1. As is customary on occasions like this one, I've drawn up a few notes about myself as a writer. It may well be that what seemed right and appropriate to me last night, as I prepared, might not seem so tonight. On the one hand I'm consistent and conscientious; on the other I'm always a kind of medium. But this is a quality that's good for poetry, and good for one as a poet — the capacity for change.

2. There's a difference between writing a good poem and being a poet.
   It's possible to learn how to write a good poem. There are models,
   and one can work out variations on them within a certain range.
   But to be a poet is something else and altogether different. Keats
   called it negative capability. I call it the cultivation of continuity. To
   continue, to establish continuity, means to always make and say
   something different.

3. And that isn't necessarily pleasant. On the one hand I love poetry,
   and over the course of many years it has become an essential part
   of me. So it's clear that I'm expected to play a certain role, and
   I understand when they tell me: "Behave yourself, show a little
   respect!" But the fact is that I'm not "respectable" — I'm notorious.
   The audience is thirsty for respectability, for legitimacy, for cultural authority, all the more so here in Israel, in a place where the
   absence of legitimacy and respect are so glaring. But now, facing an
   audience grown so accustomed to being obedient, and docile, one
   wants to say, of all things, something annoying and critical, to get
   under the skin of what's respectable and, yes, enjoy the vulgarity of
   it and be a little wild. Scandalous behavior has characterized the
   lyric since the days of the Dionysian *komos* (the archaic revel), and
   the iambic poems of Archilochus and Hipponax. *Iambizein* means,
   in Greek, to rebuke, to mock. The ethical function of poetry is to
   praise and approve, and so to scorn and negate. This is particularly
   conspicuous in the first two books of the *Iliad* — that it's impossible
   to praise without scorn and negation. In *King Lear,* there's a scene
   that's full of abuse, and also in *Troilus and Cressida.*

4. Poetry appeals as a product to which importance accrues. As a kind
   of boredom that bears prestige. It easily finds itself flattering an
   audience thirsty for the respectable. The demand for it is fixed, as
   an ideological given, especially when literature is written and mar-
   keted as part of a state-sponsored project of moral disregard and
   denial. It serves as a kind of hothouse (or separation wall), under
   the aegis of which it's possible to adorn oneself with a feeling of
   spiritual cleanliness. The absurd slaughter of World War I, the
   patriotism of the herd, the obtuseness, the obsequiousness of the

intellectual class, formed the background to the scandals staged during the time of Tristan Tzara and the Dadaists, to Mayakovsky's provocations, to the antipoems of Nicanor Parra.

5. As I see it, the situation here is similar today, having experienced several glorious years of "the war on terror." But in the past as well, in better times, I preferred the critical sense, humor, an idiotic simplemindedness, hyperbole, everything that was alien to "poetry" and removed the quotation marks around it. A poet first of all has to know how to stop being a poet, to go out into the street, to look at the cars, to understand that a poem in reality isn't important, that it's hypocritical to overvalue verse. Because poetry is first of all that going out, freedom, a radical gesture, as Raymond Queneau observed: "it's always something extreme / a poem." And this touches upon the difference between writing a good poem and being a poet.

6. A poet thinks, and changes, and the poem is a gesture in the direction of that change. The poem resides in that movement. It never ends; one always has to reread it, over and over, because that gesture is an answer to the ongoing need for ethical orientation (to distinguish, to decide, to move, to oppose).

7. Therefore the dynamic components of a poem are deceptive. Critics, teachers, and leaders of workshops often have trouble identifying them. It would seem, at first, that it's sufficient to choose one's words with care. This is an element that draws attention to itself. People fall in love with the words of the poem and its images, as though they were walking across a solid floor of words. But more important still are the words one *doesn't* choose. This is how gaps are formed in a poem. In the gaps between the words, which can't be guessed at, the poem takes on its character, moves, is interrupted, is saved from infatuation with its own reflection, encounters something else, receives feedback, finds otherness, absorbs critique. It navigates along these gaps and spaces, passes from one thing to another, and from one register to another. By means of these gaps the pitch is created by which what's said ascends or slides (the topography, dynamism). This also touches on

rhythm, which is the moment of life, the physical-gymnastic distinction of the poem that moves and assumes weight and authenticity by means of the timing (of each word) and within time.

8. Another important factor is appropriate dimension, or size and sense of proportion. A poem has a given size or dimension, and only within that size is it true. It's the same as with drawing and architecture. The modest airport in Cairo is built to the right proportions, likewise Schiphol Airport near Amsterdam. It's huge, granted, but entirely functional and teeming with life. The new Ben Gurion 2000 Airport near Tel Aviv (which bears the name of Israel's first prime minister) has no sense of size or proportion, and in this respect the poem I wrote about it speaks not only about the state that built it as a monument, but also about the use of hyperbole in poetry. The core of the poem is a spinelike proportional structure that appears as a vertical column of words at the start of each line: "Lord, / what a / corridor / of marble, / stone / and glass, / so high / and empty, / on the way / toward / the suitcases." The multiple repetitions in each line (see below) express the arrogance and presumption of the monument, the nouveau-riche cult of marble, glass, enormity, etc. On the other hand, on the level of poetry there's an inverse emphasis. The essential core was composed as a kind of ars poetica, along the lines of William Carlos Williams's well-known "So much depends / upon // a red wheel / barrow // glazed with rain / water // beside the white / chickens." These poetics (which have become conservative) are opened up in the poem about the new airport through a kind of Dadaistic or Gertrude Stein–like hyperbole. The poem isn't just an illustration (of the inflated and aggressive structure) but also an act that liberates the words from the burden of the ideological structure that has been imposed on them.

THE NEW BEN GURION AIRPORT

Lord Lord Lord Lord Lord Lord Lord Lord Lord
What a what a what a what a what a what a what a
corridor corridor corridor corridor corridor corridor
of marble marble marble marble marble marble marble

stone stone stone stone stone stone stone stone stone
and glass glass glass glass glass glass glass glass glass
so high high high high high high high high high
and empty empty empty empty empty empty empty
on the way the way the way the way the way the way
toward toward toward toward toward toward toward
the suitcases suitcases suitcases suitcases suitcases.

9. In terms of thought, the syntax (composition) is, as I see it, the
   most important element within the array of linguistic materials.
   What leads people astray and deceives, in a political sense, isn't
   exactly the (fraudulent, laundered) words that are chosen, but
   above all the *syntaxis,* the composition, the conception that links
   the facts. I'm sensitive first of all to composition. When the syntax
   is working, when there's composition and conception, there's a
   poem. But composition of course is linked in the wider sense to an
   understanding of the real. In order to compose, to put together, a
   poet has to possess a sound understanding of the links between
   things, between facts — emotional and ethical facts, the facts
   around him and in the world. Therefore he has to have the ability
   to judge, to form an opinion, to think, to argue and articulate a
   position. If you're obedient, you won't understand a thing; you'll
   understand only what you're supposed to understand, like a student
   in a classroom with windows along just a single wall. In order to
   understand and argue (to compose things, to draw conclusions),
   one has to have the ability to dismantle definitions, the walls and
   categories that have been constructed, and are being constructed,
   all around us as obstacles (or roadblocks), as containers of identity
   and conceptions.

10. It's possible to sum up what I've tried to say with this point: As I
    see it, the most important characteristic in poetry is the utterance,
    the argument. When I read a poem I look first of all for what is
    being claimed, for the *logos.* And this is the source of the resistance,
    of the negative capability I mentioned earlier. What is asked of us
    is that we become obedient, that we take up what is acceptable,
    that we stop thinking, which is to say, not argue. This, after all, is

the subject of Socrates' apology. He too would certainly agree that
the poet is he, or she, who possesses the *logos*.

FEBRUARY 2007

I'VE ALWAYS MISSED OUT

I've always missed out on the prettiest girls;
only after they've screwed in every hole and position
do they come to me for help with their poems, or a lesson,
and I tell them of Phoinix, whose lips dripped pearls

of wisdom and how, in exchange for the knowledge, he'd usually
get a comfortable bed with sheets of lambskin and, if he were lucky,
hear, in an adjacent tent — Patroklos
making love with Iphis, and Diomede with Akhilleus.

So I won't get to sleep with the prettiest girls.
I'll fix their lines, put up with their stupid chatter,
and, late at night, comfort myself as I stick my finger

into my rear then pull it out and know, lifting it up to my nose,
that the biggest, blackest, and totally most mysterious
dick in the world is lying here in this bed writing my poems.

1994

THE REASON TO LIVE HERE

This country is turning into the private estate of twenty families.

Look at its fattened political arm, at the thick neck of its bloated
    bureaucracy:
these are the officers of Samaria.

There's no need to consult the oracle:
What the capitalist swine leaves behind, the nationalist hyena
    shreds with its teeth.

When the Governor of the Bank of Israel raises the interest-rate
    by half-a-percent,
the rich are provided with backyard pools by the poor.

The soldier at the outpost guards the usurer, who'll put a lien
    on his home
when he's laid off from the privatized factory and falls behind on
    his mortgage payments.

The pure words I suckled from my mother's breasts: Man, Child,
    Justice, Mercy, and so on,
are dispossessed before our eyes, imprisoned in ghettos, murdered
    at checkpoints.

And yet, there's still good reason to stay on and live here —
to hide the surviving words in the kitchen, in the basement, or the
    bathroom.

The prophet Melampus saved twin orphaned snakes from the hand
    of his slaves:
they slithered toward his bed while he slept, then licked the auricles
    of his ears.
When he woke with a fright, he found he could follow the speech
    of birds —

so Hebrew delivered will lick the walls of our hearts.

1998

[PC]

Meir Wieseltier

(b. 1941)

A brutal observer of his society and its dominant myths, Meir Wieseltier
came into prominence very early in his writing career with several collections
of poetry that immediately established him as the leading figure of what
would come to be informally known as the Tel Aviv school of poets (which
included, among others, Yona Wallach). At its ironic best, Wieseltier's work
takes the reader into the dark heart of that city's life and landscapes—as its
peeling plaster and seamy sweatshops open onto the "dull khaki light" of the
country's larger cultural prospect. That wide-angle view is the subject of his
searing political poems of the 1970s and '80s, which examine both the militar-
ism that came to characterize Israeli society and the price the country has paid
for it. Asked once by a group of American college students why he wrote
about politics in his poems, Wieseltier answered: "That's like asking a Greek
poet who lives on an island why he writes about the wind."

Born in Moscow just before the German invasion of Russia, Wieseltier,
while still an infant, was taken by his mother and older sisters to southwestern
Siberia. His father was killed while serving in the Red Army in Leningrad. The
family spent two years in Poland, Germany, and France before emigrating to
Israel. Wieseltier has lived in Tel Aviv since 1955.

In addition to his numerous volumes of poetry, Wieseltier has published
Hebrew translations of four Shakespeare tragedies and novels by Virginia
Woolf, Charles Dickens, E. M. Forster, and Malcolm Lowry.

A Word on Rhyming

When you come to rhyme, consider the tree-tops.
The tree-tops are not the forest;
the forest is bound by earth, the cold roots
underground, moving boulders, the trunk
bearing branches and leaves, the winds
wafting pollen.
The forest is insects,
lichen, rodents, mushrooms, parasites,
climbing vines, birds,
the sky above — the tree-top
is only a sign for the eye
to stop, instruction for the neck's movement.
It's soft or sharp,
evident or evanescent,
pliable or resistant —
the lone tree's dome is recorded in memory,
though in the forest it is nothing but
a sign of modesty on high.

1986

Untitled

And again I write
what you won't want to read,
or can't. Not due to obscurity
or excessive length,
but — because of a refusal
to knock materials together and listen
to their sounds and hear, to lay
things down and consider
their inner wisdom and its results
because of the structure that overturns and stretches
from what *is* toward its defeat in time.

1981

UNTITLED

From a deep sleep I wake with a love of words.
Unexpectedly, an old love awakens to smooth
a wrinkle in memory.

And in my haste I've already said:
the form became matter, the spirit flesh.

And the flesh is trapped —
biology:
history:
a plot, then death.

1981

[RTB]

UNTITLED

The believer in what words can do
believes in what they did to him. He who has climbed
steep wordy slopes
to the top of a cliff or descended
into dark caverns while
clutching their brittle projections
and imagining he'd find in their crevices
a mystic illumination,
the face of God, or hear
voices of the dead or voices
of the not-yet-born,
stands on the embers of words
and is silent.

2000

[SK]

Yona Wallach

(1944–1985)

Yona Wallach is Hebrew's quintessential Dionysian poet, a demonic writer who, as Aharon Shabtai put it, introduced into Hebrew the language of the self and its manic dismemberment. "She shattered the scarecrow of the I," wrote Shabtai, "as a self-contained object whose contents and qualities precede language." In Wallach's poetry the self pummeled by psychosis, drugs, and the burden of a singular sensibility splinters into discrete characters and shifts from gender to gender. An Artaud-like specter of instability and mental illness (which plagued her throughout her life) hovered over all she did, as though she were an actress in his "theater of cruelty."

Wallach was born in Israel and never once left it before her death, from cancer, at age forty-one. Within a short time, however, she exerted a powerful influence on the language and its literature, and one that has lasted in the work of her successors. Brash and unabashed, Wallach often went beyond the blasphemous in her efforts to seek untapped sources of poetic power: in one of her most famous poems she employs ritual phylacteries (*tefillin*)— the black straps in which Jewish men wrap their arms and forehead as part of the weekday morning prayer—as an S&M-like sexual aid. In a sense, the religiously transgressive Wallach did with (the masculine culture's) Hebrew what she did with the phylacteries of male devotion. The often-wounded figures of her poems, with their strangely Christian names and surrealist fantasies, ride the edge of coherence and take Hebrew verse to a place it had never been before.

The interview from which excerpts follow was conducted by Helit Yeshurun in the hospital, not long before Wallach died.

I'VE DEVELOPED TECHNIQUES

What has changed in you, Yona?

I've developed techniques. Once material would slip through my fingers. Today, I know how to analyze it before I write. Things I once thought inappropriate for poetry, things I didn't know how to exploit, or that I thought had no point, things here in the hospital with the nurses, I can turn into material for poetry [. . .] into gold, and that's as it should be, too, since that's my experience. And other doors opened before me. [. . .] Besides that, I change tenses. That's one of the techniques I've found here recently. I write in the future tense, not the present or the past. A kind of language that's time, somehow an imagined time.

What brought this about?

Less fear. Fewer secrets. More knowledge. More time. I'm more open today to discover life, I have a much greater ability to give. Once, I was sunk in a paranoia where it seemed that people were always stealing from me and being influenced by me. I got over it — that "it's mine." What stinginess! Who sewed what you're wearing? Stand up for a minute. Let's see.

What is the most important thing to you in writing?

To write. [. . .]

Do you distinguish between feminine poetry and masculine poetry? Something that distinguishes poetry by a woman?

It's a totally different world. A woman poet will examine the difference between herself and a man, and she'll write as a woman. Where I see pink, a man sees blue. The optics are different. But a man and a woman look the same. Grow a man's hair, dye it, put makeup on him, you'll turn him into a very, very delicate person; turn a woman into a strong person, remove all her complexes, you'll see that what distinguishes them is tits, a penis, and a womb. It isn't such a big difference. But there is a difference. A woman creates life, a man creates sex. That's a big difference.

Does that find expression in poetry also?

I would think so. A woman is much more life itself. A man can't reach that same sort of creation of life that a woman can.

Most of the great poets were men.

They were mostly feminine. Most were homosexual. From a genetic standpoint, they were women; most of the great artists were women, not men at all. What I'm saying is pretty strong, and aggressive, isn't it?

You have a powerful need to create theories around every subject, and you hold to them tenaciously and with a kind of finality. Is there anything that you're not sure about?

I like the word *tenaciously.* I don't like the word *finality.* The word *finality* arouses a certain antagonism, no?

Not necessarily; it's part of your annoying charm. Why is it so important to you?

It's absolutely necessary to create theories around everything. Without that, you won't know anything, you won't know where you are, you won't have any direction at all. Otherwise, you'll be completely scattered and won't be able to defend your opinions. It's power. It's knowledge. It strengthens you. Otherwise, you won't know anything about your life. If you don't deal with phenomenology and don't create theories and define things, you won't have any continuum of knowledge — you'll be like a plane flying in the sky without a navigator or with a drunken pilot. You have to know where you are, precisely, point by point. That's the continuum of existence. You also have to defend yourself before someone confuses you. You have to land the first blow, always, otherwise catastrophes happen, and you become disoriented emotionally. I worked for years and lived with a very severe sense of persecution. Casting doubt is part of the technique — until you know something. Still, I'd prefer to have fewer doubts than I have.

What is your relationship to women poets?

Dahlia Ravikovitch doesn't deal enough with sex. She's not revolutionary enough. She doesn't pay attention to how differently she writes from me. She isn't a feminist.

Have you felt a need to fight for feminism?

I struggle for my life daily. I've never been enough of a woman. I was always half a boy. I had to dress like a boy, and act like a boy.

You had to or you wanted to?

I didn't want to. It was forced on me. Without my sensing it. It's the need to identify with something much stronger than I was, in my female surroundings. I learned like every woman to hate women, to hate weakness and to love men, to be half a boy, and it ruined my life. For everyone.

And the way out of that?

The way out of it is to love it, to remain a woman and not deny everything you are and not be half a penis. Why shouldn't I beat my breast now? I have the right to reveal the truth about myself at any moment.

The figure of the doe returns from time to time in your poems — "the monster doe," and not long ago "a doe, what do I have to do with her?" Who is the doe?

The doe comprises states of consciousness. It's an image of consciousness and not identity. It's a moment of life, or recurrent situations. An image of a state of consciousness and of a dream. It isn't me, at most it's me at that moment. My reincarnation at that moment. These things happen. For a moment I was a doe, once I was a lamb, and sometimes I'm a tree trunk — with a head above it and a pink ribbon. The brain sends pictures of the state of things about how you are. I love those animals. [. . .]

How did you see the Hebrew poetry and literature in which you were raised?

First of all, I hated Hebrew poetry and literature. It seemed to me to be one big fraud. I loved Baudelaire and Walt Whitman. It seems to me that Hebrew poetry missed the point. Also because they hid everything from us. They didn't speak to us about Brenner like that, they didn't talk about suffering. They spoke to us about plump and self-satisfied Bialik whom the whole nation admired, but they didn't speak to us about madness. Everything was self-satisfied, everything was national. [. . .] I hated Shlonsky and Alterman and all that poetry. I hated Amichai, I was afraid he would steal from me.

Bialik as plump and pleased with himself—that's a charge you could level at the curriculum, but what kept you from reading on your own?

It bothered me that I didn't understand what a work was, and I didn't understand what it grew from, it bothered me that I didn't understand what this reality was at all. It bothered me that only at age twenty did I begin to understand that the work is reality itself, and that reality is the source of the work and the need to solve the problems of ourselves — that's what bothered me, that only at age twenty did I discover reality and start to take up the banner, that the work is life itself. All that I'd read was disconnected from life. Only later did I begin to understand how close Bialik was to life, but what I was taught in high school wasn't close to my life, and I didn't learn anything from it about my life. That's what was so urgent for me — to understand my life. Literature should help us understand our lives, and instead it turned out to be a traitor, addressing the needs of the nation and skipping over everything personal and private. They hid all the life stories of the artists and the extraordinary people in this country who sacrificed their lives for the human experience, not for the national experience. Later, I began to study art and met people who were like me, people who answered my deepest, emotional needs — to explore existence, to find the secrets of existence.

APRIL 1984

[LZ]

Anton Shammas

(b. 1950)

The wild card in the deck of Hebrew literature, Anton Shammas has
employed a kind of Joycean cunning and exile, if not quite silence, in
achieving a leverage within the language that hasn't been matched by
any other contemporary Israeli writer. Born and raised in the northern
Galilee village of Fassuta, Shammas moved with his family to Haifa in the
early 1960s. He studied art history and both Arabic and English literature
at the Hebrew University in Jerusalem, then published several volumes of
poetry (in Arabic and Hebrew) as a young man while also editing an
important Arabic-language literary journal. He began translating works of
Palestinian literature into Hebrew, and Hebrew works into Arabic, and was
also an active participant in the more general Israeli cultural conversation.

In 1986 Shammas published to considerable acclaim what is to date his
only novel, *Arabesques.* Written in an accomplished and resonant Hebrew, the
book smuggles into the language a quietly subversive portrait of Palestinian
village life, as it examines the role of exile in the developing consciousness of
one unusual (yet somehow representative) writer, whose name in this fiction is
Anton Shammas. With the publication of the English translation of the book
in 1988, Shammas became a prominent figure on the international intellectual
scene, writing frequently for the *New York Review of Books* and engaging
in spirited debate with leading figures in the Jewish world, including Cynthia

Ozick and A. B. Yehoshua (the fire in whose famous story "Facing the Forests" Shammas alludes to at the start of the piece that follows). The essential irritation at the heart of that debate was Shammas's decision to write in what he calls his "stepmother tongue" and thereby de-Judaize Hebrew—the official language of the state. By writing with such force in Hebrew, Shammas was also able to tilt the national screaming match around his best-selling book toward the question of what it means to be Israeli and whether or not Israel might ever be, truly, "a state of all its citizens." Also contributing throughout this time to Shammas's effectiveness as a destabilizing voice were his masterful Hebrew versions of important works of Palestinian literature, the riches of which were, and remain, little known to the Jewish majority of the country's reading public. His translations of the fiction of Emile Habiby, in particular, were major contributions to Hebrew culture, and he also introduced the poetry of Taha Muhammad Ali to both the Arabic and the Hebrew literary communities.

In the moving 1984 essay "The Meeting That Was, the Meeting That Wasn't"—a work that, in a private communication, the writer has said no longer represents his views ("the context has been so radically reconfigured that I have abandoned all hope," he said, "in the most Dantesque sense")— Shammas looks at the role of the two literatures at the heart of his writing life, Arabic and Hebrew, and the chances of their ever coming together. Since 1987 Shammas has taught at the University of Michigan.

The Meeting That Was, the Meeting That Wasn't

I've begun the writing of what will follow in a small village in the Taunus Mountains, in Germany, facing a forest that has been stricken with a mysterious blight, as happens with forests, a blight that threatens to wipe it out (as it says in the Passover hymn). The forest before me is wrapped in a cold and rainy morning's fog; I imagine an old Arab whose tongue has been cut out, on the first floor, sitting and thinking (Arabs always think while sitting) of the great fire. As a poet once put it: "For a long time now I've resisted owning up to myself. / I sit. And walk. And stand. And each is a lonely act."

I'm thinking, while sitting, as the Arabs do: *owning up to myself* — which means defining that area of intersecting circles within my bilingual being, that no-man's-land between Arabic literature, or culture, and Hebrew literature, or culture (I am not using, for now, the term Israeli), and I'm thinking: Am I, in my owning up to myself, contributing something to Hebrew literature — or Israeli literature? Or, alternatively, and indirectly, to Arabic literature? And if you add the dimension of the Other, the German, you'll be able to fathom, if only barely, the nature of that no-man's-land: An Arab, whose step-mother tongue is Hebrew, sits in Germany and writes about "Arabic literature, the view from within, and Hebrew literature, with Arab eyes — and the points of meeting between them," if there are any. On the plane, an Australian woman, next to whom an Australian rabbi had refused to sit — so I was called to the rescue — tells me that from my nose and the sad look in my eyes, she'd been certain that I was a Jew. And now, I'm no longer sure which look I'll use when I turn to these two literatures.

In the village we had a bookcase, set within a thick wall, its doors the color of the green olive. It was always locked. My mother used to put the key in the same pink glass plate she served baked goods in, things she'd made with her own two hands, which she would offer to guests. The plate was hidden in the clothes closet, behind the mirror. The mirrored door was also locked, and where the key was hidden we didn't know. But we had a way of getting through the mirror and to the sweets and the key to the locked-away books, and this by lifting, as it happened, the left corner of the mirror. And so I reached my first books: Lebanese textbooks, literary journals, novels and books of poetry that my mother had brought with her from Lebanon, and a few books in Hebrew, reading material my father had gotten hold of in order to decipher the secrets of the new language that had befallen us, the language of military permits and notifications of liens, of the brand-new world that stretched beyond the horizon of our small village, at once threatening and tempting, closed-off and open. The Lebanese schoolbooks, *al-Mushawaq,* which remain to this day the finest of their kind I've ever encountered, these books contained passages of poetry and prose and many translations from world literature. I knew whole swatches of them by heart, though I didn't understand a word. Passages from a work by the Lebanese writer Amin Nakhleh, *The Village Journal,* cast a particular spell on me. It is, to my mind, the most beautiful book in all of modern Arabic literature. Nakhleh's Arabic constituted a magic formula that combined the thrill of the classical style with the beat of modern times, tight passages of prose about life in the Lebanese village, the fragrance of orchards, the clay jar that broke, and the goat that prayed with tremendous fervor that it not be sent to the slaughterhouse in the big city. Later, when I went to Jerusalem, the big city, I bought this book on the east side of town. I soon discovered, despite the magic that remained, hidden between its lines, the trait that would put me off of most of Egyptian literature, especially that of the early fifties: the feeling that the words had been written from behind the table, that the Beirut effendi who was writing about the pleasure of the village in fact had never set his hand to a plow, as had, for example, the Hebrew poet Esther Raab, who also wrote of working the land.

And there was in that bookcase a volume by the name of *Cadmus,* a poetic drama by the Lebanese writer Sa'id Aqal, about Cadmus the Phoenician, who sets out for Greece to rescue his kidnapped sister, Europa. Arabic like this one doesn't encounter every day. An almost Jabotinskian majesty. In time, that same Sa'id Aqal, who in my youth I'd so admired, appeared on the screen of Israel TV and spoke of the final solution to the Palestinian problem in Lebanon. Also on the shelf was a translated novel, which, later on, I'd reread at least once a year: *My Ántonia,* by Willa Cather; it had been translated in the forties by the Egyptian writer Suhair al-Qalamawi, and told the story of an adolescent boy in the midwestern United States, during the days of the first pioneers, when the land was still covered by the red grass of the prairie. That was the first novel I ever read. When I eventually got to the English original, I still preferred the translation, a wistful homage, perhaps, to those days beside the bookcase, and in honor of the translator's profession, which later still would draw me into Hebrew.

Apart from the Egyptians Naghib Mahfouz and Yusuf Idris, my literary loves have, to this day, remained northern, Levantine. I take greater pleasure in the late-nineteenth-century Arabic translations of the Psalms, which were done in Lebanon, than I do in the works of many "southern" writers. The boy I was, who would take his place in church each morning to participate in the sacred service, would read these translations, and not the works of Taha Hussein. A wise Englishman once said, in the manner of the English, that the further south toward the equator one travels, the fewer the pictures one sees on the walls of homes. I can say that the further south I travel in my reading, the fewer the works of literature I love. The wise, perhaps, will know what I'm missing.

At the beginning of the sixties, leaving the buried bookcase behind, the family moved to Haifa in a kind of procession as though behind the village's coffin. And there I emerged, for the first time, from those perspective-granting furrows that decorated the texts which served my father in his never-ending and, in the final analysis, not particularly Jacob-like struggle with the angel of the Hebrew language. I emerged from those furrows and went out toward the new reality of the new language in the new city. The plow my child's hand had held was exchanged for a heavy tractor that left behind it new and many more furrows. My first serious encounter with Hebrew literature came about when my Hebrew teacher — to whom I owe a serious debt of gratitude to this day for the ongoing mess she got me into — encouraged me to write a final paper (in place of the matriculation exam) on the image of the Arab peasant, or fallah, in pre-State Hebrew literature. And so I discovered the romantic plow of Khawajah Musa (Moshe Smilansky) and Burla and Stavi, and Yitzhaq Shami, who in *The Vengeance of the Fathers* had Arab protagonists from Nablus and Hebron weave the plot some fifty years before the smile of David Grossman's lamb — which was or wasn't. (I mean, of course, the lamb.)

After that I entered Hebrew's chamber of translation. The wealth of translations from world literature into Hebrew left me stunned. The door that opened before me, through the Hebrew language, brought me to regions that would have been blocked before the village child I was. And again, that same spell of translation, of that transfer from language to language, of that perverse pleasure taken in shifting the cultural boundary-line. And here, perhaps, is the place to briefly address this problem of translation, which is, in the end, my principle activity, in the no-man's-land between the two tongues. [. . .]

I come from a culture of words, also in the Greek sense of the term, the *logos.* The Arab in me still feels the power of words. Reality for the Arab consists of words, and words are reality's final word. This is why, I think, classical Arabic dictionaries are arranged alphabetically by word endings, and not by their initial letters. On the other hand, the Christian in me — though my Christianity is a battered and threadbare thing — the Christian in me believes in the sanctity of the *logos,* the sacredness of words. The schizophrenic in me, the person who's writing these words now in Hebrew, knows that my invasion of that language resembles a guest who comes to dinner and who, then, at the end of the meal, you find in the kitchen doing the dishes, with the almost Pinteresque pleasure of someone who could, at any moment, unintentionally break an exquisite bowl. Which is also to say — he might, just might, choose to stay for the night. What is one supposed to do?

Words drive the sleep from my eyes. I prefer to get to them the way one gets to sleep: by counting sheep. Round and round and round. One waits, until the word and its vigilance weaken; and then one attacks, as though with an Indian's arrow.

In the transfer from language to language I usually prefer to pass through English. This passage through a third language accelerates the word and neutralizes its Semitic residue; it grants it the power to free itself from that extra burden. I check the word by returning it to Arabic, via the Arabic translations of the Bible that were done by a marvelous translator in the 1870s, Ibrahim al-Yazji. The copy I have belonged to my father, who used a fine aluminum-foil bookmark he'd made from a pack of cigarettes, so as not to have to fold back the delicate pages, and to keep them from having ears.

My own ears opened to Hebrew literature, increasingly, as over the years I translated Hebrew literary works and entered the language's kitchen, where extraordinary dishes were being concocted, and others were being ruined, and where the threads of the warp and woof were unraveled and rewoven in another tongue, sometimes out of a tangle of threads which could not be undone. There was in this act something of the loneliness of a one-way street: writers with whom I'd been in contact during the course of the translation couldn't understand a single word in the new language that now enveloped their work. One writer threw a fit over the fact that her work in translation ended with an exclamation point, instead of the normal period. Later I realized that I'd sent her a copy of a work by another writer altogether. A. B. Yehoshua once said, apropos Naim, the character in his novel *The Lover,* that for a Hebrew writer to write about a Japanese peasant empathy is enough. He might be right, in his way. But in this context, Yitzhaq Shami's *Vengeance of the Fathers* is very different from Grossman's *Smile of the Lamb.* And if you'd like a specific example, one can imagine that Yitzhaq Shami, who was born in Hebron, knew that the phrase *kan yama kan,* with which traditional Arabic tales begin, does not mean "There was or there wasn't," as Grossman has it, but "There was, oh, how there was . . ." This, it seems, is the difference between the Israeli literature (let us call it) that emerged during the pre-State years and the Hebrew literature that begins, as I see it, with the so-called Palmach generation, or the writers who fought in the '48 War and came of age with the founding of the state. And here, perhaps, I've touched on the first point of the encounter that was missed out on over the years.

The new Hebrew literature draws on the work of Yosef Haim Brenner, the great angry skeptic, the father of "There was or there wasn't," and not on the continuation of the pre-State romantics (Smilansky, Burla, Shami). And perhaps it was only right that the literature deviated from that pre-State line and adopted the Jewish tack. The red grass that covered the endless expanses of the American Midwest in Cather's *My Ántonia* soon gave way to fields of corn. The red grass that covered Palestine, or didn't, was replaced by the pine forest of A. B. Yehoshua's story, or by Pinhas Sadeh's "the red grass burns slowly, the green river forever flows." Today we can speak of American literature, but it's doubtful that we can speak of its Israeli equivalent. Hebrew, or Jewish literature, exists — in the form of works by Brenner, Smilansky, Amos Oz, and Grossman. Israeli literature according to the other model, which saw the red grass and was held in its spell, and sought to preserve it as a whispering flame, this sort of literature does *not* exist, apart perhaps from the work of Sami Michael and Shimon Ballas, and a very few others, who arrived in these precincts from another direction, the East, and not through Smilansky and the members of his generation.

My intention here isn't to judge these two models in terms of their quality, or to defend the Eretz-Israeli (or, if you will, the Palestinian) trend. After all, no one would argue with me that the work of S. Yizhar (Smilansky's nephew) is far more important than that of his uncle, or that the Brenner of Hebrew literature is much more important for his successors than is Yitzhaq Shami. But all of the above is noted in relation to our subject: points of encounter, if there were any. And in this respect I feel closer to the work of David Shahar than I do to that of Ya'aqov Shabtai. I'm inclined to assume that the work of the former is "Israeli," or "Eretz-Israeli," as opposed to the Hebrew-Jewish literature of Shabtai — though Shabtai's work occupies a very special place in my heart as well. Not long ago I spent some time studying a certain winter night in Jerusalem — November of 1917, the eve of Allenby's entrance into the city. Alter Levine, a Jerusalem poet, a wealthy insurance man and an American national, had sought refuge from the Ottoman authorities (the charges against him are not clear) in the home of the writer and educator Khalil al-Sakakini, who would in time become a member of the Arab Higher Committee. Both were exiled to Damascus because of al-Sakakini's having taken his Jewish friend in and both were — at the last minute — spared the hangman's rope. Throughout his life, al-Sakakini kept marvelous journals, which were published posthumously, and they cover nearly half a century of life in Eretz Israel, which is to say, his Palestine, and they are what brought me to study this affair.

Alter Levine, who'd escaped the hangman's rope, would lower it with his own two hands around his neck some sixteen years later. Al-Sakakini, who had a magnificent home on what is now called Yordei HaSira Street in the Jerusalem neighborhood of Qatamon, would die in exile in Cairo in 1953.

From Sakakini's journals, Damascus, Monday, December 24, 1917:

> I have no contact with the prisoners, apart from my brother in distress, in fact the cause of my distress, Khawajah Alter Levine. Despite his broad-mindedness, and our lengthy acquaintance, I do not understand him, nor does he understand me. If not for honor's sake, I would cut off all relations with him. I will, however, not allow myself to resent him, or to show him even the slightest hint of enmity, or let him feel however indirectly that he has brought this trouble upon me. On the contrary, from the day we left Jerusalem I have not kept from him feelings of compassion, as though he were my brother, nor have I wearied of trying to please him and blaming fate for what has befallen us.

And I quote from a letter sent by Levine from Bab al-Jabiyya Prison, in Damascus, around that time:

> I have been stolen away from the land of the Hebrews although I have done not a thing. . . . How great is my grief. But how sweet is this ancient Hebrew sorrow, the suffering of the generations, the eternal grief of our people, for thousands of years.

Alter Levine, as mentioned, would take his own life sixteen years later. Natan Zach once wrote about Ya'aqov Shabtai's *Past Continuous:*

> A writer who can't manage with his world, and that includes a writer conflicted with himself, kills off first and foremost his own protagonists. Only later, and sometimes much later, also himself.

Brenner, of course, was killed by the Arabs. High blood pressure killed Ya'aqov Shabtai. But who is Hebrew literature killing?

It's hard to think of a stranger pair than Khalil al-Sakakini and the Polish-American Alter Levine. Harder still is imagining a fictional encounter between al-Sakakini and Brenner, Amos Oz, David Grossman, and others. It's doubtful that they'd find anything to talk about. Al-Sakakini was, as I see it, and despite his never having written "literary" works, the finest Palestinian writer to date. His journals are perhaps the best evidence of what a writer was capable of writing and did not write, the best evidence for the existence of a point of meeting that was missed out on, a point that "wasn't."

There was, or there wasn't. We live today, it seems, in those same precincts of great doubt, from which there is no going back. And it seems, too, that there are no points where the circles of Hebrew and Arabic literature intersect, the Western orientation of both notwithstanding. If only I were mistaken. The circle of Arabic literature in the Israel of the green line nowhere touches, let alone intersects with, that of Hebrew literature. Arabic literature within that green line is a literature taking its first steps. It's the literature of a minority within a minority within a majority, babushka-style. I love limited parts of it very much, within the bilingual stance I've adopted. And this, sometimes, grieves me. But it seems that my Levantine innocence, in the best sense, has been lost forever. This is an innocent literature that has to be approached from within, and — for the most part — great disappointment awaits those who approach it from without. For it's a literature that is asked to take root without ground, without land. The land, as is well known, was confiscated. So, too, the contours of the landscape. Ishaq Musa al-Husseini, a Jerusalem writer and friend of al-Sakakini, in 1955:

> I accompanied [al-Sakakini] once on a visit, and when we left he said to me: Let's go into the Old City through Damascus Gate. He led me through narrow alleys and steps until we reached the Christian Quarter. He stood beside an old house and said: Look at that room under the eaves, that's the room where I was born. Lord! I can sense the fragrance of the bread rising up from within the cupboard in which my mother would place it. He inhaled deeply. . . . Then my luck changed. I visited him in Cairo after the disaster [of '48], and accompanied him to a café he used to frequent. He was stooped, in body and soul, and suddenly stopped, as though remembering that same walk in Jerusalem. And he said to me: Where is my mother's cupboard, my friend? Where is my home? . . .

Al-Sakakini and al-Husseini wind up at the place where David Shahar begins. The cupboard that's broken, the house that was blown to pieces, could, it seems, be found in Shahar's novel *The Palace of the Shattered Vessels.* But modern Hebrew literature, by and large, is more inclined to deal with the dream and its shattering, at daybreak, than with the shattered vessels. The dream is essentially European, which is dreamed from left to right. It clashed, and clashes still, with the experience of the Levant, which flows, as is known, from right to left. *Will two walk together, without having met?* (Amos 3:3). Perhaps. But it isn't possible if they are not walking in the same direction.

October 1984

[PC]

David Grossman

(b. 1954)

One of contemporary Israel's most popular writers, David Grossman took the Hebrew literary scene by storm with the publication of his 1986 novel, *See Under: Love.* That formally ambitious work, which has since been translated into some thirteen languages, tells the story of Momik, whom we first meet as an earnest nine-year-old child of Holocaust survivors who are traumatized still by the horrors of the war. We encounter him again as an adult who lives in the shadows of his parents' ghosts. In an attempt to wrestle with his demons, Momik takes up writing and produces a series of stories that, together with Grossman's frame story, constitute a sophisticated attempt to grasp the ungraspable and the hellish in what might best be described as "fairy-tale terms." Momik/Grossman dreams his way into the skin of several highly imaginative characters who are tried, and eventually crushed, by the Nazis. In the passage that follows, which is drawn from one of the protagonist's own fictions, Momik attempts to describe the anxiety that attends to writing—both his own, and that of the great Polish-Jewish writer Bruno Schulz, who plays a central role in the book.

In addition to *See Under: Love,* Grossman, who is himself the child of Holocaust survivors, has published eight novels, multiple children's books, and a collection of stories, as well as several important nonfiction works about Palestinian life in the Occupied Territories and Arabs within the borders

of pre-1967 Israel. As a soldier and as a young man, Grossman also worked
as a radio journalist, and he is often turned to today as a spokesman for the
liberal peace camp in Israel.

FROM *SEE UNDER: LOVE*

Now listen.

You mentioned how hard it was for him to laugh, and I'll tell you about
his fears. About the loneliness his character and talent ordained for him.
There was the fear of the bonds of love and friendship, the fear of the abyss
between one minute and the next, and of what he would discover on the
page after it was touched by his magical magnetic pen, which sucked up the
magma of ancient truth, that rose steadily upward through layers of caution
and self-defense — and then he would stop and scream in fear, because what
he had written seemed to come from someone else, and he began to suspect
that he, too, formed the weak link through which irresistible human longings burst forth into the world, and then my Bruno stood up and paced
around the room, taunting himself that he was suffering from megalomania,
and had lost the ability to distinguish between his real life and his stories,
and that through a nyedoenga, like him, a shlimazel, only abstract essences
of preposterous errors and blunders — could possibly —

But he knew, and was afraid. And it drove him to cheat at times: he would
pay social calls, write sentimental letters (he almost believed the sentimentality himself), feign candor, and address acquaintances in the intimate
"thou" form (though he rarely addressed people thus in writing, perhaps
because he couldn't pretend in writing). He agreed to give lectures and occasionally allowed himself to be dragged to parties and fancy balls, where he
would smile awkwardly while he let people get him drunk in order not to dis-
appoint them, and even chuckled when they clapped him jovially on the
shoulder, wearing an attentive expression on his ironic face, as they
explained from experience that to know Despair ("Despair!" they shouted in
his ear, clutching their hearts as he never needed to do because he remembered where it was) and "write with authenticity, like a genuine writer," you

had to commit a little suicide or at least go insane, and in daily life as well, Pan Schulz, you have to come out of your isolation and feel "the pulse of humanity," the "sorrows of life," so don't be such a hermit. Bruno tried his best to be convinced, he really and truly tried to achieve the commonplace despair they prattled about; he struggled to reach it out of the darkness into which he had sunk, if only to escape the eel-like fear that coiled damply around him whenever he looked at what he had written, or wondered what the future held in store. But my Bruno was too honest for the suicide-insanity routine, and he could not dissolve his loneliness in the crowd because he knew the crowd offered no haven from imminent danger. He would have to keep to himself, sit in his chair, abandoning himself to his razor-keen awareness and the two big searchlights — longing and despair — converging in his head, and to bear the mark of Cain on endless wanderings; and he also knew that nowhere except his simple room, at his simple desk, writing in a schoolboy's notebook, would he be able to feel his body tensing on the rack of an inquisition unequaled in cruelty and pleasure, till his flesh and bones were stretched so flat that every ounce of flesh was infinitely diluted in the dimension of distance and dream, and only then, as a single fluttering membrane, would he be able to feel the beating of the big drum at the foundations, the feverish, despairing embrace of savage tongues and putrefying grammars, with no one left to understand them, and helter-skelter Bruno's pen sketches the impressions this secret world has left upon his parchment body, pasting them onto the palpable and visible, and Bruno's stories, his longings and laments for a banished Eden, are wrenched out of him into a frozen secondhand world of exact science, classified language, and tame clock time; see how he droops at his desk, biting his lip, his chin pointed, writing with the same upsurge of violence, frenzy, and obliviousness he knew inside you throughout the daring voyage. See him use his pen to parry the savage apparitions which have not yet fully materialized, evoking ages of genius for one brief moment, taking care never to perforate the thin membrane with his pen, to keep it all from bursting through, and dissolving away, yes dissolving: because the world is not yet ready for the life that flickers beyond Bruno: here life is congealed in human bodies, like molten lava. And only at the end of his journey did he define and dissect and compose his lost story, *The Messiah,* capering wildly inside you, and now that we've reached this particular point purely by chance, I had better shut up and let you talk about the story, and give me a hint or two, no more.

No, I won't. But I will tell you about Guruk's *torag.*

Guruk? Who's Guruk? I don't want to hear about Guruk! I want to hear about the Age of Genius! I want to hear about *The Messiah*! Now! Right now!

Okay! Be silent!

And after a pause:

My, you're obtuse. You've just told me things that are terrible and true. How do you understand him the way you do? I hate you for being able to guess like that. I know how you do it, too: you look at yourself and say the opposite. You —

Enough!

No! I want to speak, because you're merciless, too. You have to say everything, don't you! You have to know everything! You hurt me to death. You're so mean and so right about everything! I'll tell you something: While he was inside me I licked him and learned that he was falling to pieces. Many strange creatures, Neuman, nasty little creatures swam inside him like fish in a sinking ship . . .

But did he succeed? Did he succeed in the end?

For the life of me I can't understand why of all the people who love Bruno I had to meet up with you?! Now lie still! You want to hear about succeeding? I'll tell you about succeeding. Lie down! Stop wriggling! The way you swim, dearest, I bet you can't dance worth a damn, am I right?

You really enjoy putting me down, don't you?

I was just angry. The things you said . . .

He wasn't right for you.

By all the easterlies! You bastard —

He was only right for himself. Don't be angry. It hurts me as much as it hurts you. Maybe for different reasons, but it hurts just the same.

Now, please tell me about him. Tell me anything you want. Just tell me.

Shut up, will you. Shut up and let me think in peace. Guruk's *torag,* I was saying . . .

[BR]

Ronit Matalon

(b. 1959)

Ronit Matalon describes herself as an Israeli who is "attracted to the cultural
and moral richness of the wandering Jew, who does not have one nationality
or one country, has many languages, is open to everything human, and does
not always close herself off from [foreign] influences." This "Levantine option
of live and let live," she has said, represents "the opposite of Zionism," and so
it is that she has come to be considered one of the leading "post-Zionist"
writers on the contemporary Israeli scene.

That broad cultural perspective—and with it the experience of cultural
displacement—informs nearly all of Matalon's writing. Her well-received first
novel, for instance, is "a kaleidoscopic family saga" that ranges from Central
Africa to Egypt to New York to Israel. Her second and more directly political
novel artfully moves between Paris, Gaza, and Israel—between Judaisms of
the Diaspora, the Occupation, and very comfortable Tel Aviv. In her fiction
and essays, in other words, Matalon regularly shifts back and forth across
the political, social, and ethnic borders that run through the heart of Israeli
society and, to an extent, through that of the Middle East as a whole.

Matalon was born in Israel into a Jewish family of Egyptian descent. She
studied at Tel Aviv University and, in addition to teaching at a variety of Israeli
universities, has worked as both a print and television journalist, covering the
first Intifada in Gaza and the West Bank for the Israeli daily *Ha'aretz*. She is

the author of three volumes of fiction, a book for children, and a volume of essays, *Reading and Writing,* from which what follows is taken.

READING AND WRITING

I have a brother who likes to buy cars that are up on blocks. He's crazy about American cars from the '70s, and every time he hears about one, he rushes out to see it. On Saturday afternoon, the entourage gathers: my brother, his brother-in-law, his wife, his two little girls, my mother who always hands over the check for the first down-payment, the gloomy mechanic Menashe, and me. We all pile into his old American car, the one that's already given its best, and we drive out to the field, among the boulders, weeds, and thistles.

There at the edge of the field, on four blocks and slightly tilted, the car crouches: blue, wide, with sharp and shiny wings at its sides, its windows wide open. The owner's waiting there, without any great anticipation. He has all the time in the world, he explains, until the right person comes along: it isn't everyone who knows how to appreciate what's what and who's who.

For several minutes we circle the car, our feet sinking into the dust. Mother blinks her weak eyes, watching my brother expectantly, waiting for him to tell us already what we should be thinking. Menashe the mechanic crawls under the car. Two crows hop onto the smooth American roof, then fly into the car, landing on the white leather seats with their white innards bursting, overflowing like froth. An ant creeps between my sandal strap and my ankle and bites me. This isn't a car, I say, it's a chicken coop.

My brother lifts his eyes toward me. I'll never forget that look: amazement, filled with animosity and scorn. You, he says, you have no imagination, no imagination at all. I was twelve and he was twenty-six. When I dreamt then about the future, I didn't see stacks of papers, I saw shiny American cars — not in the middle of a field, but where they should be, outside the cool entrances to consular apartments and upscale hotels. I wanted to be a diplomat, one who's just passing through, who's always coming and going, floating by on the hem of her coat, belonging to nothing and no one. With contempt I rejected the concreteness that offended my imagination. My brother in turn felt offended by me on behalf of imagination's relation to that concreteness. That's the way the world is, full of offenders and the offended.

But over the years, it seems to me, my poetic understanding and that of my brother have come closer to one another: more and more we're engaged in the question of the imagination in a similar fashion. Less the haze of diplomacy and coat hems, more the reality of used cars on blocks.

My brother doesn't read what I write. He lacks too many things for that: reading habits, patience, the time, one eye (and with the second one he can barely see). His daughters tell him a little about what I write, and he's always surprised. His surprise is a combination of pleasure and disappointment: Why do you write about what *is*? Why don't you make things up?

I do make things up, I protest. I make things up big time.

Not that way, he says dismissively: There are writers who make up whole adventures in their heads. Do you know what kind of stories there are out there? When you read them, you laugh and cry at once.

But you don't even read, I argue.

I get by with what I hear, my brother says, sinking into the couch in front of the National Geographic channel.

The quiet antelopes before us, we move on to other matters. He tells me about something that happened at work. A few weeks ago he did some renovations on a small house, and they asked him to paint the wall around it. They gave him a paint gun, so the job would go more quickly. He sprayed and sprayed, and apparently didn't really see what he was doing. Suddenly all the cars parked on the street were splattered with paint too. The car-owners came out of the houses and the nearby offices, tearing their hair. What a mess, what a mess, he told me, his eyes growing bright — each one pulled me over to his car, saying "clean here," "clean here." For two hours I ran around among the cars with a rag and a bucket of water.

You should have seen it, he says, glowing with pleasure.

I can imagine, I say sourly. In my head, I start the tally: loss of time, money, small claims damages — and again he'd earned nothing, or almost nothing, from a job.

What are you thinking about? he goads me. All you see is black, everything with you is black.

That's imagination too, I counter, to see black. You think that isn't imagination?

That's not imagination, it's misanthropy, he says, dismissing me.

I ask myself if he's right. I know that in some way he *is* right, but what way is that?

I don't have such theological thoughts when I'm writing. I barely have thoughts at all. I try to stay as close as possible to the task at hand, which will lead me to the next one. I want to keep it moving. In *Sarah Sarah,* the task was to stay close to evil. Not that the people were evil, but the experience was. Harnessing your imaginative powers to the experience of evil is not a pleasurable task. Sometimes you find yourself asking, like my brother, if you too haven't been infected by evil. It's possible through the imagination to get carried away by evil, to resort to hyperbole. That isn't my way. Hyperbole, in my opinion, reflects a complete failure of one's imaginative powers, like a woman who overdresses and all you can see on her is money, money, money.

This too is an imagining of evil: to always say what *isn't.* But what *is?* I don't always know, certainly not in advance. The *is* reveals itself, if it does, after a long, almost endless list of negations, of options that weren't chosen.

My brother is horrified: if you were a judge, everyone would wind up in the electric chair, he says.

Not all of them, not everyone; two or three of them wouldn't, my sister-in-law interjects. Her name is Sarah, my sister-in-law. What, you wrote a book about Sarah, my brother says, astonished — you had so much to write about her?

It's not about this Sarah, it's about a different Sarah, I say: only the name is the same, not the person.

So who is this Sarah? He looks at me warily, with his one, almost healthy eye.

Over the years the distance between our perspectives has become more and more tangible: he can, and does, say, "What a sweet ride this car will be in the end" — while I can barely say "car."

It isn't that you can't, it's that you won't, my brother says.

That's true. Time, years, the lines that come together and those that don't, have all taught me respect for the unfathomable resistance and recalcitrance of the hand that writes. Like a beast of burden that balks in the middle of the path, for no apparent reason, and its owner whips it. But there is a reason. Obstacles, limitations — they're the reason. The limitations of language, the limitations of the other, within which the imagination operates and makes itself felt. That's the imagination that interests me in all I read and write, and which limits me and is limited by me; the imagination of the other, the imagination in relation to the language.

2001

[RTB]

Sami Shalom Chetrit

(b. 1960)

Sami Shalom Chetrit was born in Morocco and came to Israel with his family
three years later. He was raised in an immigrant neighborhood in the blue-
collar port city of Ashdod, and his work has, from the start, been closely
identified with the Israeli "underclass" and with Mizrahi (Middle Eastern
or Arab-Jewish) culture as a whole. Chetrit has also long been an educator
and advocate of social justice. One of the founders of Kedma, an alternative
organization that works for equality in education, he has served as principal
of its Tel Aviv high school and was also a founding member of the Mizrahi
Democratic Rainbow Coalition. He now lives in New York City.

"I write you poems / in Ashdodi," says Chetrit, in one of his more defiant
passages, "so you won't understand a word" — and confrontation, clearly, is
central to his literary strategy. What he wants to confront is the smugness
and often the outright racism of the Ashkenazi political and cultural establishment. "We do not want Israelis to become Arabs," said David Ben-Gurion,
one of the country's founding fathers and its first (and longtime) prime
minister. "We are bound by duty to fight against the spirit of the Levant
that corrupts individuals and society." Ben-Gurion was far from alone in
these sentiments. In time, Eastern Jews began to protest the treatment they
were accorded. That protest was led, initially, with the notorious Israeli Black
Panther movement of the 1970s. Chetrit follows out this line of resistance

in his potent work, taking his cues from African American protest poetry
and injecting Hebrew literature with precisely that spirit of the Levant that
Ben-Gurion sought to eradicate.

To Write in Ashdodi

*One of the most prominent features of your poetry is its political dimension. Your
poems express an ideological worldview and touch on the most central dilemmas in
Israeli political life. For most of the poets writing in Hebrew today, poetry is something untainted by politics. They maintain that poetry should deal with matters of
the spirit and the soul only. For them, politics and poetry exist as a dichotomy. Do you
accept that dichotomy?*

The question is what preoccupies you as a writer. I can't separate my private and intimate life from the political, in the widest sense of the term. The
personal is political, the feminists declared long ago, and I embrace that
idea. Therefore, I reject the dichotomy. There is, in fact, no dichotomy even
among those who claim there is: they are simply not political people, or they
haven't yet emerged from their shells, or someone is coddling them a little
too snugly. I don't know. Of course there's a fear among those who write
political poetry that the politics in a poem might come at the expense of its
poetics. There is something to that, but what does such a dilemma really
amount to? It's a matter of what your objective is when you write a poem,
other than finding a substitute for expensive therapy. Brecht, for example,
wrote almost exclusively political poetry and many of his poems are no more
than placards; but in his day they served a noble purpose, and they still do.
Good political poetry can also be indirect. [. . .]

As a student, I read modern Ashkenazi poetry and didn't find much
protest in it. There was the solitary Hanoch Levin and a little of Natan Zach,
and Meir Wieseltier. Only after the Lebanon War did political poetry begin
to emerge among the Ashkenazi poets — among what is known as "The
Generation of the State," and also the younger generation — because the
left-wing Ashkenazi poets allowed themselves to speak out in protest only
against the Likud government and its terrible war. [. . .] After the assassina-

tion of Yitzhaq Rabin, this wave of protest rose even higher. But there is one thing you'll never see there — the Mizrahi [Middle Eastern] Jews don't exist in that poetic world, not in the allusions, images, tones, and colors of all those poets, almost without exception. Dahlia Ravikovitch writes a powerful poem about a small Arab shepherdess among the rocks and crevices of the eastern hills ("Hovering at a Low Altitude"), but a little Mizrahi girl in a southern ghost town doesn't exist in her consciousness at all, nor in Natan Zach's or Meir Wieseltier's, though I love all their poetry. [. . .] Later I started reading African American poets and also white American political poets — Maya Angelou, Amiri Baraka, Ginsberg, and others. Even Langston Hughes, from an earlier generation, moved me greatly, and the poems he wrote in the '30s, '40s, and '50s are much more radical than those of the Mizrahi poets whom I met at the end of the 1970s. [. . .]

Your poem says: "so you won't understand a word". . .

> *I write you poems / in Ashdodi / kus em em emkum / khlla daar bukum — / screw you all / so you won't understand a word. / So what? / So who? / Who gives a fuck, / uwlad al-haraam / one by one / when have you ever cared / you who are / like this / like that / so great. / I write you poems / in Ashdodi — / so you won't understand a word.*

Do you think you can start speaking or writing in "Ashdodi" today because there's some support for it now? In music, literature, and film, too — increasingly — we're hearing the voices that come from beyond the dominant center and, as you say, you need backing to be heard.

Without a doubt in today's world of multiculturalism, real or imagined, of postmodernism that's open to everything, and of political correctness which is sometimes obnoxious, many editors feel an existential need to "open their doors to the east," to let "Mizrahi voices" be heard — and that, of course, fixes them even more firmly in the category of "the other." Therefore, we have to re-create ourselves every day, and speak Ashdodi, in order to free ourselves of the image that was created for us yesterday. This is a very difficult and almost Sisyphean mission, but one can already see the real impact on the culture unfolding here. Today you can't speak of music, film, literature without Mizrahi voices. As those voices grow — those independent images and sounds — so will the possibility of Mizrahi Jews liberating themselves from self-hatred and liberating all of Israel from the Ashkenazi ghetto complex. Ashdodi is antithetical to the ghetto, to the homogeneous, to seclusion, to the phenomenon of the melting pot.

Then why do you say, "so you won't understand a word"?

I don't delude myself. This is a call from the Mizrahi margins toward the hegemonic Ashkenazi center; actually, I'm declaring that in order to understand this language you'll have to learn it; that I'm beyond your control and your understanding. You'll have to move closer to "Ashdod" in every way, culturally, socially, and religiously. And Ashdod here involves an entire world. So in fact it becomes an invitation, an opening of a door, despite the [Moroccan and Arabic] curses that play an integral role in the poem. One of the curses there — *kus emak* [Arabic for, literally, your mother's cunt] — is easily understood, since it's part of Israeli slang; but the curses in Moroccan demand unpacking in order to be understood: "*khlla daar bukum*" [Moroccan] — May your houses be destroyed. Defamiliarizing the language, in the end, opens up possibilities and choices: you can start disengaging from your violent, racist discourse, or you'll lose the ability to understand what is going on here. This is your last chance.

Your poems employ various linguistic registers. There is the biblical register, the register of modern Hebrew, and the language of Ashdod.

Today I try to write from within all those registers at once, as though I were drawing from one large amalgam, or reservoir, without determining if the language is poetic (that is, elevated), biblical, or of the street. I used to choose registers of speech very consciously — today it just flows. Of course when the language sends me to the Bible, or to the Midrash, I delve in and try to be accurate.

What, for example, has constituted the poetic layer for you?

I've found that poetic language in every form is restrained, limiting. It utilizes unconventional verb structures. [. . .] Today I don't make these choices consciously; everything comes from the same place. I'm trying to break free of all my inhibitions. That's why I titled this collection *Poems in Ashdodian*. Ashdodian, or Ashdodi, is, I believe, the Hebrew of today. Ashdodi, according to the *Even-Shoshan* dictionary is "foreign language, language intermingled with foreign elements. Dialect." Actually, I like that, that definition makes me happy.

Ashdodi is also associated with "Canaanite." Have you taken that into account?

It connects up perhaps to that same Ashdodi from the vantage point of Ratosh and company, who sought a non-Jewish Hebrew — that is, a Holy Language without God — and of course they failed in their search. But my Ashdodi isn't another Canaanite experiment, nor is it an attempt to free the language of its Jewishness. On the contrary: the more I draw from my Jewishness, the stronger Ashdodi becomes for me, because my Jewishness contains my Moroccan identity.

Do you think that anything from the liturgical tradition has entered into your poetry? And along the same lines — an additional layer in your poetry involves biblical imagery. The question is: Are these the biblical images that Zionist discourse appropriated for itself, or are these biblical images that you took from your home and that in fact conflict with the Zionist discourse?

In most cases these images come to me from the Jewish language of my home, from the weekly Torah portion, from prayers, from the liturgy I've heard. As to prayer — there are prayers that I read as sublime poetry and when I hear them sung by a chorus of three hundred Moroccans — *Lekhu renanana*, for instance, in the Friday evening service — I'm moved to tears. In no way is that an orthodox religious experience, though it is religious in the spiritual sense of the word. For example, in the poem "Children's Wishes" I write about my forefathers who would at times turn to God and say [in the hymn recited at the end of every prayer service], *Aleinu leshabe'ah l'adon hakol* ("It is our duty to praise the Lord of all"). I could have written that in simple Hebrew, but it wouldn't have flowed that way through my memory. On the other hand, a poem like "Hey, Jeep" is written in a very calculated, even mathematical way — so there I chose biblical myths carefully; it didn't flow automatically, "the Sacrifice" of the Isaac story, the story of Ishmael, the admonitions of Amos, the phrase "Thou shalt love thy neighbor as thyself" — all of these I set in opposition to Zionist Israeliness as represented by the words of the pre-State Palmach's "Song of the Jeep" and the story of the jeep itself from the pre-State days to the Intifada. I can't write without biblical motifs; they aren't just part of my memory, but part of my soul too, part of my essence as a writer. That's why I'll never write a poem in English.

When did you know you were a political poet, a political person?

It started at the university. I met left-wing people and started to absorb what they had to say. [. . .] I wrote my very first poems about the war with a political awareness, but two to three years later I wrote almost all the poems in the book *Opening,* including "Bus #18," "A Moroccan Woman," "After the Opera" — poems I then thought the height of protest. Only in 1988 did I write the poem which, as far as I'm concerned, embodies full political awareness — "Hey, Jeep" — which was written at the end of the first year of the [first] Intifada. In 1984, for example, while I didn't vote for a Zionist party in the elections, I was still an entirely private person and didn't yet dare say anything against Zionism in public. In the beginning I put a black slip in the ballot box; this was a private invention of mine, a protest against the white slip, or blank ballot. Later, for many years I voted for Hadash [the Communist party] until Azmi Bashari founded Balad [the National Democratic Assembly, which describes itself as "a democratic progressive national party for the Palestinian citizens of Israel"]. My political crisis reached its peak when we fled to study in America, and for three and a half years I refused to visit Israel or even to read an Israeli newspaper! In America I wrote almost all the poems in the collection *Freiha's a Beautiful Name* [Freiha — a common woman's name in Moroccan, but a word that in Israeli slang has come to mean something like "bimbo"]. In New York, through distance and perspective, everything came into sharper focus for me. All those poems were written from that distance, which finally freed me. Suddenly I could place the story of the Holocaust against the backdrop of the occupation, though still gingerly, as in the poem "Mass Media."

MASS MEDIA

On an evening documentary, / on American TV, / [poet] Abba Kovner tells of the Jewish Partisans — / the few who dared / against the many, / against the mighty, / against injustice / . . . while the world watched in silence. // In the *LA Times* that same day: / "Rabbi Levinger will stand trial / for murdering an Arab / a year ago. / . . . the Rabbi shot the man with a submachine gun / from the distance of twelve yards . . ."

This poem was liberation from Big Brother, from the vigilant eye of hegemonic Hebrew. Suddenly I understood that no one was watching me, no one was checking to find out what I was saying or not saying. At least that's how I felt at the start. Later, when for the first time I saw a poem of mine translated into English in an American journal, I felt like the poem was completely free, even more than I was; I envied it a bit, because in Hebrew I'm always trapped in a thicket of conflicting worlds.

It's surprising that you say you feel trapped in Hebrew, because you don't come to Hebrew from within the dominant culture, from the memory of "the founding fathers" and their ethos; you're free of that bind. What you're actually saying is that the language on its own brings with it all those mechanisms of control.

Someone here controls the language, controls the discourse, controls what we say or don't say. Or the way we speak. Discourse isn't a matter of diagrams — it's language, memory, borders, definitions, culture, creation, erasure. That's why I'm so comfortable in opinion pieces where I can, you might say, cut loose in Hebrew, and try to shatter everything in the dominant discourse. But when I write a poem, suddenly the sacredness of the language closes in on me. Within the context of the dominant discourse, every poem is a real triumph for me. Essays are no big deal. Today, when I'm abroad again most of the year, the poetry is set free once more and moves toward the front line of my writing. One could say that sometimes I write in Hebrew against Hebrew. It's a bit crazy.

Like "I write you poems in Ashdodi . . . so you won't understand a word"?

Yes, it's a type of schizophrenia. That's why I return to my roots again and again, to reinvent my Hebrew from within the confines of that European Hebrew which is the language of the master; and that's why I return to prayer, to the Bible, to Ashdodi, to what is Moroccan. In contrast, when I write in English, it feels very technical and functional, because English for me is a tool, it's superficial for me, and has no roots in me; it hasn't been absorbed in my soul with multiple registers and through endless allusions. Even when I translate something of mine from Hebrew to English, I feel a kind of release in the text; suddenly it becomes lighter. It's a strange feeling — and I'm still not certain whether that's only good or also bad.

2004

[RTB]

Haviva Pedaya

(b. 1967)

Haviva Pedaya was born and raised in Jerusalem, within a religious environment. Her family descends from a line of Torah and Qabbala scholars who
were central pillars of the Iraqi-Jewish community. The musical legacy of the
family is also rich. Pedaya herself—who teaches at Ben Gurion University in
Be'er Sheva and also serves as the musical director of the Yona Ensemble for
Jewish Music of the East—has written extensively on Jewish mysticism. Her
poetry is spun directly and powerfully out of that often-esoteric world, as
well as out of the literary heritage of Jewish Spain: she speaks of a particular
affinity for the poet Shelomo Ibn Gabirol, that tormented master and one of
the four or five major poets of the Hebrew Golden Age. In part because of the
matrix of her work, the surface of her poetry is unlike anyone else's in Hebrew
today, and it also resists translation more than most. No one in Hebrew more
forcefully fuses the impulse within Judaism's linguistic mysticism with the
formal and emotional knowledge that poetry bestows. Nor is any other poet
of note as clearly rooted in the Eastern religious tradition.

A recipient of the President's Prize for Literature, Pedaya—who is
religiously observant—is the author of two volumes of verse and several
volumes of scholarly work treating the mystical Literature of the Palaces,
the Spanish Qabbala, and eighteenth-century Hasidism. In what follows,

Pedaya discusses the conjunction of several worlds in her work: poetry and religion, politics and faith, scholarship and art, East and West.

GIVING UP ON HOLDING ON

Is poetry for you a way of getting to the same places that mysticism seeks to reach?

There are poems in which that miracle happens, in which there are no boundaries between experience and language. I've been writing for as long as I can remember myself, and the first years of my writing life were passed under the stress of silence and a sense of strangeness in the world. When I got to the university I felt very palpably the tension between the place I was in and the path I wanted to follow — the tension between the reality I knew, as a forgetting, and the memory I hoped to reach, through the language, and only through the language. And I thought that I would never get there. At a certain point, things calmed down. Maybe because I went on learning. And by learning here I don't mean academic writing and research. It was a matter of survival, of being nourished by what I was studying. The spiritual development I sought took place when, at a certain moment, that study gave birth to what I'd wanted from the language.

But I have a certain aversion to the word *mysticism*. [. . .] I don't want it to sound as though I'm having mystical experiences. [. . .]

Does the poem help you understand something that you hadn't understood before?

Most of my poems, not all, were written in a state of tremendous despair, of — literally — fear and trembling, as though the poem were the last respite in the face of something desperate. The poem let me understand where I was. Sometimes the opposite happens, and those insights accompany me in a new period [. . .] and yet it doesn't come out in a poem. I try not to hurry anything. Not to control these moments. Not to interfere. [. . .]

You've written that "not only is the concrete or literal level of textual interpretation nourished by the mystical level, but the mystical is also nourished by the literal." Do you try to maintain this back and forth in your poetry?

Yes, the movement between them is critical. From the moment that movement exists in life it also exists in the poem. There were stages at which

I tried to shirk off that mystical level, and there were stages when I tried to accept it or reject it. At a certain point, I realized what a disaster the neutralization of the mystical dimension is. The understanding of the way in which that might destroy me or what it might bring me to, in every respect, stopped me, and I gradually began to work with the literal and the mystical in a new way. When I look at a poem, I'm prepared to see a considerable mystical dimension in it, so long as it doesn't depend on that alone. Because a poem can't be dependent on any extrapoetic esoteric code. Not a personal one, and not one that comes from certain texts that one has read. It has to stand on its own, but if it does, and can contain that other dimension — then that's a good thing. It doesn't take away from it.

What enables a poem to stand on its own? When does it do that?

It's like a kind of glazed pottery that's exposed to fire and then immersed in cold water. There's a certain agitation or raising of the temperature out of which the poem emerges. That's the immersion in fire. After that, sometimes right after that, and at other times only after several weeks, there develops an ability to see the poem coldly and from an utterly alien perspective. That's the immersion in water. And that's when you sense whether or not it can stand on its own. The poem comes wrapped in materials that may have been vital for its existence prior to separation, like the amniotic fluid and placenta, but later on it may well be that they're not necessary and may in fact get in the way. Sometimes it's extremely hard to arrive at that objective perspective within just a few days or weeks, and so it takes longer. Each poem is different. [. . .]

How do you relate to the image? To what extent is it fed by texts you're reading and working with as a scholar?

I don't try to invent things. The images of mine that are influenced by mysticism — it's simply a matter of religion, of these things being part of religiosity, and of having a long lifeline within the Hebrew language. [. . .] I'm not satisfied with metaphors and imagery. I'm also looking for a way to restore the story to poetry, and the sense of mystery. To make room for forms that derive from mythology and from allegory, to lessen the impact of the "I," so that there won't always be a dominant personal perspective in the picture, or not always the perspective of the moment of observation or the moment of occurrence. Sometimes that view is from afar, or distinctly belated, and subsumes other, more contemporary perspectives, or still earlier perspectives. I try to leave hints of memory's movement. That doesn't necessarily assume the form of an image, since there is much less simile in my work than there is reality, continuity, and the conjunction of distinct registers. But even when I do make use of "images," they're usually part of a broader story or perspective.

Sometimes one senses a certain inflation in the use of images, when, for instance, the image alone anchors a poem. Sometimes it's just a matter of language, in which case it's empty. And that characterizes a good part of contemporary Israeli poetry.

The danger of images is prevalent for you in particular, as a scholar of the Zohar, which is one of the great poems of all time.

And in fact I nearly collapsed under the weight of it. Because I didn't want to make use of that wealth, and I wanted to write poetry. As a result, I lost all sense of form for a while — ancient and modern alike. But this is also why I chose as the title for my first book *MeTeiva Setuma* (From a Sealed Ark) — as though I were daring to approach that wealth once again, and to speak from the place of hidden discourse. [. . .] When in a certain early poem of mine — in fact, the first poem in my first book — words floated in that could easily have come from the *Zohar,* I accepted them because I felt that they had passed through an entire process of assimilation; [. . .] I hadn't simply plucked out for myself a choice turn of phrase here and an image there. And if at a later and "colder" stage of composition I see that this in fact is what has happened, I'll cross out what I've written without thinking twice about it. For the most part, I feel, at this point, that this is my language.

This is a risk that's faced by all religious poets, who are surrounded by extraordinarily powerful materials.

Just as habit and the quotidian endanger the performance of the *mitzvot,* or commandments, so too religious language faces the danger of being taken for granted. Clichés. Dissipation. Rashi says of the *mitzvot:* "Don't let them be in your eyes like an old letter, but like a new letter." That is, don't read what's written as you would an old piece of correspondence that you already knew and had just taken out of a box; read it as though it were a new letter that has just reached you. Religious language passes repeatedly through a filter or the mediation of a certain socioreligious context, and that involves a narrowing and limiting, but it's also a source of considerable distress. The text should be read without any connection to the religiosity of the social or collective plane. Often one sees literary critics or editors of literary journals gathering a group of poems that seems to them "religious," when in fact the actual content of the poetry isn't religious at all; it's simply that they've been written by people who observe the commandments and are, at least outwardly, "religious."

You distinguish between religious poets and poets who "observe the command-ments." Can you accept that poetry by a nonreligious person, an apostate, can also be religious?

Religious poetry is not necessarily — and often one can say that it has lit-tle or nothing to do with — poetry written by those who observe the com-mandments. And that's because religious experience per se doesn't really concern them. A poem can be full of images based on the tallit (the prayer shawl) and tefillin (phylacteries), or even turn to address God, without being a religious poem. I'm not talking about those poems that intentionally pro-fane or desecrate; I'm talking about poetry that contains the *language* of reli-gion but not religious *experience*. On the contrary, a poem that contains not a single "religious" image might be a deeply religious poem. Likewise poetry that brings religious imagery into confrontation with the profane world isn't always religious, in the true sense — and this without relating to its quality as poetry, to whether it's good poetry or not. The materials themselves do not establish the degree of religiosity so much as do the intention and impulse. Poetry in which the presence of God exists, a poetry whose trials and joys are linked to the thirst for the divine and a longing for metaphysical grace and consolation. It makes no difference whether the form of that meta-physical presence is transcendent or immanent. [. . .]

In many of your poems one feels that your aspiration is downward rather than upward.

That's interesting, because both of these axes exist in myth — the cults of the one god or the cults of the heavens and cults of the earth, which are usu-ally external (that is, outside the temple or shrine). It's true that some sort of flickering, or shimmering, of external light causes me to drill inward. That is true. I wouldn't have put it that way. But it reminds me of the mystics of the Heikhalot literature of late antiquity, the Poetry of the Palaces; to this day we don't know why they were called the "*Descenders* of the Chariot." [. . .]

Do you see yourself as continuing a given tradition in poetry?

I see myself as someone who lives in the poetic reality of the Hebrew poetry of medieval Spain and the Heikhalot poetry, and the Bible, and all the mystical texts I read. I would like to think that I'm bringing them forward into a contemporary place. I've also gotten a great deal from the new Hebrew poetry. That's the line I'm in.

Do you feel a particular affinity for any of the Israeli poets? Or any of the earlier Hebrew poets?

I'm extremely close to the Spanish-Hebrew poet Shelomo Ibn Gabirol. From childhood. I've identified with the exposed and vulnerable speaking voice in his poems. "My flesh is devoured from seeking wisdom" — that was mine. Almost everything in his poetry spoke to me, even his writing about the fact that illness has made his cheeks red and people think that he's flush with contentment. That exists in me too. Also the combination of shyness and arrogance, which is particularly conspicuous in his work. The desperate search for form — he's one of the great innovators. And you feel how he processes an inner reality in front of the mirror of the outside world. [. . .]

But I can't make do with only the Heikhalot poetry, or the poetry of the *Zohar* or the middle ages. I can't get by without them — that's my poetry — but whoever needs poetry, needs it in relation to the present reality as well. There's always a certain hope in contemporary poetry, but I prefer it when it opens onto broader depths. Not every dimension of Hebrew has to be present in every poem, but when that depth is missing, it's hard. [. . .]

How do you hear contemporary Hebrew in relation to the Hebrew of earlier periods?

The language today is undergoing a process of extermination from every angle, and that goes beyond the imposition of the messianic-Zionist voice, and the cultic-military voice, which has stolen for itself a word like *le-tahair* (to cleanse, to purify). I'm not talking only about overdetermination, or overloading, but about determination that freezes, or paralyzes, meaning. Often the price is in the reduction of a word's area of subsistence through complex conceptual and religious concepts, which is to say, in an emptying out and cheapening of their meaning. As with the word *ge'ula* (redemption).

But the determination comes from another direction as well. The imposition of the language of the street also brings about an emptying. Every superfluous word that's invented destroys another word. The invention of superfluous words, words that lack all resonance, is sometimes brought about in order to blur our view of the injustice that's being perpetrated in a given reality; it constitutes a kind of violence against the language. People think that just because they understand the nature of Hebrew grammar, etymology, and morphology, they can make up words. And often that's done so as to distance one from what the word that should have been used would call for, if only it had been uttered. One says *hisuf* (bare-ification) instead of "cutting down trees and saplings" and "destroying homes" and "confiscating property." Why does one have to take the entirely normal and useful word *hasifa* (to make vulnerable, to expose, to lay bare) and turn it into the neologism *hisuf*? The word *hisuf* is empty, it lacks all connotation, it has no resonance, no depth; at most it has the aggressiveness of the intensifying form and declension of the verb. But if we say *hasifa* (to lay bare or expose), someone might start to think: Why should we be "exposing" land? Exposing it to what? What happens when roots are exposed? The neologism is designed to keep us from the real words, which will one day rise up and rebel. That's why God can remain silent: He has never uttered a word like *hisuf*. [. . .]

Who is your ideal reader? And what should he or she be familiar with before starting to read?

He doesn't need to be familiar with anything. If he wants to make himself familiar with things, that's fine — but it isn't important. But he doesn't need to come equipped with a diving suit to lower himself into my poems. The more one knows, the more one gets from them. But the poem has to be able to stand on its own, on the surface.

I don't know if I want to make things easier or harder for the reader. A poem might initially repel a reader, but one shouldn't be afraid of that. The question is, How long will the interval be between that initial repulsion and the subsequent attraction? It's a matter of whether or not you're drawn back in to clarify for yourself and explore that depth, the surface of which had at first driven you off and been so hard to absorb. To the same degree, sometimes a poetry that you took in without any difficulty, and without any back-and-forth, stays with you for a while, then slides off you and is gone.

2003

[PC]

Translators

Rachel Tzvia Back
Dalya Bilu
Chana Bloch
Jonathan Chipman
Peter Cole
Nicholas de Lange
Jeffrey Green
Aloma Halter
Kathryn Hellerstein

Shirley Kaufman
Chana Kronfeld
Gabriel Levin
Betsy Rosenberg
Jacob Sloan
Marsha Weinstein
Linda Zisquit

SH (several hands)

Permissions

Every effort has been made to identify the copyright holders of previously published materials included in this collection; any incorrect attributions will be corrected in subsequent printings upon notification to the publisher.

S. Y. AGNON, "The Nobel Address" (Stockholm: The Nobel Foundation, 1966). Copyright © 1966 by the Nobel Foundation. English translation by several hands.

NATAN ALTERMAN, "On the Incomprehensible in Poetry," from *BaMa'agal* (Tel Aviv: HaKibbutz HaMeuchad, 1975). English translation © 2008 by Trinity University Press. Published by permission of HaKibbutz HaMeuchad Publishing House.

YEHUDA AMICHAI, "How Do You Get to the Poem?" (Interview with Yehuda Amichai, by Helit Yeshurun), from *Hadarim* 6 (Tel Aviv: Gordon Gallery, 1987). English translation © 2008 by Peter Cole. Published by permission of Helit Yeshurun.

AHARON APPELFELD, from *A Table for One* (New Milford: Toby Press, 2004). English translation © 2004 by the Toby Press. Published by permission of the Toby Press.

DAVID AVIDAN, "Something for Someone," from *Mashehu Bishvil Mishehu* (Tel Aviv: HaKibbutz HaMeuchad, 2005). English translation © 2008 by Trinity University Press. Published by permission of the author's estate.

DEVORA BARON, from *By the Way*, from *Agav Orha* (Tel Aviv: Sifriat Poalim and HaKibbutz HaMeuchad, 1960). English translation © 2008 by Trinity University Press. Published by permission of HaKibbutz HaMeuchad Publishing House.

AVRAHAM BEN YITZHAQ, "Blessed Are They Who Sow and Do Not Reap," from *Collected Poems* (Jerusalem: Ibis Editions, 2003). English translation © 2003 by Ibis Editions. Published by permission of Ibis Editions.

HAIM NAHMAN BIALIK, "Revealment and Concealment in Language," from *Revealment and Concealment: Five Essays* (Jerusalem: Ibis Editions, 2000). English translation © 1950 by Jacob Sloan. Published by permission of Ibis Editions.

RONIT MATALON, "Reading and Writing," from *Kro u'Khtov* (Tel Aviv: HaKibbutz HaMeuchad, 2001). English translation © 2008 by Trinity University Press. Published by permission of the author.

SAMI MICHAEL, from "I'd Come Back from Work, Wash Off the Mud, and Sit Down at My Desk" (Tel Aviv: Haaretz, 2005). English translation © 2008 by Trinity University Press. Published by permission of the author.

AMOS OZ, from *A Tale of Love and Darkness* (New York: Harcourt, 2004). English translation © 2004 by Nicholas de Lange. Published by permission of Harcourt.

DAN PAGIS, "For a Literary Survey," "Exercises in Practical Hebrew," from *Kol HaShirim* (Tel Aviv: HaKibbutz HaMeuchad, 1991). English translation © 2008 by Peter Cole. Published by permission of the author's estate.

HAVIVA PEDAYA, "Giving Up on Holding On" (Interview with Haviva Pedaya, by Helit Yeshurun), from *Hadarim* 15 (Tel Aviv: Gordon Gallery, 2003). English translation © 2008 by Peter Cole. Published by permission of Helit Yeshurun. First published in *World Literature Today* 82.5 (September-October 2008).

GABRIEL PREIL, "On Nature as a Source in the Poem," from "Der Yohk un di Monung fun a Lid," *Svive* 5 (New York, February 1962). English translation © 2008 by Trinity University Press.

ESTHER RAAB, "Words Like Rare Birds," from *Kol HaProza* (Petach Tikva: Astrolog, 1994). English translation © 2008 by Trinity University Press. Published by permission of Ehud Ben-Ezer.

RAHEL, "On the Order of the Day," from *Shirat Rahel* (Tel Aviv: Davar, 1965). English translation © 2008 by Trinity University Press.

YONATAN RATOSH (URIEL SHELAH), "Israeli or Jewish Literature?" from *Sifrut Yehudit baLashon HaIvrit* (Tel Aviv: Hadar, 1982). All rights reserved. English translation © 2008 by Trinity University Press. Published by permission of Acum and the author's estate.

DAHLIA RAVIKOVITCH, "Surely You Remember," "The Hope of the Poet," from *Hovering at a Low Altitude: The Collected Poetry of Dahlia Ravikovitch* (New York: W.W. Norton, forthcoming). English translation © 2008 by Chana Bloch and Chana Kronfeld. Published by permission of the translators.

HAROLD SCHIMMEL, from *Qasida* (Jerusalem: Ibis Editions, 1997). English translation © 1997 by Peter Cole. Published by permission of the author and the publisher.

GERSHOM SCHOLEM, "Thoughts about Our Language," from *On the Possibility of Jewish Mysticism in Our Time* (Philadelphia: Jewish Publication Society, 1997). English translation © 1997 by Gershom Scholem. Published by permission of the Jewish Publication Society.

AHARON SHABTAI, "The Good Poem, the Good Poet." Copyright © 2008 by Aharon Shabtai. English translation © 2008 by Peter Cole. Published by permission of the author.

Writers/Works Index

PETER COLE's most recent book of poems is *Things on Which I've Stumbled*. His previous work is collected in *What Is Doubled: Poems 1981–1998*, and his many volumes of translations from Hebrew and Arabic include *The Dream of the Poem: Hebrew Poetry from Muslim and Christian Spain, 950–1492* and *J'Accuse,* by Aharon Shabtai. Cole has received numerous awards for his work, including the PEN Translation Prize for Poetry and fellowships from the NEA, the NEH, and the Guggenheim Memorial Foundation. A 2007 MacArthur Foundation fellow, he lives in Jerusalem, where he co-edits Ibis Editions.